TOGETHER WE ASPIRE TOGETHER WE ACHIEVE

Created and Directed by Hans Höfer

INSIGHT
GUIDES

TRINIDAD & TOBAGO

Edited by Elizabeth Saft
Photography by Junia Browne,
Bill Wassman and others

APA PUBLICATIONS

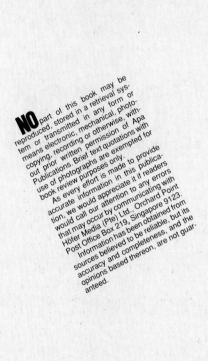
TRINIDAD & TOBAGO

First Edition (2nd Reprint)
© 1992 APA PUBLICATIONS (HK) LTD
All Rights Reserved
Printed in Singapore by Höfer Press Pte. Ltd

ABOUT THIS BOOK

Joining Apa Publications' collection of award-winning *Insight Guides* series is *Insight Guide: Trinidad and Tobago*, the first travel publication devoted entirely to the sister islands of Trinidad and Tobago. This is the result of the spirit, verve and hard work of the editors, writers, and photographers that helped capture the quintessence of the Trinidadian people, their lifestyles and culture, and transformed it into a visual commentary which is both informative and stimulating.

Apa Publications' innovative approach to creating travel chronicles has been honored throughout the world since publisher **Hans Höfer** established Apa in 1970. His first book, *Insight Guide: Bali*, set the precedent for the distinctive style that is to be evident in all future *Insight Guides*. This new concept offers a more insightful look at a country than traditional books. It calls for each book to have clear, frank journalistic writing illustrated with fine photographs, with the total look reflecting Höfer's training in the Bauhaus tradition of book design, production and photography.

Heading the team for *Insight Guide: Trinidad and Tobago* was project editor, **Elizabeth Saft**. Prior to embarking on this project, Saft had just finished a stint in the editorial department of a major New York publisher. By then, she was keen to return to her earlier wandering ways traveling in America, the Caribbean and Europe, and hence welcomed with enthusiasm the opportunity to immerse herself in a culture so richly dissimilar though parallel to her own culture.

The comprehensive and provocative history section was written by **Kim Nicholas Johnson**, a graduate of the University of the West Indies. Johnson's passion for the culture and politics of T&T has also resulted in the book *Festivals in the Caribbean*, as well as numerous articles in regional journals and papers.

Johnson's involvement led Saft to **Merle Hodge**, whose article "People" is an invaluable aid to newcomers to T&T society. With the disarming straightforwardness of so many of her fellow countrypeople, Hodge gives the lie to stereotypical views of Trinidadians while elucidating the origins of their distinctiveness. Hodge comes multiply qualified for this project, with numerous scholarly articles to her credit, as well as many contributions to books on T&T and the Caribbean, and a long career of public service in the form of research projects on all aspects of Caribbean culture.

The impressionistic sections on carnival and other festivals were the work of **Molly Ahye**, a Trinidadian who began her career as a dancer. She founded a modern and folk dance troupe and is the author of two volumes on Caribbean dance forms.

Therese Mills brings her familiarity as a lifelong resident of Port of Spain and a journalist and editor at the *Trinidad Guardian* to the travel section on Trinidad's capital city. She also contributed to "Roti on the Run" and the Travel Tips.

Clara Rosa de Lima picks up where Mills leaves off, covering all corners of the bigger island. Owner of Art Creators art gallery in Port of Spain, de Lima is also the author of three books of verse, five novels, many magazine and newspaper articles, and a daily commentary on Radio Trinidad.

"Above and Below the Water" was compiled by **Ian Lambie**, who serves as Presi-

Saft

Browne

dent of the Asa Wright Nature Centre. As a naturalist and nature photographer, Lambie also lectures widely on T&T's flora and fauna, and breeds fish in his spare time.

The in-depth article on Trinidad and Tobago's musical past and present was the work of **Ernest Brown**, an assistant professor of Music and African-American studies at Boston's Northeastern Univeristy. Widely traveled in Africa and the Caribbean, Brown has previously written articles on jazz and on children's gamesongs, as well as on Caribbean music.

Newsweek editor **Knolly Moses** was born and raised in Trinidad and has lived in the United States for over 10 years. He is widely published in Caribbean and American magazines. "Local tastes" is a subject close to his heart, as food and cooking are a long-time hobby of his. Aptly, he wrote the article "Roti on the Run."

The Photographers

Photographer **Junia Browne**, an enthusiastic and tireless chronicler of the landscape and culture of his country, made it his mission to ensure that Trinidad and Tobago were beautifully, fairly and thoroughly represented in this book. For over 20 years, Browne has been photographing current events and natural beauties for three local newspapers. He has also acted as chief photographer for the Trinidad & Tobago Tourism Development Authority for more than 10 years. Besides contributing a large portion of the photographs for this book, his work has also been published in numerous books and brochures on Trinidad & Tobago and the Caribbean.

In addition to Browne's photographs, many of **Bill Wassman's** images are reproduced in this volume as well. Wassman is a resident of New York whose work first attracted international attention in *Insight Guide: Nepal*. Wassman spent months poking his Leicas into every part of Trinidad and Tobago, gathering literally mountains of pictures despite incurring misfortune upon misfortune during his long expedition through the landscape, greatest of which was the temperamental behavior of his rented motorcycle. A graduate of Indiana Univeristy in comparative literature and anthropology, Wassman worked as an assistant to photographers Eric Meola and Peter Turner in 1973 and 1974 before establishing his own reputation.

Photographs were also contributed by **John Hill**, an Englishman who has lived in Trinidad since 1979. Trained as an architect, he has been a successful commercial photographer since 1983.

Photographer **Richard Spence** is a native Trinidadian who studied the art in Rhode Island and now works as a professional photographer in Port of Spain.

Thanks go to the officials and employees of the Trinidad & Tobago Tourism Development Authority, the Hilton Hotel and Lee Johnson of McCann, Erickson Trinidad.

Individuals who contributed in one or many ways are **Peter Post**, who edited a number of pieces; **Zorina Shah**, who worked quickly and thoroughly on "Trinidad"; and **Robert Hadow**.

To all who have helped make this book a success, we wish to acknowlege their contributions and efforts with thanks.

—APA Publications

Wassman

Johnson

Mosses

History & People

Places

Features

Maps

TRAVEL TIPS

**For detailed Information
See Page 261**

WELCOME TO TRINIDAD AND TOBAGO

Sir Walter Raleigh envisioned it as the gateway to the gold of El Dorado; Robinson Crusoe sustained himself on the fruits of its earth and sea; 18th-Century Europeans traveled thousands of arduous miles in the hopes of becoming as "rich as a Tobago planter." For hundreds of years the beauty and fecundity of these paradisical islands have entranced and inspired dreamers, visitors and inhabitants alike.

Southernmost of the islands in the Caribbean archipelago, the Republic of Trinidad and Tobago lies only seven miles from the South American mainland, just off the coastal plains of Venezuela. And unlike other Caribbean islands, Trinidad and Tobago are not the remnants of ancient volcanoes but rather the serendipitous result of a gradual and gentle breech between South America and a small, mountainous region on her northeastern coast. This geological fact creates a sea of difference between these two islands and those further north, with a geography, flora and fauna as multiform as that of the great continent.

And though for eons these islands lay in relative obscurity in an elysian corner of the uncharted world, in the few hundred years they have been on the European map, the peoples and lands of Trinidad and Tobago have exerted a subtle influence on the culture and history of lands all over the world.

When Trinidad and Tobago were "discovered" by European man, the promise they held of riches and beauty brought four of the most powerful nations in the Western world to struggle with one another for her control. Kings, Princes and Dukes staked out her lands as their own, and in their greed involved even more distant peoples in her future. The cruel commerce of slavery transplanted the people of many African nations to these islands, and when, only 150 years ago, that practice was ceased, laborers from India, China and the Middle East were compelled by both despair and hope to make new homes in Trinidad.

Indirectly, Trinidad and Tobago were involved in the United States Civil War, and since then, the Trini people and their music have filtered northwards to entwine themselves in the growth of America and 20th-Century American music. Calypso and steel drums have brought their rhythms to folk songs, jazz, big band music, R&B and rock 'n' roll, while hundreds of thousands of Trinidadians have made themselves an integral part of American life.

After so many years of foreign control, those immigrants who made Trinidad and Tobago their permanent home forged an independent and original nation, and since declaring themselves in 1956, the Republic has made a concerted effort to consolidate its culture without the constant intrusion of Europe and America. It has only been in the last few years that the T&T government has felt ready to invite tourists in large numbers to savor the delights of Trini life, and so the natural beauty and indigenous culture is still unspoiled by the requirements of tourism. Those who come to enjoy her scintillating beaches and lilting music also discover a land and peoples as diverse as that of countries many times her size, and a population eager to welcome the traveler and the tourist to a unique and vibrant culture.

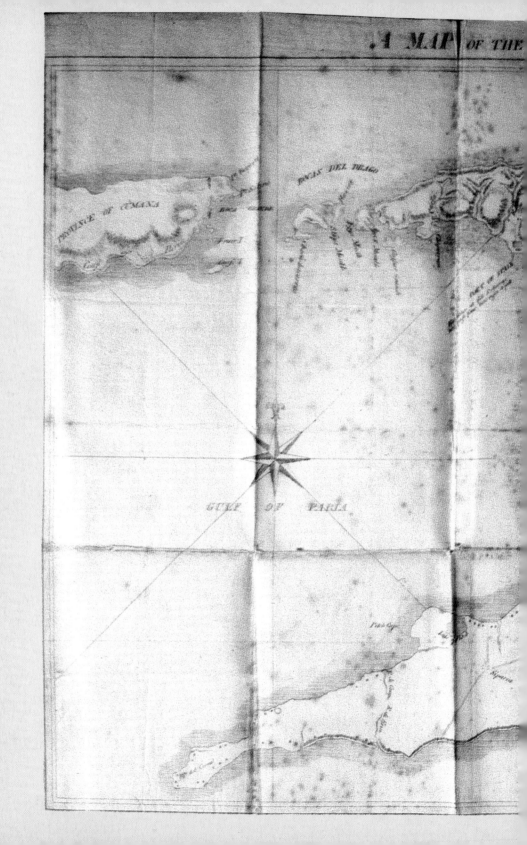

IN THE BEGINNING

When the Meso-Indians established communities in Trinidad, they made it the first settled island in the Caribbean, hunting, fishing and gathering in the swampy coastal areas. Their tools of stone, bone and shell were left behind like fingerprints.

Around 300 BC Neo-Indians of the Saladoid people arrived again from the mainland and their skills were even greater. They could spin and weave, make nicely painted pottery, cultivate sweet potato and cassava and process the latter into a long-lasting bread. These people eventually colonized the lesser Antilles, the Virgin Islands and Puerto Rico, but around the time of Christ they were only in Tobago. The two peoples were joined around 250 AD by the Barrancoid people, and Saladoid pottery was replaced by Barrancoid. (The names come from archaeological sites in Venezuela.)

A sharp break occurred around 1000 AD when central and southern Trinidad developed close cultural links with the Paria coast of Venezuela. Tobago and north Trinidad kept their ties with the Windward Islands to the north. Formerly, all of the tribes of Trinidad and Tobago had spoken Arawakan dialects, but after the caesura, Cariban dialects were probably introduced. And for the next 500 years more immigrants arrived from the mainland to settle on what was then called 'Ieri,' land of the humming bird, eventually, perhaps to move on up the Caribbean archipelago.

So when Columbus arrived in 1498, who was there? Shebaio and Arawak tribes were on the south coast, Nepoio on the southeast and east coasts, and Yao on the southwest coast. In the northwest were the Carinepagoto who, like the Yao and Nepoio, spoke Cariban dialects, along with the Kalina of Tobago. All in all, they totalled about 35,000.

The Trinidad and Tobago Amerindians were described by the Spanish as well-proportioned and of fairer complexion than the Island Caribs. They went naked but for girdles and head bands, painted their bodies red and wore feathers for decoration. Chiefs wore crowns and ornaments of gold while normal folk contented themselves with beaded decorations of stone and bone and teeth.

Living in villages of no more than a few hundred inhabitants, they moved their bell-shaped thatch houses regularly. Theirs were loose societies, and chiefs, who held little secular power, were easily replaced. This arrangement allowed them to resist the Spaniards much more successfully than the rigidly hierarchic Incas and Aztecs of Central and South America, for the death of a chief did not immobilize the tribe.

Cannibal Chiefs?: The main social divisions were between men and women: men cleared the forest, hunted and fished; women planted, weeded, harvested and prepared meals. The economy was based on the shifting cultivation of cassava, maize, tobacco, beans, squashes and peppers for food, cotton for clothes and hammocks, and annatto for body paint. They fished, hunted and gathered shells, crabs and turtle eggs. And they traded and made war.

Villages fought with one another, formed and dissolved alliances, and captured slaves. Their weapons were darts, stones, bows and poisoned arrows. Yet most war expeditions resulted in no more than a minor skirmish which never interrupted the mutual commerce between otherwise hostile villages.

What of the notorious man-eating habits of the Caribs, whose very name has given us the word cannibal? Undoubtedly most Amerindian tribes in the region practiced some form of ritual cannibalism, eating bits of the heart of a courageous enemy or a beloved chieftain. Certainly there existed nothing like the voracious flesh-eaters with a taste for the human as portrayed in many history books. This scurrilous myth was the creation of Spanish slave traders who sought to justify to their Queen their very un-Christian activities.

In 1510 there were declared to be no peaceful Indians along the coast of Tierra Firme, except in Trinidad. The King of Spain forbade slave raiding from the island. In 1511, however, Trinidad was categorized as Carib. Las Casas protested vociferously, and an investigation was made. When the report was presented in 1520, Trinidad was excluded from the list of Carib islands. In 1532 Sedeno nonetheless asked for permission to catch slaves in Trinidad, for the inhabitants were "Caribs and people who eat human flesh and have other rites and evil customs and are very warlike." And so on.

The Amerindians in Trinidad and Tobago participated in a trade network that stretched for thousands of miles to include the three

Preceding pages: the Trinidad and Tobago coat of arms; a young Carnival beauty; a Carnival band; Trinidadian schoolchildren at River Estate in Petit Valley; Manzanilla beach; Tobagonian roadblock; Trinidad coastline; and an early British rendering of Trinidad. Left, one of the remaining Carib Indians poses for a 19th-Century guidebook.

Guianas, northeastern Venezuela and the Orinoco basin. Each tribe had its specialty products which it traded for those of others. Feasts were held for the initiation of chiefs or their burials, or as part of war preparations. But feasts also integrated several villages for trade in a fair-like atmosphere where products were bartered: cassava graters for salt, pearls for axes, trumpets for hammocks. The last were produced by a tribe called Lokono, whose villages were found in Trinidad and along the Orinoco. Lokono specialized in trade, traveling hundreds of miles up the river with the wares of other tribes, for water in those days did not separate people but brought them closer. One particular Lokono village, located on the left bank of the lower Orinoco, was larger than the others because of its admirable position for trade upriver and

island that Christopher Columbus sighted on July 31, 1498. This was the Admiral's third trip to the New World, and a harrowing one it had been. Becalmed at the equator, he changed his plans out of desperation and sailed due west and north. It was on this course, just as the water on his ships was about to run out, that they sighted three peaks joined at their base. Overjoyed at their deliverance he named the land 'La Trinite,' or, Trinidad.

Columbus cruised along the south coast for an anchorage and found one at Punta de la Playa (now Erin) where he landed. His men met only footprints in the sand. He continued along the coast, to the southwestern tip, dropping names along the way like a god. Next day his ship was approached by a pirogue containing about twenty Amerindians. Men from the two

downstream along the coasts. This 'town' was called by its inhabitants 'Arucay' and supplied many a Spanish expedition with food. This earned the Arawaks, as they were called, the title "friends of the Christians." Spanish dependence on the Lokono, and especially those from Arucay, enhanced the latter's economic strength, for they had access to the coveted iron tools. It also exempted Lokono from Spanish slave raiding, so that all Lokono, and other tribes as well, found it expedient to describe themselves as Arawak. A reverse logic worked for the Spanish slave raiders for whom it was convenient to find as few 'friends of Christians' as possible, and as many cannibals as there were Amerindians.

Spanish Trinidad: It was a well populated

worlds stared at one another for some time until the Spaniards began singing and dancing on their deck. The Indians let loose a flight of arrows and the Spaniards responded in kind. The Indians approached one of the caravelles and invited the pilot to come ashore, but then lost their nerve and fled. And the Admiral departed, never to land again on the island, content with leaving a few more names before heading on to Santo Domingo where he'd deposited settlers on an earlier voyage. En route he espied two islands to which he gave the names 'Concepcion' and 'Assumpcion.' They were Grenada and Tobago.

God or Man?: Further Spanish incursions into Trinidad began as a search, in the 16th Century, for slaves to work the nearby pearl islands

20

of Cubagua and Margarita. The story is told that once the Indians had grown tired of the Spaniards' burdensome presence, the decision was made to chase them off. The problem was, could these white people be killed, or were they really supernatural beings? A skeptical chief named Brayoan devised a plan: they found a Spaniard passing through their lands and offered to escort him. Once the group arrived at a river the Indians courteously offered to take the Spaniard across on their shoulders, but in the deepest part they threw him off and held him under the water until he was still. Then they dragged him to the bank and wept copious tears, apologizing for keeping him so long under, for it was only a joke. The chief then came and inspected the corpse; once it was proven to be indeed dead, they knew it was possible to wage war against the Spaniards.

Sir Walter and the Spaniards: Otherwise, Trinidad was used as a starting point for expeditions into Guyana in search of El Dorado—the mythical city of gold—and the first Spanish settlement wasn't established until 1592 by Domingo de Vera at St. Jospeh. He marked out the sites of the church, the Governor's residence, the Cabildo (town council) and the prison. And so was founded a colony which, for the next two centuries would be characterized by poverty and anarchy, and which would be repeatedly attacked by foreign adventurers, including Sir Walter Raleigh heading for the mainland in search of El Dorado. Just passing through, he sacked the town and put its occupants to the sword because, "to leave a garrison in my back interested in the same enterprize, who also dayly expected supplies out of Spaine, I should have savoured very much of the asse." Raleigh then freed the Indians held prisoner by the Spaniards, and told them of his "Queene, who was the great casique of the North, and a virgine." Another, less sanguine, invasion, by the Dutch this time, merely took all of the Spaniards' belongings, including their clothes: Trinidad was turned into a nudist colony until clothing could be sent from Margarita.

Missions and Malaise: Having staked their claim, the Spaniards then allotted a certain number of Amerindians to privileged colonists in four *encomiendas* (plantations). The failure of these to see to the Indians' conversion led to the setting up of Catholic missions. In 1699 the Indians at Arenales (the site is marked at San Rafael) rebelled and killed the missionaries along with the Governor and several soldiers who came to restore order. They were pursued

Left, Sir Walter Raleigh, on his way to El Dorado, sets free five Indian kings and, right, Caribbean priests breathe courage into their native subjects.

by a vengeful army to Toco where, rather than surrender to the Spaniards, they leapt off a cliff to their deaths. By then, however, the missions had fallen afoul of the planters who wanted labor, not devotion. They were eventually abolished in 1708, although four survived the 18th Century as Amerindian villages: Savana Grande (Princes Town), Guayria (Naparima), Savanetta and Montserrate.

The early Spanish settlers grew tobacco, an Amerindian drug for which Europeans had acquired a taste. They produced for the illegal trade with the Dutch and English, and when word got back to Madrid an investigation was set up. A general pardon was recommended because, "all would have to be punished down to the children of ten years old." But Spanish naval policing (in 1610 a fleet destroyed all

foreign ships in the Gulf) and competition from North America ended that industry. Next cocoa was produced and it soon became the major industry, cultivated by Indian laborers on Spanish plantations. Then in 1725 a disease wiped out the cocoa farmers, and in 1739 a smallpox epidemic ended all pretense of civilized life: the settlers abandoned the town of St. Joseph, and surrendered to a subsistence life in the bush from which they emerged to intrigue against the Governor. The Cabildo even staged a coup in 1745 and imprisoned one Governor until a force was sent to the rescue from Venezuela. Eventually, in 1757, the representative of the Spanish state abandoned St. Joseph to set up office at Puerto de España: a fishing village on the coast consisting of about 30 houses.

ENTER FRANCE AND BRITAIN, EXIT SPAIN

The intrigues continued but the winds of change had begun to blow, even through the moribund Spanish state, even through sleepy Port of Spain, described in 1777 as "several cannons on a battery, a church, and about 80 houses covered with straw." Trade within the empire was liberalized (though foreigners were still excluded) and under the influence of his French allies, Charles III sought to strengthen the empire's defenses by developing the more neglected provinces. In 1776 Manuel Falquez was appointed Governor with instructions to attract Trinidad Roman Catholic immigrants, especially French planters, by offering land grants and tax incentives. But it was the Africans, whose labor had enriched islands such as Barbados and Haiti, who were really in demand.

The first trickle of immigrants came from Grenada, where the French suffered discrimination under a new British Government. One such man was Romme de St. Laurent; this energetic planter supported the scheme by lobbying in Caracas and Madrid for its expansion. In 1783 his opinions were embodied in a Cedula of Population issued from Madrid offering very generous terms to planters willing to immigrate with their slaves to this wilderness. Every white immigrant was entitled to approximately 130 acres of land for each member of his family and half as much for each slave he brought with him, and there were tax exemptions as well. Free colored and free black settlers were granted half as much. The settlers only had to be Roman Catholic and from a nation friendly to Spain.

It is a strange coincidence that Tobago, kicked around between different metropolitan countries for the previous two centuries, was at this time in the hands of the French, who pursued a similar immigration policy to that of Trinidad: a French colony was offering money bribes to attract French settlers from a Spanish colony.

By 1784 in Trinidad there was a total of almost 4,500 non-native people and only 1,495 Amerindians. By 1797 there were 16,000 non-natives, including Europeans, slaves and people of mixed blood, and only 1,000 or so Amerindians. Trinidad was not yet a plantation society based on African slavery in the way the other islands were, but it was getting there, with a slave population that nearly twice outnumbered the freemen.

Left, slaves landing from the ships and, right, a rebel slave complete with musket.

The man in charge was Governor Don José Maria Chacon, an educated multilingual Spaniard with a black mistress and mulatto children. Chacon set about encouraging new colonists to the detriment of the old Spanish settlers. A decree was passed forfeiting to the Crown lands left uncultivated, for Chacon thought the old Spanish settlers lazy and crooked. His advisers were Spaniards from Spain or the mainland and French settlers, and by 1788 six out of nine members of the Cabildo were foreign. As Trinidad grew less like the mainland colonies in social structure, Chacon's powers

grew more autonomous and extensive and Trinidad's links with the captaincy-general of Venezuela, under whose jurisdiction the island lay, grew weaker. It was as if the antediluvian connection with the mainland, continued in an Amerindian cultural unity and a Spanish administrative unity, had at last been broken. And so the old Spanish and Amerindian society became superseded and its members left the historical stage for new actors to strut and fret their hour.

Building the Plantations: Very soon, Trinidad was a colony whose mind and heart were French. French planters filled the important public offices such as the Commissioner of Population, the Commandant of Quarters and the members of the Cabildo; the predominant language was French or French patois, and social customs were French as well. This was when Carnival, which lasted then from Christmas to Ash Wednesday, was introduced. And while French and patois would die out in the 20th Century, Carnival would grow from an exclusively white festival to one inclusive of all races and classes, providing an idiom for the Trinidad social mind in general and a wellspring of the nation's arts.

The leaders of society were all wealthy white planters, but in the 1790s, as the fortunes of the French Revolution waxed and waned in the Caribbean, immigrants in Trinidad reflected the entire ideological spectrum, much to the dismay of the Governor and the planters: "The seeds of revolutionary principles," stated the Cabildo, "have not only taken root but in several instances have been seen to send forth shoots." Republicans and Royalists of every shade, fleeing from this or that colony, landed in Trinidad to fill the grogshops with argument and conspiracy.

More numerous than the whites were the free coloreds, who fled the older French slave colonies such as Grenada, where they had been systematically discriminated against. In Trinidad, although they were given no public posts, coloreds faced no public apartheid as in British and French colonies. Some were wealthy slave-owning planters, some were republicans. Most were petit bourgeois smallholders and artisans with no more ideology than a desire for equality. Already they possessed the contemporary characteristics of large numbers, beautiful women

and deep conservatism. But they were tarred with the same brush as the free coloreds of Haiti, and every colored man claiming equality was seen as a wild revolutionary, forever willing to foment disorder.

The largest group of immigrants, however, were the African slaves. Roman Catholic, patois-speaking, at first they came with their owners. Some were bought or kidnapped from neighboring colonies. But the development of the colony required more slaves and soon the slave trade was introduced to Trinidad and declared open to all nationalities in 1790.

It is sometimes argued that Spanish slavery was less harsh than in the French and British islands. The Spanish Slave Code of 1789 was quite liberal. But Spanish laws were implemented in Trinidad by French planters, and

the mortality of slaves in Trinidad was higher than the birth rate, especially in the early phase of clearing the land. Yet the scarcity of slaves, the accessibility of the bush, and the influence of Latin culture, made for a more intimate master-slave relationship than that found in other territories. The issue is clouded, but certainly the Roman Catholics tolerated, even encouraged, much of the Africans' culture in a way not found in Protestant colonies.

British at the Controls: For Governor Chacon the 1790s were the worst of times. His nightmare was that of all slave-owners in the age of revolution. He wrote Madrid: "the contact which our coloured people and our Negro slaves have had with the French and the Republicans, has made them dream of liberty and equality." Britain and France were fighting the Napoleonic wars, which often spilled into Spanish colonial territories, especially the poorly defended island of Trinidad. French privateers and British warships battled in the Gulf of Paria, and in May 1796 open fighting broke out in Port of Spain between British sailors from the *Alarm*, which had just sunk some privateers in the Gulf of Paria, and French inhabitants.

In these troubled times Chacon did what he could: he organized a militia, armed a few Amerindians with bows and arrows, and pleaded with Madrid for reinforcements. But when French Jacobin emissary Victor Hughes offered his assistance, Chacon demurred: "Should the King send me aid, I will do my duty to preserve his Crown to this colony; if not, it must fall into the hands of the English who I believe to be

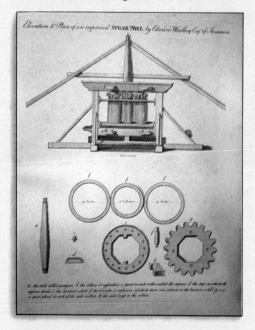

generous enemies, and are more to be trusted than treacherous friends."

In September 1796 a Spanish squadron of five ships commanded by Admiral Apodaca arrived in Trinidad from Puerto Rico with 740 soldiers, many of whom immediately fell ill with yellow fever. In October Spain declared war on Britain; the *Alarm* incident was mentioned. A corvette bringing money and ammunitions from Puerto Rico had been captured by the British who had long set their eyes on Trinidad, and now intended to make no mistake about it. And

Left, a cartload of sugarcane to be used as cattle fodder and, right, a type of sugar mill in use throughout the West Indies.

on Feb. 16, 1797 their invasion force sailed into the Gulf: eighteen ships to Apodaca's five, seven thousand soldiers to Chacon's two thousand (most of whom deserted, if healthy enough). That night the Spaniards burnt their own ships. The next day they surrendered to the British with hardly a shot. For this Chacon would be later vilified by the Trinidad planters and humiliated by the King of Spain.

The terms of the capitulation offered by Sir Ralph Abercromby were generous: Chacon's soldiers were to surrender and would be allowed to return to Spain—but not to take up arms against Britain; officers in the judiciary and administration were allowed to remain at their posts and Spanish law was to be maintained; everyone, except the prisoners of war, was to swear allegiance to Britain and, having done so, was allowed to retain his property; men of property were allowed to keep their weapons; and those who considered themselves to be citizens of the French Republic were to be given safe conduct to some French, Dutch or Spanish colony. Abercromby next appointed one of his officers, Thomas Picton, as Governor with near absolute powers. "Do justice according to your conscience," ordered Abercromby, and then he left the island. The results were horrendous.

Thomas Picton was a harsh soldier who had been early advised to rule with an iron rod because the island was full of revolutionaries and assassins. "If those men do not fear you," explained a Spanish official and landowner, "they will despise you." Picton responded with vigor. In the next few months he preemptorily executed several people—a Spanish peasant, an Irish sergeant, and a colored sea captain among them—on the slightest pretext and the flimsiest evidence. Arbitrary imprisonment and execution, judicial torture and mutilation were the hallmarks of Picton's six-year reign, and slaves and free coloreds bore the brunt of it. The blunt soldier with the frightening laugh had overnight become an absolute dictator and a planter; his cruelty was merely the logic of his position.

Picton's transformation was a gradual departure from British policy: when they first captured the island, their aim, apart from the tactical one, was to foster an illegal trade with Venezuela by two methods. First would be to encourage the contraband trade through Port of Spain, up the Orinoco and into Venezuela. The second plan was to encourage the embryonic nationalist revolution on the mainland, knowing that a liberated Venezuela would trade openly with Britain. For a while, Picton diligently assisted the Venezuelan revolutionaries, turning Port of Spain into a den of spies and conspirators, much to the dismay of the Governor of Cumana: he offered 20,000 dollars for Picton's head. Picton offered 20 for the Governor of Cumana's. Eventually, however, London's lukewarm support for his activities opened Picton's eyes to a greater cynicism.

Praised in 1801 for his 'zeal,' by 1802 Picton was an embarrassment to the British Government, for he had promoted a slave colony; London wanted a colony of free white settlers. There lay Picton's great mistake, and a Commission was set up to govern the colony. Picton, William Fullarton and Samuel Hood were its three members, but the first two became involved in a sordid feud over Picton's methods of government. The Commission dissolved, Fullarton secured an indictment against Picton for torturing a colored girl, and the problem of how to rule the country was, in 1803, once again painfully raised.

Meanwhile, Over In Tobago: In the same year,

arrived in 1625. The Indians wiped them out, but Britain claimed the island anyway. The Dutch landed settlers in 1628, but a Spanish and Indian force from Trinidad invaded in canoes and put them to the sword: as Eric Williams explains, "Trinidad and Tobago went to war." The English landed again in 1639, and again the Indians chased them off. A British monarch gave the island to his infant godson, the Duke of Courland (Latvia), as a christening present, so another settlement was attempted in 1642, this time by Courlanders. Indians chased them off, along with a party from Barbados. Courlanders returned in 1650, and again in 1654. The Dutch came again and suppressed them. Louis IV of France gave the island to the victorious Dutch, who were expelled by the British, who were in turn driven off by the French. That last

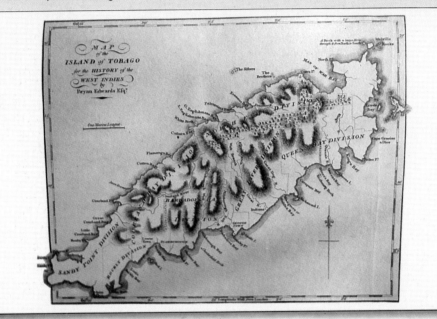

1803, a British force took Tobago away from the French without any opposition. Tobago, the region's most knocked-about island, had changed hands for the last time, and Britain's ownership was confirmed in 1815 at the Congress of Vienna, never to be challenged until Independence. But let us start at the beginning.

At the time of Columbus the island was probably occupied by Kalina Indians, and in the 17th Century there was immigration of Kalinas from St. Vincent. Although the Admiral had named the island 'Assumpcion,' in passing, as it were, it later came to be called Tavaco after an Indian smoking instrument, so it is sometimes told.

Whatever the name, it was a nominally Spanish island on which the first British settlers

bunch razed the settlement and abandoned the island.

By 1674, when Tobago was ceded to the Dutch, the island had changed flags over a dozen times, and so it continued — Dutch, French, Latvian, English, Dutch, French, English — even the Americans took a chance in 1778 at capturing the half-deserted, undeveloped island which was for most of the time just a nest of pirates.

Rum and Rebellion: European policy for Tobago was that the island should be "so laid waste as will hinder all settlement," partly to appease other colonies fearing competition. The British began to encourage settlers once again in 1764, and by 1769, 23,000 acres were under cultivation. The colony developed rapidly and seven years after the first shipment of sugar was exported, Tobago was producing 1,200 tons of sugar, 1,600,000 gallons of rum, 1,500,000 pounds of cotton, and 5,000 pounds of indigo. The corollary of this expansion was that by the early 1770s slaves outnumbered whites by 20:1. It was a ratio higher than anywhere else in the British West Indies, and, as a result, Tobago, up until 1774, experienced almost annual slave revolts on a small scale. These were mostly inconclusive, in that a few whites and a few blacks were killed, and the rest of the rebels fled to Spanish Trinidad. One rebellion in 1774 brought savage punishments on the captured rebels, and after that Tobago simmered down for the rest of the 18th Century.

The French captured Tobago again in 1781 and proceeded to sponsor immigration from the other islands by offering incentives similar to those offered by the Spanish in Trinidad around the same time. And sugar production began in earnest: Tobago's population rose from 5,084 in 1771 to 15,020 in 1791; 14,170 of these were black slaves. Only five Amerindians could be found. But the black-white ratio had fallen to a less dangerous level, or so the planters thought.

The British and the French made Tobago productive and populous, an exporter of sugar and cotton, at the cost of creating a typical West Indian slave society. Nevertheless, Tobago planters also displayed a remarkable if futile perspicacity. By 1780 they had reduced the ratio of free to unfree by half, and reduced the number of African slaves in favor of Creoles. Then in 1798 a Legislative Committee in Tobago produced a report on the state of the slaves unique for its liberality.

In summary, land was to be distributed to the slaves and time to cultivate it allowed, more food was to be given them, slave imports were discouraged (!) and the Creole population to be increased naturally. Matrimony was to be encouraged, children and pregnant mothers protected, and midwives paid by planters. And Guardians of the Rights of Negroes were to be appointed in every parish.

The planters were pleased with themselves and confident of their slaves. Early in 1801 Sir William Young, a local grandee, stated that, "here the planters talk of their Negroes as their resort to be depended on against either a licentious garrison, an arbitrary Governor, or the mad democracy of French hucksters." Imagine their surprise when a Christian slave exposed a massive plan for insurrection, scheduled for

Left, a map of Tobago showing British divisions and, right, freed slaves celebrate Emancipation on the first of August.

Christmas Day 1801.

Martial law was declared and 200 suspects were rounded up. And the whole conspiracy lay exposed. The slaves of 16 estates were involved: Roger, a driver at Belvedere estate, was the "governor," and Thomas, a cooper, the "colonel." There were five "captains" on various estates and five "chiefs" in Scarborough. These men had formed companies of slaves and the plan was to set alight five estates, killing any whites who came to control the fire. In the town, the Governor and the Commander in Chief of the garrison were to be assassinated. It was expected that the whole slave population would then arise in revolt.

By Jan. 4, 1802, sentences had been handed down and the whole affair finished. For this reason only six rebel leaders were executed. Four

other rebels were banished, and the rest sent back to work after a severe flogging. And Tobago was quiet for the next 60 years.

The Experimental Colony: In 1812 it was written, "Trinidad is a subject for an anatomy school or rather a poor patient in a country hospital on which all sorts of surgical experiments are tried, to be given up if they fail and to be practised on others if they succeed."

The first experiment sought to discover what kind of government the colony should have. The issue had been forced by the Governor who'd replaced Picton, Thomas Hislop. He became embroiled in a struggle with Chief Justice George Smith, an irascible man whose rigorous application of Spanish laws angered the planters. Chief Justice Smith despised them in return. "Generally colonies are peopled by the refuse of the Mother Country," he said, "but Trinidad is peopled by the refuse of the other colonies." Hislop, his Council of Advice and the Cabildo all petitioned the King in 1810 for a British Constitution and British laws.

Britain, however, was less willing to grant British laws to new colonies than in the 18th Century. London had grown too familiar with the difficulties and obstructions of which West Indian colonial assemblies were capable, but they could not ignore as unanimous a demand as came from Trinidad. Just then the free coloreds petitioned for consideration on the matter. They were uneasy that a local assembly would merely entrench the power of a small and bigoted elite. Hislop was furious, the secretary of state elated. Smith reasoned that if the free coloreds were excluded from an assembly there would be difficulties, so there could be no assembly. No third possibility of including the free coloreds, not even the wealthiest, was considered and the matter was closed: Trinidad would be a Crown Colony under direct supervision of Britain. This signaled the beginning of the end of colonial self-government in the British West Indies.

The second experiment faced the problem of development. Trinidad was mostly under forest and large slave-owning plantations were rare. The planters wanted more slaves although their number had doubled in Picton's time but the British Parliament was under pressure from abolitionists to make no extensions of the slave trade. Other sugar colonies agreed with the abolitionists because they feared competition. So Britain suggested a scheme of free laborers, but implemented it halfheartedly. In 1806 the slave trade was prohibited to new colonies and in the following year it was completely abolished. Trinidad never became a mature slave society like the other West Indian territories, although sugar came to dominate land use and exports.

The third experiment sought to solve the problem of illegal importation of slaves. "The poor patient has to go through some very severe operations. She is now actually bound down for a most painful one — a registry of slaves, prescribed by (abolitionist) Dr Stephen." Every slave was to be registered within a month of March 1812 and no unregistered person could be held as a slave. The Registrar was a slaveowner and both he and the Governor, Sir Ralph Woodford, hardly implemented the Order at all. The deadline was ignored or extended and the whole exercise rendered useless. Slave smuggling continued, many brought in as 'domestics' from other territories and sold in Trinidad where the prices were high. A new Governor, Sir Lewis Grant, prosecuted many who had illegally imported slaves but too late — only a year before Emancipation in 1833.

A fourth experiment tested whether harshness of slavery could be ameliorated by legislative measures. In 1824 an Order in Council was passed restricting an owner's right to punish his slaves and giving slaves certain legal, religious and social rights: no more whipping of women; for men no more than 25 strokes; no more Sunday labor; manumission must be facilitated, even without the owner's consent; slave evidence was admissible in court; and a Protector of Slaves was to act on their behalf.

Howls of protest went up from the planters and, as with the Registration Act, the planters subverted the Amelioration Act and made it nugatory. By 1830 this was apparent to the British government and a tougher Order was drawn up. Planter reaction grew hysterical as they resisted with the assistance of officials, especially those in the Cabildo. In so doing they paved the way for the abolition of Spanish laws and the Cabildo in the 1840s. But more importantly, the planters themselves convinced the Imperial Parliament that it was time to end slavery completely. Or the slaves would do so, as the 1831 Jamaican rebellion had shown everyone.

The Great Emancipation: And so the Act of Emancipation — the 'Great Experiment' — was passed in August 1833 to take effect on Aug. 1, 1834. Slave-owners were compensated for their loss of property; field slaves were apprenticed to their former owners for six years, other slaves for four; special magistrates were appointed to administer the system. On the big day, hundreds of slaves assembled in Port of Spain to protest the apprenticeship period. The militia was called out, arrests made, and the darkest era of Caribbean history came to a close.

Or did it? On June 17, 1837 a Yoruba African called Daaga led a mutiny of liberated Africans from the 1st West Indian Regiment. The mutineers, under Daaga's inspiration, attacked and fired on the barracks at St. Joseph. They then set off to walk back to Africa. After days of skirmishing with the regular forces the rebels were put down, and within a week the whole affair was over, having cost 40 lives, most of them rebels. And on the morning of Aug. 16, 1837, Daaga and two others were executed in the mists of St. Joseph by firing squad. And in 1971 another man with flashing eyes and a deep voice, the leader of a "Black Power" movement which had also inspired an unsuccessful mutiny in the army, changed his name from Geddes Granger to Makandal Daaga.

Right, a letter from the Governor of Trinidad is an amusing mixture of fear and paternal reassurance.

THE HISTORICAL SOCIETY OF TRINIDAD AND TOBAGO.

Publication No. 882.

General Hislop to the Under Secretary of State.

Source:- Public Record Office. State Papers Colonial. C. O. 295/14.

Published by the courtesy of the Master of the Rolls and the Deputy Keeper of the Public Records.

Private.   Trinidad.
                                            8th January 1806.
Dear Sir

X   X   X

You will learn from my public dispatches which are forwarded by this packet, of the alarming situation into which the Colony has recently been thrown, and in which it still exists to a certain degree.

Our neighbouring Island of Tobago, is also under Martial Law in consequence of a discovery of an intention to poison the cistern of the garrison. It is also reported that a plan of an insurrection among the negroes in Guadeloupe has fortunately been discovered; and that General Evreux caused six of the Chiefs to be burnt alive. They were said to belong to San Domingo.

I can assure you that our situation is far from being pleasant but I trust that with proper examples in the first instance and a strict observance of discipline in the next, we shall succeed in preserving the Colony from a recurrence of so shocking a state as that from which it has so miraculously escaped.

THE PROBLEMS OF FREEDOM

Apprenticeship of the ex-slaves ended two years before schedule, in 1838, because of the insistence of abolitionists in Britain and the intransigence of the ex-slaves who decided to not work after Aug. 1, 1838. On that day the old society died, and the future offered only the challenge of building freedom.

For the ex-slaves, freedom meant choosing how they wished to live: culturally, socially and, most important, economically. It involved no retreat to the bush—largely the preserve of Spanish-Amerindian peons—and any movements were to the urban areas. Most of all, in an island where labor was scarce, freedom for the ex-slaves meant using their bargaining power to improve their economic conditions, and that they did successfully. The average wage per task throughout the Caribbean was 30 cents; in Trinidad it was 50. In 1841 the planters tried to collectively reduce wages to 30 cents, but the workers withdrew their labor and the planters backed down, scoring a success for Trinidad's first strike.

Planters sought to retain a dependable labor force by allowing ex-slaves to occupy estate huts and provision grounds, but most left the estate anyway. Many settled in or around the towns and a large internal trade network grew up. For others, land was abundant and if they were unable to meet the price they squatted illegally. The Crown showed no inclination to distribute land to the landless, but couldn't stop the squatting.

This pull and tug was interrupted in 1846 when the Sugar Duties Act was passed in Britain, allowing cheaper foreign sugar into the mother country. West Indians howled; many estates were abandoned and wages fell. The industry recovered in a few years but two important changes had been precipitated: first, in 1848 the British Government agreed to sponsor the immigration of indentured laborers from India, and, second, the sugar industry would be modernized but in the hands of large British companies.

The 1860s and 1870s saw two important and closely related developments. Under Governor A.H. Gordon, Crown lands were opened up to smallholders. His predecessor, Lord Harris, had sought to prevent ex-slaves from becoming landowners by authorizing the sale of large lots of land only and at high prices. In 1869 Gordon

Left, a young indentured laborer from India on her arrival in Trinidad.

reduced the smallest lot to five acres, the price to one pound, and conveyance costs to a minimum. Many of the most intransigent squatters, it was discovered, were willing purchasers, and Gordon even offered land to the Indians who had served their indenture in lieu of a return passage to India.

The second change was the expansion of cocoa cultivation. Completely owned by locals and often in peasant hands, it had always been cultivated in Trinidad in small quantities. But chocolate touched the English sweet tooth in the 1860s, the market opened up, and cocoa blossomed in Trinidad to become the largest export. It was an achievement mainly of the peons, although blacks and Indians later contributed. These peasants bought small plots of Crown land, then cleared and planted them with cocoa. When the trees began to bear they sold the plots to a plantation and were paid for both land and trees. They then repeated the process. Or, the plantation, already owning the land, contracted with peons for its clearing and cultivation. They did so but simultaneously used it for cash crops. At the end they were paid for each tree and moved on. This is how the French Creole elite shifted their wealth from depressed sugar to buoyant cocoa, and cocoa made them even wealthier up until the 1920s, when the cocoa market crashed.

Tobago's Travail: Tobago, a more classic plantation society than Trinidad, found itself bankrupt on Emancipation Day. "This Colony," stated an 1823 petition, "has now arrived at a pitch of distress of a deeper nature than we can possibly detail." As everywhere else in the British West Indies, in Tobago the labor force lost its tractability once freed, so again the common solution: planters sought to encourage immigration; English convicts, Barbadians, Africans from Sierra Leone, free blacks from America. But wages were too low to be an incentive, half the level of Trinidad, and the treasury could not afford to pay for immigration. A hurricane in 1847 devastated the island and made prospects more grim. Even the British capitalists, usually willing to buy out bankrupt estates at knockdown prices, considered Tobago a bad deal. A different approach was required, and the planters looked to St. Lucia and Antigua for inspiration. What they came up with was known as the Metairie System.

It was an arrangement whereby the workers took no pay for their labor but instead shared the crop with the owner. An oral agreement, it worked well enough until, in the late 1870s, the sugar industry declined further. Then planters began to renege on their agreements and the almost feudal relationship showed its cracks.

Life had never been easy for the workers and riots broke out in May 1876 at Roxborough Estate: there had been fires on the estate — arson by Barbadian workers, it was said. Cpl. Belmanna and five privates were sent to arrest the alleged incendiaries but as the warrants were being executed, the people grew restive. The Corporal was knocked down and he shot a woman. She died, and the flame of justice was set alight: the Manager's House was gutted, and the people besieged the Court House. The police released their prisoners, but Belmanna, especially hated by the people, was beaten to death. A warship was sent from Grenada and many constables sworn in.

As the Morant Bay Rebellion did for the Jamaican planters in 1865, the Belmanna Riots scared the Tobago planters into surrendering their self-government in favor of Crown Colony government. So at the beginning of 1877 the 215 eligible voters in Tobago lost their democratic right to elect representatives, and Tobago became a Crown Colony.

A Royal Commission was appointed in 1882 to look into the impoverishment of Tobago (and other colonies). The Commission found an empty Treasury, but it was the laborers who felt the pinch hardest.

In 1886 a métayer, Joseph Franks, was evicted by a planter from his plantation. The 73-year-old Franks, an ex-slave, took the planter to court, and lost the case. He appealed and, in February 1890, received the judgment of Sir John Gorrie, the Chief Justice of Trinidad. The judgment was a bombshell: Sir John castigated the planter for his shamelessness and upheld the old man's claim for damages. And the planters raised their tiresome voices in the same centuries-old protests: "...the labouring classes of the Island are in an unsettled state and ...this condition of affairs is attributable to an impression which has been created amongst them, with which your Honour's name is unfortunately associated." A Commission of Enquiry was set up to look into the question, and the Chief Justice was reprimanded. What was suggested instead of the Metairie System? More immigration, and if Tobago couldn't afford it, then try to inveigle some Indians over from Trinidad which had by then been wedded to Tobago.

The Commission of 1882 had recommended a federation of St. Vincent, St. Lucia, Grenada and Tobago to reduce administrative costs and to combat the (fiscal) "evils of isolation," and in 1885 this was effected, although Tobago retained its own bureaucracy. Then in 1886 Britain decided to tack the island on to Trinidad, either as a dependency or as a wholly incorporated ward. Tobago planters opted for the former, demanding fiscal autonomy. As Tobago resisted, so Britain insisted, and in 1889 a union of sorts was forced upon the two grumbling partners, although, again, Tobago retained some autonomous institutions. Eventually, tired of the whole matter, Britain decided to solve the issue by fiat, and in 1897 Tobago was made a ward of Trinidad. A shotgun marriage, yes, but only for the wealthy; for the ordinary people it was a union long before consummated by their migrations and the communities of Tobagonians on Trinidad's north coast.

The Arrivants: Labor in Trinidad had always been scarce, but after Emancipation things grew worse, for ex-slaves could no longer be compelled to work 18-hour days, and soon the planters were desperately seeking immigrants. Recruitment agents were sent to the other islands to tell of job opportunities, high wages and cheap land. Many came but few remained on the plantations. And if they brought their crafts and skills, they were still inadequate because planters wanted sugarcane fodder and nothing more. Next the United States was looked at as a source, but the few free blacks who came were even more urbanized. A colony of liberated slaves — Sierra Leone — was turned to and yielded over three thousand Africans. But although they remained discrete tribal groups — Radas in Belmont, Yoruba and Congo in Laventille — they, too, abandoned sugar. Some Europeans came but they either took overseer jobs or left for America. Portuguese came from Madeira and quickly set up as shopkeepers, as did the Chinese. Trials and errors were all of these, from the planters' point of view (for otherwise the newcomers were valuable additions to society). But eventually the planters found what they were searching for, and in May 1845 a windjammer, the *Fatel Rozack*, docked at Port of Spain, bringing 225 immigrants from Calcutta.

India was ideal. It had a large destitute population willing to migrate. Largely a British colony, it had a tropical climate, and its people were mainly agriculturalists. Transportation costs, though high, were not prohibitive. Only one problem remained: the first immigrants from India had, in Trinidad, deserted the estates. The solution was an indentureship contract which would later be described as "a new system of slavery."

A financial crisis temporarily halted the scheme between 1848 and 1851, after which a steady flow of Indians arrived in Trinidad until the Indian government stopped it in 1917. By then a total of about 144,000 Indians had come to Trinidad. Most of them were from the Gangetic plain, especially the provinces of Uttar Pradesh, Bihar and Oudh. Smaller numbers came from Bengal and the Punjab, and a tiny minority from Madras in the south.

Conditions in India were the main incentives to immigration: there were famines due to a decaying economy and exploitative ruling classes, and dislocation caused by British imperialism. In addition to extreme poverty, there was the savage repression which took place after the Indian Mutiny (1857).

The immigrant on arrival was assigned to a plantation where he was bound to work for 3 years. After that, he had 2 years to go to complete his 'industrial residence' during which he could re-indenture himself to any plantation, or pursue another occupation — provided he paid a special tax. Only after the five years was completed did he receive his 'free paper.' However, he was not yet entitled to his free return passage:

borers lived in single-room barrack ranges reminiscent of slave quarters, cramped and insanitary, and suffered from malaria, hookworm, anaemia and ground itch. Some plantation hospitals were so deplorable that the cure was often worse than the illness.

Perhaps the cruellest cut of all, at least for the men, was the imbalanced sex ratio which made women scarce and generated the notorious 19th-Century Indian crimes of passion, when Indian men murdered wives who had succumbed to the enticements or coercion of another man; between 1872 and 1900, 87 Indian women were murdered, 65 by their husbands.

On the plantations they were an isolated community, desperately poor yet despised by the wider society who thought them amoral, deceit-

he first had to remain in the colony for an additional five years. And after 1895 indentureds were forced to pay a proportion of the cost of returning to India.

Cruel Conditions: The indentureship 'contract' signed in India laid down minimum wages, working hours and working conditions. These were often ignored by planters, especially in the 1880s when the sugar industry almost collapsed. On the other hand, breaches of the contract by the indentured laborers were treated as criminal offenses punishable by imprisonment.

Conditions were wretched. Indentured la-

Above, farm workers breaking cocoa around the turn of this century.

ful, revengeful, barbarous and dirty. Their customs were considered 'degrading practices,' 'vile' and 'painted devilry.' Even the black ex-slaves held the Indians in contempt for their languages, their customs, their appearance, their poverty and their bondage.

And yet most remained once their indentureship contracts had expired, perhaps for reasons of both optimism and inertia.

Once released, many Indians remained as laborers on the plantations. Some picked up the crafts they'd practiced in India (they were famous for their skills in jewelry-making) while others became petty traders. Moneylending made a few rich but many more subsisted as laborers, gardeners, porters, scavengers, domestics and a host of other menial 'coolie' jobs.

And, most importantly, they became peasant proprietors, growing 'wet' rice, sugarcane and vegetables on land received in lieu of a return trip or purchased from the Crown. By 1905 a Labour Committee could find that they "are industrious and useful citizens."

The creation of an Indian peasantry allowed them to recreate their customs as best they could, and if the caste system survived only in vestiges, by the last quarter of the century the countryside would be dotted with Hindu temples. By then an Indian sense of community with middle-class leadership had been formed. In 1897 the East Indian National Association was created to protest the discrimination suffered by Indians, and in 1898, the Indian *Kohinoor Gazette* was published—the first Indian newspaper.

Conflict between the two groups took the form of local versus foreign whites, or merchants and planters versus government officials, but most consistently it was French lined up against British, the latter wanting to Anglicize the colony in language and manners, the former wanting some say in government policies. Otherwise the two groups were very similar in their outlook, and by the end of the century their antagonism appeared to have been a storm in a teacup.

Yet this sparring had important consequences. First was the creation in the 1850s, under the Anglicizing Governor Lord Harris, of a series of free (primary) Ward Schools and (teacher training) Normal Schools. Second was the fact that when, in the 1880s, the Government sought to abolish the black Carnival

AVENUE OF PALMS, QUEEN'S PARK, SAVANNA.

Creole Contradictions: At the top of Trinidadian society there were the whites, the ruling class who controlled the wealth and power. Yet whites did not form a single homogenous group, but were divided between English and 'French Creoles.' Today 'French Creole' refers to any white person whose family has been resident in Trinidad for some generations. In the 19th Century it was a different matter. The French Creoles then were Roman Catholic, French speaking and descended mainly from Royalist French settlers. They were racially exclusive and saw themselves as an aristocracy, even when the blood of their forebears was actually quite common.

The English on the islands were Protestant, often born abroad and employed by the state.

because of its rowdiness, the French Creoles protested. Finally, there was established a tradition of French Creole opposition to government, a tradition which produced men like Philip Rostant and Capt. Cipriani.

When Lord Harris' Normal Schools began taking in graduates from the Ward Schools, most black children remained outside of those doors, but for a few of the brightest the state-funded Ward Schools provided the means of social mobility. They could, on graduation, study to become teachers in the Normal Schools and make the first faltering steps out of manual labor. Thus was begun the formation of an educated black and colored middle class. A smaller group of fortunates won free places in the secondary schools, which qualified them to become junior clerks, journalists and store assistants. And every few years one of these sons of the respectable working class won the College Exhibition Scholarship to study abroad, from whence they returned doctors and lawyers to the man. Two notable 20th-Century exceptions read literature and history: they were V.S. Naipaul and Eric Williams.

But it was the teachers who formed the backbone of this class, producing even at an early stage men such as John Jacob Thomas, a philologist of international repute.

Even among the Indian community, largely ignored by the state, the Canadian Mission began to set up schools in 1868, creating a parallel Indian middle class in embryo.

The largest sector of the population was the black laboring classes, however. Predominantly

Company Villages), the demobilized soldiers of the West Indian regiment, and the freed Africans who numbered about 8,000. In common they held their poverty, lack of education and exclusion from political power.

Yet Trinidad was a rapidly urbanizing colony and Port of Spain at the turn of the century contained a quarter of the population. The urban black plebeians were found in various menial jobs, as domestics, messengers, washerwomen, longshoremen, petty traders. Many practiced trades as artisans, carpenters, masons, tailors, printers and mechanics. Many were periodically or permanently unemployed and they all lived in overcrowded, squalid barrack houses in the city or the labyrinthine hills of Laventille and Belmont, racked with dysentry, malaria, sometimes cholera and smallpox,

rural, they worked as agricultural laborers, small farmers and tradesmen. In the sugar industry they were replaced by Indians in the fields but kept many of the skilled jobs in the factories. In the Northern Range, shaded by immortelle trees, they worked on cocoa estates as laborers, contractors, or smallholders alongside the Mestiso-black peons known today as 'cocoa payols.' Even within the black community there were discrete groups: those who spoke French patois and the immigrants who spoke English, the 'Americans' (demobilized U.S. soldiers in the

Left, urban blacks enjoy Port of Spain's largest park around 1903 and, right, young farm hands pause in a cornfield.

camping, as Earl Lovelace puts it, "on the eyebrow of the enemy." This population exhibited the symptoms of urban unemployment: juvenile delinquency, vagrancy, prostitution, petty crime and gang warfare. They also practiced their African and syncretic religions, indistinguishable in respectable eyes from the illegal obeah (witchcraft) of slavery times. It was a tightly packed community with an exuberant demi-monde and intense loyalties.

The Years of Revolt: The closing years of the 19th Century saw the various classes and the factions within them stretching to adjust to the new places they now occupied in the society. In some cases the exercise was painless. The French Creole elite and the British governing class grew closer, with only two slight obstacles to the process. The first was a land distribution policy of Governor Gordon (1866-1870) who allowed the peasants to buy plots of Crown land — the planters were displeased. Second was the impartiality of Chief Justice Gorrie who reformed judicial procedure to make the courts more accessible to the lower classes — even the Governor didn't like that. Otherwise the planters and the Government exchanged not a harsh word.

Things went differently for the lower-class blacks, the Indians and the rising middle class. In the first case, the blacks, and in particular the urban working class, felt the brunt of upper-class fear and loathing from the long end of a police baton, wielded more often than not by "Barbadian rowdies," according to J.J. Thomas, "whose bitter hatred of the older residents had been often brutally exemplified." The law interdicted lower-class music and religion, frowned upon their sexual mores and language, and punished even trivial offenses with stripes.

Needless to say, the most outrageous were the *jamets*, described in the *San Fernando Gazette* as "hordes of men and women, youthful in years but matured in every vice that perverts and degrades humanity, (who) dwell together in all the rude licentiousness of barbarian life." The *jamets* had taken over the Carnival celebrations in recent years with their sexual horseplay, gang warfare, ribald songs and drumming. At the Canboulay procession on the Sunday before Carnival Monday, gangs tramped around with lit torches (Canboulay from the French *cannes brulee*, meaning burning cane), singing and dancing and challenging rivals to duels in *kalenda*, a traditional martial art performed with sticks.

In 1877 the Inspector-Commandant of Police, Capt. Baker, decided to destroy the *kalenda* gangs and reform Carnival. The next two years he clamped down and in 1880 called on all marchers to surrender their torches, sticks and drums. Taken by surprise, they complied. The next year they planned for him. In 1881 he armed the force with clubs and tried the same tactic, but the *jamets* were ready with bottles and stones and sticks, and a riot started. The Governor conciliated the revelers and confined the police to barracks until things cooled down. Three years later the Canboulay was made illegal and warfare erupted in San Fernando. Two gangs laid siege to the police station; police shot into the crowd leaving two dead and five wounded. Thus ended the *jamet* Carnival, and the respectable classes joined the fête once more. Noticeably, throughout it all, the French Creoles, despite their high moral tone, criticized Baker's high-handedness and condemned any intention on the part of the Government to ban Carnival.

A similar fate befell Hosay, a Shiite Muslim festival in which bands of masqueraders, carrying a large ornate tomb, reenact a famous battle of Islamic history. Despite its origins, this celebration was mainly supported by Hindus, and by the 1870s it had become "a sort of national Indian demonstration." Gatka — an Indian martial art with staves — was performed and Hosay bands from different estates competed with one another. In the 1880s the festival grew more riotous, more a demonstration of class and ethnic solidarity, because of worsening conditions in the sugar industry. In 1884 regulations were passed to exclude Hosay bands from San Fernando and Port of Spain and to stop the *jamets* from joining the festival as they were accustomed to doing. The bands ignored the order and the police opened fire, killing 12 and injuring 104. The festival became, after that, a more domesticated affair.

The emergent middle class also sought changes, but politely, in the reform movement actually started in the 1880s by Philip Rostant, a white French Creole journalist. Rostant organized meetings and a petition in favor of elected members for the Legislative Council, but the Colonial Office in 1889 rejected the idea. Thereafter the banner was carried by black and colored professionals such as C.P. David, Henry Alcazar, J.S. de Bourg and Emmanuel Lazare. These men linked constitutional change with a reduction of the selfish influence of the planters in Government. "Men who are selected for the business of Government from a particular class," complained a middle-class paper, "will naturally be prone to give undue prominence to their exclusive interests." The reform movement appeared a useless passion, however: the suffrage sought was exclusive and the tactics used were courteous, but the Secretary of State for the Colonies, the indomitable Joseph Chamberlain, put an end to the matter in 1895 by refusing point blank. The point was emphasized in 1898 when he abolished both the Borough Council and the unofficial majority in the Legislative Council.

Nevertheless, the reform movement was not simply sound and fury, and in years to come some of its members would engage in black nationalist and working class politics, foreshadowing key developments of the 20th Century. In 1897 Walter Mills, a druggist, formed the Trinidad Workingmen's Association, and in London a Trinidadian lawyer, Henry Sylvester Williams, formed the Pan-African Association which opened enthusiastic branches at home in 1901.

Right, the French aristocracy watches while slaves enjoy their own festival.

36

POLITICAL AND ECONOMIC BEGINNINGS

A Baptism of Fire: Amazing scenes were witnessed in Port of Spain on Monday, March 23, 1903, when the Red House, seat of Government in the colony, was burnt to the ground in the course of a riot over water.

In the previous months, the Government had announced its intention to control the wastage of water by installing a metering system in houses (for the wealthy were known to bathe indulgently), and by visiting homes to cut off the water supply to leaking taps. The culprits were unrepentant: "We know that rheumatics is the only evil resulting from the use of these House, and the crowd outside roared. A woman threw a rock, and a rain of stones fell on the building; Governor Maloney hid with one official and the rest fled. The Red House was set alight, and the RPA leaders of the crowd decamped; the hidden official escaped, disguised as a policeman but the Governor had to be escorted by the police, under a shower of stones, away from the conflagration. Firemen came to the rescue, but were repelled by the crowd. The Riot Act was read and the police fired into the crowd and charged with bayonets, leaving 18 dead and 42 wounded. And the Red House was

Fig 19.2 *Crowds gathering in Port of Spain during the protest against new water charges. Later the same day the Red House, the large building on the right, was burned down.*

baths," complained one writer. Besides, Government inefficiency was thought to be the cause of much wastage anyway. But the underlying issue was really the middle-class demand for a more representative and less high-handed government.

The objectors forced the Government to postpone its water legislation in 1902, then again in February 1903, and yet again on March 16. Leading the struggle was the Rate Payers Association (RPA), a middle- and upper-class group led by reform agitators of the 1890s. This time, however, they were supported by the lower class (who had no interest in the matter but felt strongly on the issue).

Tension mounted. The RPA leaders were denied entry to the Council Chamber in the Red burnt to the ground.

An investigative Commission absolved the police, and found the riots unrelated to the issue of representative government. Joseph Chamberlain, the Secretary of State for the Colonies, was more perceptive. He told the Governor to begin talks for the restoration of the abolished Borough Council, and in 1913 it was agreed that an elected Council would be created.

Ten years — the change had taken long to arrive, and the franchise was limited, but on the Borough Council local politicians now had a platform. Significantly, in the waiting the RPA disappeared but the older Trinidad Workingmen's Association (TWA) grew in the struggle, only to lapse once the 1914 franchise excluded its members.

Nineteen Fourteen: It was in the same year Europe entered World War I and the first oil refinery in Trinidad was opened at Pointe-à-Pierre.

The history of the oil industry in Trinidad dates from 1857 when the first oil well in the world was drilled by the Merrimac Oil Company at La Brea in Southern Trinidad. The company folded soon after that pioneering effort and two other 19th-Century outfits were no more successful. Then in the 1890s the internal combustion engine became a commercial proposition. Things were never the same

to prospect for a British company. His successful drilling prompted a conference at 10 Downing St. with the Governor of Trinidad and representatives of the Colonial Office and the Admiralty in 1909. The Navy, which was converting to oil-powered ships, had become interested. In 1910 Trinidad Oilfields Ltd. was formed, to be joined in 1913 by United British Oilfields of Trinidad and Trinidad Leaseholds Ltd.

Drilling for oil in those days was hard work. The fields which were found in Guayaguayare, Palo Seco, Rousillac, Siparia, Erin and Taba-

again.

The oil industry was pioneered by an Englishman called Randolph Rust who had migrated to Trinidad in 1881. Rust sought to explore for oil in the Guayaguayare forests with local backing: none was forthcoming, so he obtained Canadian capital and the first well was drilled in 1902, followed by eight others in the next five years. He lobbied tirelessly, in Port of Spain and London, for Government support, and in 1905 an engineer was sent from England

Right, the original Red House and, left, the beginning of the water riot that left the Red House in ashes and 17 people dead.

quite had to be wrested from dense jungle through which heavy equipment was dragged. It was, in Rust's words, "one terrible fight against nature." Blowouts, gushers, fires, explosions, all of these were common occurrences and as late as 1929 a fire killed several people near Fyzabad. It was one of the last, however, and technology and safety standards improved rapidly thereafter.

The Dockworkers' Strike: World War I revolutionized Russia; in Trinidad and Tobago there were less spectacular changes but important nevertheless. The war years and after were hard, inflation was high, especially for basic foods, and wages remained low. The diet of the laboring classes became, in the words of the Surgeon General, "somewhat deficient in protein." A strike in oil and asphalt in 1917 resulted in imprisonment for the leaders and for a Seventh-Day Adventist who had displayed a placard saying "Awake ye Stevedores and be men." The East Indian Destitute League was formed only to have its founder deported in 1918; Indian immigration was curtailed because of agitation against it in India.

So the Government drafted the infamous Habitual Idlers Ordinance (although widespread opposition delayed its passage until 1920) in an attempt to keep the Indians tied to the estates. The Colonial Secretary thought that the law went "considerably beyond anything in the UK, in that it makes the mere fact of refusing to work and being without visible means of subsistence a punishable offence." It was eventually passed anyway. It tells much of the society

Some were sent to Egypt where a few, briefly, saw action against Turkish troops; most performed labor services, like the others who'd gone to Europe, digging trenches and carrying ammunition. November 11, 1918, and the War ended. The British West Indian Regiment was sent to Taranto, Italy, for demobilization under a South African camp commander. There they were made to wash linen and clean latrines, and work for labor units, because "the men were only niggers." When they refused to do it, several were court-martialed and sentenced to from 15 months to three years. In postscript some West Indian soldiers created the clandestine Caribbean League, which advocated economic, social and political reforms for the West Indies. The League was reported to the authorities and disbanded, and its members closely observed on

that in 1911, the year of Eric Williams' birth, 62,000 pounds were spent on education, and £66,000 on the police, £18,000 on prisons and £4,000 on the local military.

The British West Indian soldiers had fared no better in Europe. As good British subjects, they'd volunteered to fight for the Empire, but the British Government refused to let blacks serve, and only when the King interceded did the War Office agree to a West Indian contingent. They formed a separate regiment, not part of the British Army, with lower pay and lower allowances; and only those of "unmixed European blood" were eligible for commissions. Furthermore, perhaps to preserve them from acquiring a taste for white blood, they were excluded from actual combat with Europeans.

returning to their islands. But ideas leavened with experience cannot so easily be set aside, and the soldiers, especially Capt. Arthur Andrew Cipriani, returned home to make their mark on the times.

In July 1919 there were anti-black demonstrations in Britain, and news of this inflamed the returned soldiers. British Honduras saw rioting. In Trinidad, soldiers boycotted the victory celebrations held on July 19, and a few British marines from the *HMS Dartmouth* were knocked about. White businessmen requested arms from the Governor. They also sought the suppression of the paper which informed the public of conditions in Britain. *The Argos* was a paper for the colored middle class which, along with Marcus Garvey's paper, *Negro*

World, advocated race pride.

In 1918 the TWA had come under new and more radical leadership: James Braithwaite and David Headley, two dockers influenced by international socialism, J.S. de Bourg from the reform movement, and Howard Bishop, a journalist. From early 1919 the revamped TWA had participated in agitation for higher wages, supporting a wave of strikes throughout the island. Workers on the railways, city council employees, electricity and telephone workers, and laborers at the Pitch Lake, all called strikes in 1919. But it was the laborers at the Port of Spain docks who changed the tempo.

Called the "scum of the wharves" by the *Trinidad Guardian*, the dockers were the most well-informed and cosmopolitan workers in the colony. Many had traveled abroad as sailors,

their tools in support. Even the black police, thought the Governor, "could not be relied upon." He formed a conciliation board which, on December 3, offered the dockers a 25 percent wage increase.

The same day, around noon, the *HMS Calcutta* steamed into the harbor, and the tide of conciliation turned to one of repression. The Government, backed up by the British troops and a white volunteer force of colonial vigilantes, cracked down on the strikers. Ninety-nine people were arrested, 82 imprisoned and four leading TWA members deported.

On December 6, a crowd attacked the Government wireless station in Tobago with bottles and stones. But it was already too late for that kind of behavior—the troops had imposed order next door the day before. Em-

and all had access to smuggled literature and new ideas. In November 1919 they went on strike. Led by the TWA, the dockers demanded wage increases. When the shippers refused to negotiate, they walked off the job. The shippers brought in scab labor, and on December 1 the dockers retaliated: they smashed warehouses, driving off the scabs. Then they marched through the city, closing businesses and encouraging other workers to join them. And the workers throughout the colony downed

Left, sailboats at anchor in Port of Spain harbor and, right, a passenger ship steaming into port while dockhands and greeters watch.

boldened, the police fired on the crowd, killing one and wounding six. The marines came soon after to mop up.

Rise of the Captain: The immediate outcome of the 1919 dockworkers' strike, which had almost become a general strike, was repression. The Government passed the Strikes and Lockouts Ordinance, and the Industrial Court Ordinance, which made strikes illegal. The *Trinidad Guardian* expressed "profound gratitude." The Government also wrote to the TWA threatening deportation for anyone who started strikes. Next the Sedition Ordinance was passed which banned Garveyite and socialist literature, and saw to the closure of the *Argos*. A Wages Committee, set up when conciliation was necessary, recommended a minimum wage of

68 cents for men and 45 cents for women. The Government threw out the report.

Although a Colonial Officer had described the dockers as "the most gentlemanly rioters I have ever heard of," the planters revived a fear which had possessed them since the 18th-Century Haitian Revolution: the crazed fear of a black millennium. People spoke of a secret organization led by six foreigners, dedicated to the destruction of organized Government, and the "elimination of the white population".

Out of this turmoil rose the Captain. Arthur Andrew Cipriani was born in 1875 to Albert Cipriani, a white planter of Corsican stock and with blood ties with the Bonaparte family. Arthur lost both parents very early, by the time he was seven, and was brought up by an aunt. He left school at 16, distinguished only by atrocious handwriting. His next 25 years were equally unremarkable, divided between managing cocoa estates and horse racing.

A few months before his 40th birthday, World War I broke out. Cipriani lobbied for a West Indian contingent and eventually found himself a Captain in the British West Indian Regiment, stationed in Egypt. There he earned the respect of his compatriots by defending them against army racism. He wrote letters, sent off protests, argued at courts-martial, and continued to do so until demobilization. By the time Capt. Cipriani returned to Trinidad in 1918 he was loved as a man of the people, both because, and in spite of, his white planter background.

Capt. Cipriani, who retained his army title, joined the TWA in 1919 and became its president in 1923. The organization had shifted its focus from trade union struggle to political agitation; and Cipriani, the white planter who sided with the "unwashed and unsoaped barefooted men," was seen to be the perfect man for the job.

In 1925 he won a seat in the first Legislative Council elections, despite an extremely limited franchise, on a platform favoring workmen's compensation, an eight-hour day, abolition of child labor, compulsory education, competitive examinations for entry into the Civil Service and repeal of the Sedition Ordinance. The demands changed over the years; the seat he kept until his death in 1945.

Cipriani was autocratic but an effective speaker and under his joint leadership with Howard Bishop the TWA grew, boasting 33,000 members in 1928. And although the organization was predominantly urban, black and strongly influenced by Garveyism, the TWA also attracted support from the Indians. Sarran Teelucksingh and Timothy Roodal, two Indian leaders elected to the Legislative Council, joined the TWA. Krishna Deonarine, later

known as Adrian Cola Rienzi, was president of its San Fernando branch in 1925, years after he became Butler's emissary.

Cipriani sacrificed trade unionism on the altar of reformist politics. Worsening economic conditions in the 1930s made many followers disillusioned with his limited ambition "to propose and oppose legislation." Two incidents foreshadowed this. In 1931 the Government proposed a Divorce Bill which was hotly opposed by the Roman Catholic French Creoles. The TWA was neutral but Cipriani broke ranks in favor of the French Creoles. Howard Bishop criticized him in the *Labour Leader*, the TWA organ. The paper was closed in 1932. Then in 1932 came the Trade Union Ordinance which gave limited rights to trade unions. After two years of consultation with the British TUC,

Cipriani decided not to register the TWA as a union: the Association was renamed the Trinidad Labour Party. Again his colleagues grumbled; having given a colonial people an awareness of politics, Cipriani's star began to fall.

Cultural Evenings: The 1930s began with dark clouds on the horizon. The world economy was depressed, and fascism ascendant. In Trinidad unemployment rose and planters tightened the

Above, Capt. Arthur Andrew Cipriani, champion of the rights of people of color, children and workers.

screw, lowering wages and extending tasks. In Tobago the peasants, "wrestled with the earth with their bare hands for sustenance." So wrote their poet, Eric Roach, of a people who were "like figures in bas-relief, half-emerged from the heavy clay of our tragic past."

In this context a cultural movement was started by men such as C.L.R. James, Alfred Mendes, Albert Gomes and Ralph de Boissiere, men influenced by World War I and the Russian Revolution.

"Those were the two events in our lives at that time which drove us into writing about our islands," recalls Mendes. And this marked the beginning of West Indian creative writing. The movement began around *Trinidad*, a magazine started in 1929 by James and Mendes and folded after two issues, for the colony was just a small, philistine backwater. Then the 20-year-old Albert Gomes brought out *The Beacon* in 1931, editing and financing it through 28 issues over an heroic three years.

The Beacon published fiction and poetry, cultural criticism, political analysis and historical essays. In their "barrack yard" literature *The Beacon* group celebrated urban lower-class life for its spontaneity, and criticized the respectable classes for their hypocrisy. Nor were they merely middle-class romantics, and so *The Beacon* group also condemned the exploitation of the laboring classes.

As Gomes described it, *The Beacon* was, "the debunker of bourgeois morality, obscurantist religion and primitive capitalism." And inevitably the magazine came under attack from the establishment: the police harrassed its leading writers, and businessmen organized advertising boycotts. It folded before the end of 1934. (That was a bad year for culture, for the Government passed a law to censor calypsos.) But in its short life *The Beacon* did its job well: it created the beginning of a Trinidadian literature, and politicized men who would play leading roles in times to come.

Before the Storm: A Commission of Enquiry found working class housing in Port of Spain, "indescribable in their lack of elementary needs of decency." Conditions were worse in the rural areas where in places 80 percent of the population was infested with hookworms. From the late 1920s onwards, prices climbed with unemployment, but workers earned less in 1935 than in 1929. Like a bad joke, the Wages Advisory Board found that workers' needs were lower in 1935 than in 1920; malnutrition was epidemic. Life was even harder in Tobago, and the poet Eric Roach remembers "clinging to life by the skin of our teeth... (although we) did not realise our hardship because we knew nothing else."

By 1934 the National Unemployment Movement (NUM), formed by Jim Headley, Dudley Mahon and Elma Francois, was organizing hunger marches in Port of Spain. But it was the Indian sugarworkers who started the ball rolling. In July 1934 sugarworkers from San Fernando to Tunapuna demonstrated against their desperate situation. A hunger march fought its way from Caroni to Port of Spain, attacking bosses and policemen, burning company buildings, and looting shops. Just before the city, a police barricade halted the marchers and a delegation of 'leaders,' all unknowns, went to parley with the Governor; Cipriani's organization was completely by-passed. The situation was defused, but only for the moment.

The torch passed to workers at the Apex Oilfields. In March 1935 they downed tools and tramped to Port of Spain, protesting low wages and harsh conditions.

Cipriani had sanctioned no such action, but the workers went ahead under the leadership of John Rojas and Buzz Butler, a fire-and-brimstone preacher with a pronounced limp and a loud voice. The two broke with Cipriani, and from then on Butler began mobilizing oil workers in the South.

Bertie Percival, a friend of Butler, was an Apex worker with a talent for public speaking. He gave a speech in Port of Spain about conditions at Apex, and was invited to join a new organization, formed by Elma Francois, Jim Barrat and others, called the Negro Welfare, Cultural and Social Association (NWA). It was the successor to the NUM. Denouncing Cipriani as "Britain's best policeman in the colonies," the NWA saw to mobilizing workers in the north and establishing links with Communist organizations around the world. When in 1935 fascist Italy invaded Abyssinia, the NWA organized large demonstrations in support of the Africans.

Social Explosion! Oil was important. Trinidad supplied most of the British Navy's fuel, and the companies made large profits in the colony. White expatriate staff, some South African, lived luxuriously. Black workers, however, were treated shabbily: their wages lagged behind inflation, the bosses were insufferably racist, workers were liable to instant dismissal and a blackballing system made it difficult for a man dismissed by one company to find employment with another. There was no compensation for industrial accidents. Yet the oil workers were a concentrated modern industrial proletariat, better off than sugarworkers, and easier to mobilize.

Tubal Uriah 'Buzz' Butler was a Grenadian who came to Trinidad in 1921 to work in oil. In 1929 an industrial accident lamed him and, unfit for oil work, he turned to the Moravian Baptist Church. After the Apex strike of 1935

Butler left Cipriani's TLP to form his own party, the British Empire Workers (BEW& CHRP). By the early months of 1937 he was moving up and down the southlands, holding meetings, opening and ending each one with a hymn, rallying workers for the "heroic struggle for British justice for British Blacks in a British colony." Butler had indeed become the "Chief Servant."

On June 18, 1937, having exhausted the "prayers, petitions and bootlicking tactics of a suffering class," oil workers at Forest Reserve began a sit-down strike for better wages and working conditions. Police swarmed into the area.

On June 19, the strikers were dispersed and, at 5:30 a.m., two oil wells at Apex oilfields were set on fire. The authorities thought it was the

signal, for there was no turning back. Later, when 40 policemen attempted to recover the charred corpse, the crowd repelled them with bottles and bullets, killing another policeman.

On June 20, a platoon of policemen attempted to clean out Fyzabad but the strike had moved to other parts and the operation had to be aborted. At Point Fortin, on June 21, the police fired on strikers, killing three and wounding four. The strike moved on, closing down San Fernando and Ste. Madeleine, shutting off the power station. At the telephone station, the strike met with police who killed two and wounded eight. Another siege left one policeman dead and four civilians wounded. Yet the strike grew: it closed Waterloo Estate, Wyaby Estate, Woodford Lodge (one dead, two wounded) and received succor from the NWA

call to strike; more police were sent to the area. That evening a warrant for Butler's arrest was issued and a group of policemen traveled to Fyzabad to apprehend him. There they found Butler addressing a large crowd. The police closed in on Butler. He asked that the warrant be read. Lance-Corporal Price tried reading it, but the crowd grew restive. An officer held Butler by the arm and the crowd set on the police, chasing them off. Cpl. King, a plain-clothes officer, tried to arrest Butler. King was one of the most unpopular policemen around and the threatening crowd closed in on him. He ran into a shop and trying to escape, jumped from a high window. His leg was broken in the fall and, helpless, he was set alight by the uncontrollable crowd. That was the real

in Port of Spain where shops closed. At Rio Claro and Dinsley work stopped on the estates; police killed one man. That was June 22, the same day that *HMS Ajax* steamed into Port of Spain. *HMS Exeter* arrived the following day and by July workers were returning to work. On July 6 the *Trinidad Guardian* reported that the strike was over.

While the marines were mopping up, the Governor and the Colonial Secretary tried to appease the masses. A Mediation Committee was set up and public workers were granted an eight-hour day and a new minimum wage. Both officials castigated the employers for their rapacity: "tact and sympathy (would be) a shield far more sure than any forest of bayonets to be planted here," stated the Governor. "Industry has no right to pay dividends at all until it pays a fair wage to labour," added the Colonial Secretary. For this the Governor was recalled to London and forced to resign in December 1937, and the Colonial Secretary was transferred in 1938. The Forster Commission of Enquiry submitted a tough law-and-order report in February 1938. However, the Moyne Commission, which investigated conditions in the whole region, produced a report so damning that its publication was delayed until after the war.

Hold the Fort, for We are Coming! Butler got the ball rolling, but after June 19 he was in hiding, and so he remained until he emerged straight into the arms of the police and two years' incarceration. The man who held, or rather built, the fort in Butler's absence was Adrian Cola Rienzi.

Born Krishna Deonarine, the grandchild of indentured laborers, Rienzi left school at 14. In 1925 he was a solicitor's clerk and the President of the San Fernando branch of Cipriani's TWA. Already this young man took sufficient interest in world politics to be considered by the Governor as having "markedly seditious views." Deonarine was unimpressed. He organized protests, formed a Young Socialist League and became President of the Indian National Party. Frustrated in Trinidad, he changed his name to Adrian Cola Rienzi (fair skinned, he hoped to

Left, a woodcarving of Uriah "Buzz" Butler conveys the ferocity of the union organizer and, right, Adrian Cola Rienzi, who continued Butler's work in a more moderate vein.

pass as Spanish) and migrated to Ireland where he joined the Sinn Fein Movement, and studied jurisprudence. Then on to London where he qualified as a barrister, came under the watchful eyes of the police, and tried unsuccessfully to go to India. Frustrated again, Rienzi returned to Trinidad where he was refused admittance to the Bar until he promised to "not indulge in agitation."

Maintaining links with Butler, he gave advice, and when the strike started he operated as Butler's emissary. After the strike subsided, Rienzi was approached by a deputation of black oil workers who asked his assistance in forming an organization. Presently a group of sugarworkers approached him with the same request. In September and November were registered, respectively, the Oilfield Workers Trade Union (OWTU) and the All Trinidad Sugar Estates and Factory Workers Trade Union (ATSEFWTU). Rienzi was the President-General of both unions. Oil and sugar, African and Indian, had joined hands.

In the north, Rienzi and others organized the Transport and General Workers Union. And there were others: the dockworkers formed a union, as did the building workers and the Public Works workers. By the end of 1939 there were 12 unions, and labor was finding its voice.

All this was in keeping with numerous official recommendations which considered unions to be the best protection against social anarchy. But neither Government nor employers were convinced of that, and the police relentlessly harrassed the unionists. Albert Gomes, lecturing as a trade unionist to an absent crowd at Woodford Square, related an experience: "when we spoke to the trees and grass in the Square we were sure of an audience of one — the security officer in plain clothes... lurking furtively behind some tree."

When Butler was released from prison in May 1939, he was given a hero's welcome and an executive post as General Organizer in the OWTU. Butler's combative messianism and Rienzi's organizational discipline didn't mix, however. And when Butler began urging workers to go on strike in defiance of Executive decisions, he was expelled from the union. He took with him much support and continued his agitation. Four months later he was once again arrested for sedition. This time they kept him behind bars for the duration of the war. Rienzi, for his part, continued working with the trade unions until 1944 when he withdrew from the movement, fulfilling his own prophecy: "individuals are subordinate to the movement, would play their role, then take their exit, to be succeeded by others; but the movement itself goes on."

Working for the Yankee Dollar: The years of World War II, coming on the heels of the Butler riots, marked the end of one era and the birth of another. The Government locked up Butler and prohibited Carnival in its war effort. The people were skeptical. "This war with England and Germany, going to mean more starvation and misery," sang the Growling Tiger: "But I going plant provision and fix me affairs, and the white people could fight for a thousand years." He couldn't have been more wrong. For Churchill had leased parts of the West Indies to the United States in return for 50 old

Paria with submarines. But most importantly the Americans provided well-paid jobs for tens of thousands, and in Trinidad life changed. The Yanks paid high wages, and the people lost their servility. The Americans labored bareback, swore, got drunk and brawled, and white respectability crumbled; nightclubs and calypsonians prospered, and their music grew more risqué. Nor was it all hunky dory: the racist arrogance of the American soldiers irritated the population, and the defection of many women to the Yanks rubbed salt in the wound.

Glory Days: VE Day arrived on May 6, 1945,

destroyers. In Trinidad, the Americans chose the North West peninsula (Chaguaramas) and the Valencia district (Waller Field), and a reluctant Governor Young was eased out of office. The world of a small colony shifted orbit.

In his memoirs, calypsonian Raymond Quevedo, also known as Atilla the Hun, recounts; "We had been seeing them for months past around Macqueripe, Chaguaramas and Scotland Bay. They had been depth-testing, mapping, measuring, surveying and engineering. But now they had arrived officially." Huge military bases were built where the Americans tested their carriers and airplanes, formed their Atlantic convoys, and filtered the movement of Latin Americans to Spain and the United States. In response, the Germans infested the Gulf of

and music filled the streets of Port of Spain. But now there was a new sound. Formerly, until Carnival was prohibited in 1941, the bands tramped the streets to the thumping of bamboo pipes. Tamboo bamboo these bands were called, and they'd come into being after drums were outlawed in the 19th Century. On VE Day however, there was a ringing, clanging, booming melody being hammered on metal pans: out of the slums of eastern Port of Spain, the steel band had emerged!

Andrew Beddoe and Winston 'Spree' Simon of John John Band (now Carib Tokyo); 'Fisheye' Olivierre and Neville Jules of Hell Yard Band (now Catelli All Stars); Ellie Manette of Oval Boys (now Trintoc Invaders); these and a host of others had collectively fashioned a new music during the war years. And in the 1940s and 1950s the steel band movement grew, gaining important patrons such as Beryl McBurnie, Canon Farquhar and Lennox Pierre, and new innovators such as Bertie Marshall, Anthony Williams and Rudolph Charles. But those years of the steel band's adolescence were difficult ones. The movement was pioneered by lower-class men, direct descendants of the *jamets* of the 1880s, who faced all the hostility of respectable society. "Steel-band fanaticism is a savage and bestial cult and it must be completely wiped out," wrote one correspondent to the *Trinidad*

and their continuous practice (no seasonal bands, these) welded them into tightly-knit units: Desperadoes, Casablanca, Invaders, Destination Tokyo, Renegades, Red Army. And when bands met, a hell of bottles, stones, machetes and knives broke loose.

Steel band warfare continued sporadically until as late as 1960, but a winding down of the violence began in 1950 when Invaders and Casablanca ended their feud, the T&T Steel band Association was formed, and the Spree Simon Benefit Performance, attended by the Governor, was mounted. The following year a

Guardian, and the police backed up this attitude with batons, staging regular forays to disperse practicing steel bands.

Nor were the steel band men angels. Wilfred Harrison, a stalwart from the early days, recalls that "they were difficult boys and I renamed the band 'Desperadoes'...they were famous for their 'action.' The steel band, which then numbered about 20, was supported by numerous strong robust dangerous men who were respected in the community." They had inherited a violent rivalry from the *kalenda* (stick-fighting) days

Left, mounted police watches over a public gathering and, right, pre-fab houses being assembled on an American base.

tour was organized by the Association, and the Trinidad All Steel Percussion Orchestra performed at the Festival of Britain. "If you let this movement die," cautioned a recently returned academic, "then you drive a nail in the coffin of our aspirations." The speaker was Dr. Eric Williams.

The cultural efflorescence of the early 1930s preceded the labor riots of 1937. Similarly the nationalist movement of the late 1950s was led by an artistic exuberance of which steel band was only a part. There was also the growing confidence and professionalism of the calypso, as practiced by such men as Atilla the Hun, the Roaring Lion, King Radio, the Mighty Spoiler and Lord Kitchener. Beryl McBurnie opened the Little Carib Theatre for folk dance performances, and in literature Samuel Selvon and V.S. Naipaul, though abroad, immortalized the language and characters of Trinidad, while Edgar Mittelholzer, in Trinidad, explored their human comedy.

Birth of Parliamentary Politics: In 1946 and 1950, the first two rowdy elections were held under universal suffrage, and all of Trinidad's anarchic individualism came to the fore. Thus in 1950, 141 candidates vied for 18 seats. Ninety were without a party. It was the heyday of the independent politician, men subject to no party discipline or program, and who offered the moon to an ignorant electorate, from higher pensions to more scholarships, cleaner water to a 'better' Carnival. One vowed to abolish dog licenses while another promised to "demobilize unemployment."

These rum-and-roti politicians exploited every possible division of race, class and culture to capture votes: Butler and Rojas relied on the black trade union block; Victor Bryan on the eastern peasants; the Sinnanan brothers wooed the Indians; and Bhadase Maraj manipulated 'his' Hindu Maha Sabha; Norman Tang remained absolutely inscrutable so as to offend no one and Ajodhasingh was renowned as being a mystic masseur. Some candidates weren't above using obeah (witchcraft) in their causes. Much of the to do of these first two elections was reported by a journalist, Seepersad Naipaul, who had married into a well-known political family, the Capildeos. Years after, Seepersad's son, Vidiadhar, would relive his childhood memories to produce two brilliant satirical novels on the elections: *The Mystic Masseur* and *The Suffrage of Elvira.*

There was a left-wing United Front (1946) and a Caribbean Socialist Party (1950), but both fared badly. All eyes focussed on two men: Butler and Albert Gomes. Butler, released from gaol in 1945, challenged Gomes in his St. Ann's seat in 1946 and lost. On the industrial warpath again, Butler's popularity rose amongst workers, and he won in the south in 1950, when his coalition party held more seats in the Legislative Council than any other. Yet none of the Butlerites were nominated by the Governor onto the Executive Council. "Political blasphemy," accused Butler to no avail. The man who held the limelight was Albert Gomes.

Albert Gomes, the leader of *The Beacon* group in the early 1930s, was a Portuguese of immense girth and over 200 lbs in weight. After the 1937 riots he, along with Quintin O'Connor, built the Federated Workers Union, and went into politics as a City Counsellor. In that forum he bitterly attacked the colonial Government and Cipriani, and defended the rights of the common people. He supported the steel bands men, the calypsonians, the Shouter Baptists and many other plebeians who felt the heavy hand of the Government. One of his famous tactics was to make a scene in the Council meeting until he had to be ejected. When the police came to take him away, he prostrated himself on the floor from where he, all 15 stone, would have to be carried. "But the Captain (Cipriani) had reckoned without a technicality... The Standing Orders...did not provide against my immediate return once I had been evicted," Gomes gleefully recalls. "I, therefore, promptly returned."

When Gomes was elected to the Legislative Council and nominated to the Executive Council in 1946, his radicalism evaporated and he broke with his erstwhile comrades. "In different positions," he explained, "we were bound to assert different claims." In 1950 he was elected again, and this time was nominated to be Minister of Labour, Commerce and Industry. He was easily pulled over to the side of the Government, for the Constitution provided for only a partly responsible cabinet system: five elected representatives were put in charge of ministries at the Governor's discretion. There, in that Executive Council dominated by Britain's representative, Gomes spent his time implementing a policy of "industrialization by invitation" by restraining union demands and encouraging foreign investment. "O what a awful thing," sang the Roaring Lion, "to see Gomes in a lion skin." And although he contested the 1956 and 1961 elections, Gomes, like Butler, found himself swimming against the nationalist current, doomed to failure.

Williams the Conqueror Returns: The pace of life quickened in 1956. In the south, George Weekes, a young trade unionist, was elected President of the key Pointe-à-Pierre branch of the Oilfield Workers Trade Union. The British oil company, Trinidad Leaseholds Ltd., was bought by the American Texaco. "Money start to pass, people start to bawl," sang a new calypsonian. "Pointe-à-Pierre sell the workmen and all." The singer, using the sobriquet Mighty Sparrow, won both the Calypso King and the Road March competitions that year with a calypso titled "Jean and Dinah." He instantly became the hero of the black working class, second only to another man, Eric Williams, who also made his debut in 1956 but on the political stage.

Eric Williams was born in 1911 to a declin-

injury which would eventually render him close to deaf. In 1932 Williams left for Oxford to read History, determined to follow in the footsteps of some of the teachers whom he admired. One of his tutors at college, C.L.R. James, had gone to England a few months earlier, hoping to make his way as a writer. He stayed with a Trinidadian cricketer, Learie Constantine, and worked as a cricket correspondent. He soon became well-known as a Trotskyist and Pan Africanist speaker. He was to produce several important books, including *A History of Negro Revolt*, *Minty Alley*, *The Life of Cipriani*, *World Revolution* and *The Black Jacobins*.

Williams, meanwhile, pursued his academic career single-mindedly, studying throughout the "excessively long vacations," and graduating with First Class Honours. The chairman of the

Campaigning in Woodford Square, 1956

ing lower middle-class family ("Family fortuncs were reflected in the descent from the water closet to the cesspit.") Yet they were ambitious, and little Eric was rigorously drilled to win whichever scholarships were for the taking. At Tranquillity Primary School he won the Government Exhibition which funded him through five years at the Queen's Royal College. Then, on his second try, he won the House Scholarship which took him through until, on his third try, he won the Island Scholarship in 1931. By then, as a footballer, he had already suffered the ear

Left, soldiers enjoying the perks of the Yankee dollar and, right, Eric Williams addresses a class at the University of Woodford Square in 1956.

board of examiners asked about his interest in colonial history and Williams replied that he could not see the value of study unless there was that connection with the environment. Two years were wasted trying for an All Souls Fellowship at Oxford, and then Williams decided to undertake a research degree in history. The topic he chose, on James' advice, was the economic factors underlying the abolition of slavery. In 1939 Williams went to the United States to take up a post at Howard University. James, who had arrived in America the previous year, was engaged in leftist politics.

In America, Williams expanded his doctoral thesis into the book, *Capitalism and Slavery*. A research grant allowed him some Caribbean travel, out of which came the radical book *The*

Negro in the Caribbean. He began working part-time with the Washington based Anglo-American Commission, an organization set up by the two countries to encourage Caribbean cooperation, in the early 1940s and received his full-time appointment in 1944. He maintained his university connections, however, and continued giving guest lectures. In 1948 he was put in charge of the Commission's research—a post tenured in Port of Spain, Trinidad. He severed his ties with Howard University and returned home.

University of Woodford Square: Williams had always been interested in education. He submitted, after discussions with John Dewey, a memorandum on the proposed West Indian University to the Committee on Higher Education. But this interest really made an impact

in the World," drew ever larger crowds which spilled out of Public Library into Woodford Square. There they heard the words of the "Doctor" over a loudspeaker, and were mesmerized by his eloquence, uplifted by his scholarship, and fired by his passion. And the black masses, always admirers of education (as represented by a facility for rhetoric) and insolence, fell in love.

The first months of 1955 were quiet. The Political Education Group, a nucleus of committed supporters, had secretly crystallized around Williams to promote his entry into politics, and a People's Education Movement was formed from the teachers' association to sponsor his lectures. On June 21, Eric Williams' contract with the Caribbean Commission expired and was not renewed by the Commission. For hours that evening he told the public of the

after he'd been transferred to Port of Spain, and it was in the sphere of adult education. He started the *Caribbean Historical Review*, wrote a weekly series on Caribbean history in the *Trinidad Guardian*, and gave public lectures in the early 1950s, at the Trinidad Public Library facing Woodford Square. Under the auspices of the progressive Teachers Educational and Cultural Association, Williams lectured on a wide variety of topics: West Indian history, the sugar industry, the development of small scale farming, education in the Caribbean, John Locke, Rousseau, Toussaint L'Ouverture, Carlyle, Aristotle. But the lectures were always variations on a single theme: "the defense of the national interests against colonialism." And Williams, now dubbed the "Third Brightest Man

injustice of his dismissal: "I was fundamentally, legally, morally, intellectually right." De Wilton Rogers, one of the teachers closest to the Doctor, recalls that night: "Regional Secretaries, activists, voluntary workers, members of the Women's Council, the marshalling of intellect, of brain and brawn, the Artisan class, the shoemaker, the tailor, the apprentice, the journeyman, the housewife... they were there, and the domestics by their thousands and the laboring class and the band-leaders and steel banders and metal workers were there on the grand opening night of the longest day of the year, 1955." There Williams vowed, "I am going to let down my bucket where I am, right here with you in the British West Indies." A new series of lectures was started, and so was founded a new politics based on public education and nationalism. A speech on Constitutional Reform ended with a call to sign a petition: within weeks the embryonic party had collected almost 28,000 signatures. The cocky self-assurance of a brilliant academic had captured the black middle class and proletariat. "Now that I have resigned my position at Howard University in the USA," the Doctor promised them, "the only university in which I shall lecture in future is the University of Woodford Square and its several branches throughout the length and breadth of Trinidad and Tobago." "Master! Giant!" shouted the people.

In April 1955, elections were postponed from September 1955 for one year. On Jan. 15, 1956 the Inaugural Conference of the People's National Movement (PNM) was held. And in

Hindus, the trade unionists, and the independent politicians, the newspapers, and the Roman Catholic Church, deciding, "to eat the whole hog," as one journalist put it, "or be violently anti-pork."

The PNM's greatest threat, however, was the People's Democratic Party (PDP) led by Bhadase Maraj. Thought by many to be little short of a gangster, Maraj was nevertheless the President of the Maha Sabha, an orthodox Hindu association, and leader of the sugarworkers' union. He was viewed by rural Indians as their equivalent of Williams: a man whose achievements had elevated the entire ethnic group. And Maraj, accustomed to racial politics, categorized the PNM as "Pure Negro Men." Williams used a divide and conquer strategy against the PDP: he wooed the Muslim Indians; labeled the PDP

September 1956 elections took place.

There were independent politicians, but only 39 of them this time. Then there were seven parties. And although there were few differences between their programs, the parties all varied in style and tone, and all came to be seen as representing different social groups. The PNM, emphasized morality and discipline, intelligence, nationalism and modernity, and was considered by all to be a "black people's party," versus the rest. And the PNM, riding a wave of black nationalism, attacked the French Creoles, the

Left, the first T&T Cabinet of 1962 (Eric Williams is 3rd from left in front) and, right, young girls at the festivities welcoming Queen Elizabeth in 1983.

a racialist party akin to the Hindu Maha Sabha in India, thus alienating Muslim, Christian Indians and reformist Hindus from it; and attacked it as a Brahmin (high caste) party linked to big business.

The results of the elections surprised everyone familiar with Trinidad's politics. The PNM, an organized political party, won the majority of elective seats, 13 out of 24: from the polling results it seemed that even some of the French Creoles had voted PNM. The PDP won five, the Butler Party two, the TLP two, and the independents two. Many looked on it as "Trinidad redeeming itself," and the Governor decided to give the winning party a working majority: the Legislative Council also contained four nominated members and two officials; the

PNM was allowed to nominate two, and the rest were chosen from people not hostile to the party. A Constitution which Williams had inveighed against was invoked to give the PNM a chance to effectively govern. And the black intellectuals came to power, prompting the Mighty Sparrow to sing:

Well the way how things shaping up.
All this nigger business go stop.
I tell you, soon in the West Indies
It's please, Mister Nigger, please.

Survival of the Fittest: The years leading to independence in 1962 were acrimonious ones for the country. Peace offerings were made to the French Creoles by the PNM, who nominated two white members to the Legislative Council, and the trade unions were conspicuously ig-

arms and turned away, saying "industrial democracy is based on the right of workers to withhold their labor by way of strike, even if the community is thrown into turmoil." Britain was criticized for giving Chaguaramas to the Americans, and Williams demanded it returned to Trinidad, calling the lease "a callous anachronism." A demonstration was organized for April 22, 1960. The rain fell bucket-a-drop, but it couldn't deter the thousands who marched behind the Doctor.

Meanwhile, the DLP leadership had slipped from an ailing Maraj to Dr. Rudranath Capildeo. As a youth Capildeo was frail, sensitive and volatile, tormented by his family life. Although hopeless in English, unlike his cousin Vidiadhar, the boy was bright. In 1938 he won the Island Scholarship and left to study

nored. Not just an olive branch, this was part of the Government's continuation of Gomes' industrialization by importing foreign capital. Williams wooed the Indians as well as the Creoles but with little success. The whites and the Indians came together to form the Democratic Labour Party (DLP) which bitterly and without respite attacked the Government. The West Indies Federation, set up in 1957, held its elections in 1958. The DLP won six seats, the PNM four, and political tone sank to an even lower level. Williams was furious. C.L.R. James was invited to Trinidad and put in charge of *The Nation*, the PNM organ, and the nationalist struggle intensified. A strike in the oil industry in 1960 had businessmen clamoring for Government intervention. Williams folded his

medicine the following year. His career in England was also marked by loneliness and uncertainty, but in 1941 he could graduate with First Class Honours in Mathematics and Physics, and in 1944 was elected President of the Men's Union. In 1945 he returned home to teach. Soon however, he fell afoul of the Director of Education and Capildeo packed his bags and returned to England. By 1950 he had his Doctorate and was a Lecturer at the University of London. In the next few years he studied law, visited Trinidad, and took up a post as the principal of the Trinidad Polytechnic under the PNM government. And in March, 1960, he accepted the job of leader of the DLP. "Trinidad's Most Educated Man" had come to match knowledge with "The Third Brightest Man in the World." His astonishing suggestion that a tunnel be blasted through the Northern Range earned Capildeo another name, however: "The Mad Scientist." Capildeo wilted under the mockery; his health failed and he fled to England. There he rediscovered God through a mystical experience and returned to Trinidad some months before the 1961 elections.

The DLP began campaigning against a blistering PNM attack. Trade unions demonstrated for the PNM, and the *Trinidad Guardian* complained of the "hooligans." Williams turned a blind eye: "March where the hell you like," he said. They thought he meant "mash up what the hell you like." PNM supporters went on a rampage, looting Indian and French Creole homes and businesses, slashing car tires, breaking up DLP meetings. Capildeo

bone of contention. The Jamaicans were unenthusiastic about the idea of an economic and political alliance of 10 British islands, unwilling to financially assist the smaller islands. They were further repelled by Trinidad's proposals for a highly centralized Federal Government: the capital site was to be in Trinidad; the Federal Prime Minister, Grantley Adams, was Barbadian. A Jamaican referendum in September 1961 decided that the island would no longer participate in any Federation and would move towards independence alone. Hearing this news, Williams refused to saddle his country with the poorer islands. He ignored his objectors and decided that "one from ten leaves nought." Trinidad and Tobago would also move to independence alone. It was a bitter defeat for Pan-Caribbean idealists. "Federation boil down to

called for "bloodshed and riot, revolution or civil disobedience." On October 15 he told a large crowd to "arm yourselves with weapons in order to take over this country." His French Creole supporters quietly withdrew. Violence erupted in the east; one man was killed and a state of emergency declared. In December 1961, with the country teetering on the brink of a racial war, elections were held. The PNM won 20 out of 30 seats. Even Tobago turned to the PNM.

The West Indics Federation became the next

Left, a military regiment salutes the national flag of the Republic of Trinidad and Tobago, right.

simply this," rhymed the Mighty Sparrow: "Is dog eat dog and survival of the fittest."

Initially, the move to independence saw the PNM and the DLP still at each other's throats. The PNM drafted an independence constitution, but the DLP were critical; they wanted certain safeguards against political interference with the Elections Commission and the Judiciary. Williams turned a deaf ear. Tensions mounted again in the country. Then, at the last moment, the PNM conceded to many of the opposition's demands. Everyone heaved a sigh of relief, and at midnight, Aug. 31, 1962, the Union Jack was lowered for the last time in 165 years: Trinidad and Tobago had become a sovereign state, fully equal in the community of nations.

FORGED FROM THE LOVE OF LIBERTY

After independence, the DLP accepted its fate of permanent opposition; Capildeo, while still leader of the party, returned to his post at London University. Williams discarded the University of Woodford Square, and parliamentary politics declined.

The "industrialisation by invitation" strategy followed by the PNM entailed restraining trade unions, and encouraging foreign investment. Williams had invoked a militant nationalism amongst the black working class before the 1961 elections, but after 1962 these same people decided to translate independence into terms

dustrial Stabilisation Act (ISA), which made striking virtually illegal, was rushed through Parliament in 24 hours. It was all unnecessary: the following year the PNM won the general elections once again, and all candidates from the newly formed Workers & Farmers Party, including C.L.R. James, George Weekes, and Basdeo Panday, lost their deposits.

Development still seemed to elude Trinidad and Tobago. The favored manufacturing sector didn't perform as expected, unemployment rose, oil prices stagnated, and foreign capital was not coming in as fast as profits were being exported.

meaningful to them. A rash of strikes against foreign-owned companies prompted the government to set up a Commission of Enquiry into Subversive Activities in 1963. In 1964 the Minister of Finance observed "a developing strike consciousness" which threatened the confidence of investors. In 1965 sugarworkers went on strike, against the orders of their leader, Bhadase Maraj. They appealed to the sympathetic leader of the OWTU, George Weekes, for assistance. A confrontation within the trade union movement loomed, and the Government acted fast. The Subversive Activities Commission released its report; a state of emergency was declared in the sugar areas. C.L.R. James, who was in Trinidad to report on a cricket match, was placed under house arrest; and the In-

Independence made the poor poorer and the rich richer. The poorest 20 percent received 3.4 percent of the total wealth in 1957 and 2.2 percent in 1970; the wealthiest 10 percent increased their share from 33.3 percent to 37.8 percent in the same period. Fourteen years of PNM rule had left the 'massas' still in control of the wealth. Youths who had benefitted from the PNM's expansion of secondary education were joining a saturated job market by 1968. The clerical jobs for which they had been trained were not available to blacks, however. "We sit on pavements dreaming our dreams," wrote the young poet Roger McTair in 1965, "trying to invoke visions." By 1969 a vision of the black millennium had begun to appear for dozens of small organizations.

In April 1969 transport workers downed tools in contravention of the law. A confederation of radical groups, the National Joint Action Committee (NJAC), joined the fight. The police moved in and the union was defeated. But the workers had flexed their muscles. Three man-days lost in strikes in 1967 grew to 17,568 in 1968, 19,972 in 1969, and 99,600 in 1970.

Black Power: On Carnival Monday 1970, there appeared on the streets masquerade bands, which almost seemed to be demonstrations, portraying topics such as The Truth About

of Canada to scuffle again. Then they went to the Roman Catholic Cathedral on Independence Square. Inside the Cathedral, the demonstraters made speeches from the pulpit, and draped the statues in black. After an hour they left to tramp around the city some more, denouncing the exploiters. That day cabinet met in emergency session and on the following morning the leaders of the procession were arrested. Taken to court and refused bail, the protestors were supported by a crowd of thousands chanting "power!"

The leaders were released from gaol on

Blacks, King Sugar, and 1001 White Devils. The more sensitive noses smelled a storm, and the PNM thought to formulate a program "to achieve dignity and self-respect for the numerically dominant groups."

On the anniversary of an earlier protest against racial discrimination in Canada, the Sir George Williams University incident, NJAC took 200 marchers into Port of Spain where they tramped around for hours. They halted at the Canadian High Commission and scuffled with the police, then moved on to the Royal Bank

Left, the President's house in Port of Spain and, right, the Oilfield Workers' Trade Union building in Fyzabad with its statue of Buzz Butler.

March 4, and a disheveled generation took to the streets, marching into Shanty Town, a ghetto of cardboard and tin shacks. The Movement swelled to over 10,000 and several black power groups addressed the crowd. The following day, when Geddes Granger, one of the leaders, came up for trial for behaving without decorum near a place of worship, a massive crowd assembled. Suddenly people were running everywhere and batons were swinging. Into downtown Port of Spain the surging crowd went.

Throughout the next weeks, the Black Power Movement trudged all over the country during daylight. The Movement held enthusiastic meetings at Woodford Square, renaming it "The People's Parliament." At night, however, the Movement showed its teeth; businesses and banks were bombed.

Under pressure, the government offered concessions: unemployment relief, small businesses, a Commission of Enquiry into Racial Discrimination. "We do not want crumbs," replied the Movement: "we want the whole bread." Then the steel band movement joined the ranks. Tobago sponsored a rally, and the Deputy Prime Minister, A.N.R. Robinson, a Tobagonian, resigned from Cabinet. "The law will have to take its course," announced Williams, and the police swung into action. When the police shot Basil Davis, a young Black Power activist, the Movement brought 60,000 people to his funeral. "By God we will fight fire with fire," declared Geddes Granger: "This is war." The Movement identified Williams with the "exploiters."

The island-wide unrest culminated in a then set out for the city. The Coast Guard had a different idea: from their boats they shelled the road and blocked the rebels' passage with landslides. Some took to the hills, most remained at the army camp. Meanwhile, in Port of Spain, there was some burning and looting. One man was killed in clashes with the police, and a dusk-to-dawn curfew was imposed. The rebel soldiers eventually surrendered to the police. When everything subsided, the gaol was crammed with 87 soldiers and 54 militants.

After that, Black Power, a movement that contained much of the theatrical, lapsed into cultural concerns: African names and dashikis and pyjama suits in public; Afro hairstyles and an emphatic brogue; redemption songs from a new breed of political calypsonians, and musical extravaganzas. Even Eric Williams occasionally

series of wildcat strikes. Oilfield Workers, postal workers, water and sewerage workers, civil servants, government workers, all were being swept along by the Movement. On April 19 the sugarworkers walked off the job, and planned to march into Port of Spain on April 21. As in 1965, they called on George Weekes of the OWTU for assistance. Transport workers in another radical union planned a demonstration, also for April 21.

On April 20 a state of emergency was declared, and in the wee hours the NJAC leaders were arrested. Sugarworkers were routed by the police, and the Regiment was called out. A section of the soldiers, led by Lt. Raffique Shah and Lt. Rex Lassalle, rebelled and took over the army camp at Teteron. A convoy of the rebels surrendered his jacket-and-tie in favor of hot shirts and colorful scarves. But the movement had succeeded in politicizing a generation and removing the grossest forms of racial prejudice, especially in employment.

Unconventional Politics: The Public Order Bill was introduced by Attorney-General Karl Hudson-Phillips on Aug. 7, 1970. A draconian piece of legislation, it prohibited marches and public meetings, unless authorized by the police, unlawful oathtaking, inciting racial hatred and subversion. The Bill also gave the police wide and arbitrary powers of search and entry, and "suspected persons" could be restricted in their movements. Only the Catholic Church endorsed it, and the Bill was withdrawn. Hudson-Phillips offered his resignation, but Williams didn't accept it. Chalkdust, a school teacher calypsonian, echoed public sentiment when he sang, "Ah 'fraid, Karl." Most of the Bill's provisions, however, were eventually slipped into the statute book piece by inconspicuous piece.

But that was only one part of the confusion surrounding the elections which were due in 1971. A.N.R. Robinson, the PNM renegade, took to wearing gold chains and Nehru shirts, and formed the Action Committee of Dedicated Citizens (ACDC). The ACDC formed a merger with the DLP, now led by Vernon Jamadar. Bhadase Maraj protested: he should be the one to replace Capildeo. So he formed a new party, calling it the Democratic Liberation Party, to have an identical acronym.

Then there were the groups advocating "unconventional politics" and calling for a boycott

thodox Communist. URO's vital contribution to the times was to spearhead a "don't vote" campaign. Then there was the Tapia House Movement, a collection of intellectuals led by Dr. Lloyd Best. Often capable of a witty turn of phrase, Best nevertheless aroused no public enthusiasm.

As the elections approached, the "no vote" campaign won a last minute convert in the form of A.N.R. Robinson. The ACDC/DLP merger collapsed, and both parties called on supporters to join the boycott. As a result only the PNM, Bhadase Maraj's DLP (which offered no program), and an obscure African National Congress participated in the 1971 elections. The PNM, supported by 28 percent of the electorate, won all 36 seats. Those who questioned the results, mostly OWTU and NJAC leaders, were

of the elections. The first of these was NJAC. But NJAC's brand of revolutionary politics became identified in the public mind with anarchism and violence and tiring marches in the hot sun. Left of NJAC's radical black nationalism stood the Union of Revolutionary Organisations. This confederation contained a fluctuating membership mostly of NJAC renegades, some of whom Lloyd Best described as jumping "from the frying pan into the frying pan." Consequently, its tone varied at times from pink to scarlet, from vaguely left to or-

Left, a stream of Black Power demonstrators crossing the flyover into Port of Spain and, right, protestors chant slogans downtown.

detained under a new state of emergency. And a Commission of Enquiry was set up to look into Constitutional Reform.

Peace, Bread and Justice: On Sept. 29, 1973, at the 15th Annual Convention of the PNM, Eric Williams shocked everyone by announcing his decision to retire. He told the party to choose a new leader by December 31, claiming weariness, his daughter's pleas, and his desire to return to academic research. Two contenders offered themselves for the post: Karl Hudson-Phillips and Kamalludin Mohammed. Hudson-Phillips was the more popular. The decision was to be made on December 2. Instead, that meeting was manipulated into asking Williams to change his mind. He did so, and Hudson-Phillips was left with nowhere to go. He never

forgave Williams for the jilt.

Bhadase Sagan Maraj died in October 1971. An unlettered, violent man, he had made mischief amongst the Indian community for 25 years. As Leader of the Opposition, he made undercover deals with the PNM and vilified his own party. As President of the sugarworkers' union, he fêted with the bosses and intimidated workers who tried to go on strike. Maraj was given to displaying guns in public and flashing large rolls of dollars. So it was that when this picaresque, dangerous man died, everyone knew that big changes were in the air.

In the vacuum created by Maraj's demise three men came to the fore: Basdeo Panday, George Weekes and Raffique Shah. George Weekes was born in 1921 in the northern village of Toco to a village schoolmaster. He traveled widely when he was an officer in the Caribbean Regiment, and was influenced by Social Democrats. Returning to Trinidad, he worked in oil and became a member of Butler's union. Eventually he joined the OWTU, however, and successfully led a group of 'rebels' to remove John Rojas. In those days Weekes was a PNM supporter, but by 1966 he had become involved with C.L.R. James and the Workers & Farmers Party. Shortly before the elections that year he persuaded a young barrister, Basdeo Panday, to abandon his doctoral scholarship and join the party. Panday had recently returned from England where he'd studied drama, then law, then politics.

After losing the elections, Weekes continued as the militant leader of the OWTU, and Panday put up his shingle. He advised several unions on legal matters and after Bhadase Maraj's death, was asked to accept the presidency of the sugarworkers' union. The old executive wanted a respectable figurehead for the union. "I became the reluctant bride," recalls Panday. He immediately proceeded to undercut the old executive. In January 1974 he called a strike; the executive called it off; the workers followed Panday.

Raffique Shah had been one of the leaders of the 1970 mutiny. Sentenced to 20 years' imprisonment, he appealed and was set free in 1971 on grounds that he had not received a fair trial. In 1972 the new Islandwide Cane Farmers Trade Union needed a leader, someone well-known who could unite the scattered cane farmers against the old farmers' association identified with the PNM. ICFTU's talent scouts eventually settled for Raffique Shah and Winston Lennard. By 1974 ICFTU had the support of the cane farmers and was fighting for

recognition from sugar producers. Panday was simultaneously fighting for wage increases for sugarworkers. And Weekes was fighting Texaco for wage increases. Despite some hostility between Shah and Panday, a meeting between the three unions came up with a proposed rally. The meeting ended and members were walking out when Basdeo Panday suggested they call the rally a United Labour Front.

Over 30,000 turned up to hear the militant words of the trade union leaders who all vowed to continue their struggles. The ULF launched a campaign of public meetings. A religious march for bread, peace and justice was planned for Tuesday, March 18. The day arrived, thousands came, and the procession was led by religious men and the trade unionists. The police had a different idea: they told the marchers to disperse, and immediately clouded the air with tear gas before wading into the panic-stricken crowd, swinging truncheons. All the leaders were arrested for participating in an illegal march, and the day went down in history as Bloody Tuesday.

But the ULF couldn't be stopped so easily. On Jan. 4, 1976 a Conference of Shop Stewards of the four unions (oil workers, sugarworkers, cane farmers and transport workers) passed a resolution: "Be it resolved that the ULF, while not sacrificing the unity it represents, takes all necessary steps to bring into being with all speed a party of the working class...." Thus came together as motley a collection of leftists, radicals, trade unionists, and black nationalists as can be imagined, all under the leadership of Basdeo Panday.

Elections 1976: There were 12 parties and six independents. Many of them merely provided comic relief. Dr. Ivan Perot offered himself as a man "younger and better looking" than Dr. Williams; the two DLPs squabbled shamelessly and bitterly. The main challengers to the PNM were the ULF, A.N.R. Robinson's DAC, and Lloyd Best's Tapia House Movement. The first was vaguely socialist, but only vaguely. The PNM branded them as Communists who would confiscate people's land, while Lloyd Best thought they were only the old DLP Indian party in new guise. The grain of truth was that although the ULF was a sort of holding company for many small left groups, it had little black support. A ULF/DAC merger aimed at removing this taint was scuttled at the last minute by the mercurial Robinson. Tapia and the DAC were different from the PNM only insofar as they promised to do the job better, with less corruption, and, as the results showed, with less public support.

The surprise came from Williams. He campaigned against his party and called five PNM candidates "millstones" with a total lack of awareness. He became the PNM's most severe critic, stealing much of the other parties' thunder. "Heads will roll," promised Williams. Lloyd Best thought that the bottom had dropped out of the 1956 bucket; Robinson thought that the party was over. Williams just laughed: he was already planning for the 1981 elections. And a Carnival atmosphere pervaded the crowds who moved from meeting to meeting.

The campaign had little violence, but polling was low and many, perhaps most, voters fell back into the racial voting patterns of the 1960s. The ULF won 10 seats, the PNM won 24, and the DAC won the two Tobago seats.

Disunited Labour Front: According to Hector McLean, PNM Minister, his party's 20 years of success was because "the other side too stupid. We are winning by default." The ULF, after elec-

called, languished in its beautiful, idyllic, neglected state, lacking in social amenities. Even administrative facilities were absent, and to get land titles, birth and death certificates, planning approval, etc., Tobagonians had to go to Port of Spain. During this time Tobago passed through a Commissioner for Tobago Affairs, a Permanent Secretary, a non-resident Minister for Tobago Affairs, and a resident Minister. By 1976 Tobagonians had grown to resent their step-sister status, and, unencumbered by racial considerations, they voted the PNM out.

The DAC victory in Tobago annoyed Williams; he blamed it on a desire of seccession. "If you want to go, go," he fumed, "whatever used to be said in the past, we don't live in any world of true eternal love. The greatest thing today is the divorce celebration."

tions, made a desperate attempt to prove him correct. Panday was voted out as leader of the party by the Central Committee and Shah put in his place. The reins of the party changed hands several times in the next few months, and the *Trinidad Guardian* asked, "are we to resign ourselves to having a new Leader of the Opposition every morning?" For a while there were even two ULFs. But Panday had always been the main vote catcher, and when the dust cleared he emerged as the leader of the ULF and the Leader of the Opposition.

Tobago Breaks Away: Four years after 1961, Tobago was considered a PNM stronghold, and indeed, the 1956 Government showed an interest in the sister island. For the next 15 years, however, Crusoe's Isle, as Tobago came to be

In 1957 Williams had felt a need to "insist on the development of Tobago virtually as a self-contained unit." Robinson quoted him in order to table a motion in Parliament "that all proper and necessary steps be taken to accord to the people of Tobago internal self-government in 1977." New laws were drafted and eventually passed, despite Opposition complaints, to provide for a Tobago House of Assembly which would replace the County Council. In the interval, the PNM won a large majority in the County Council elections, and they expected to control the House of Assembly. As such, the powers granted the House were wider than the County Council's had been, although narrower than Robinson's proposals. The Assembly elections, held in November 1980 were contested with enthusiasm. The DAC took eight seats, the PNM four, and the DAC House of Assembly and central government settled down to wrangle over financial matters.

Money No Problem: It was the best of times, it was the worst of times. In 1974 the oil-exporting cartel, OPEC, hiked up the price of oil to astronomical heights. Trinidad and Tobago's economy ballooned: the visible balance of trade changed from a deficit of TT$188,638 in 1973 to a surplus of TT$387,872 in 1974 and TT$2,158,368 in the peak year of 1980. Over 90 percent came from petroleum exports, production of which was in the hands of U.S. companies. Through taxation the government coffers filled up, and in 1977 Eric Williams announced that "money is no problem."

The Government invested lavishly in many costly and ambitious projects. Wages increased, inflation increased, public and private expenditure increased, import bills increased, and millionaires were made overnight as oil money lubricated a freewheeling economy. Every street had its chicken and chip outlet, every home a video; no road without its traffic jam, no big shot without his house in Miami. On the other hand, productivity fell, agriculture disappeared, and inefficiency and corruption clogged the arteries of society. The massive Special Works Program for the unemployed burgeoned into the flaccid Development and Environment Works Division. Trinidad plunged into an obscene and philistine materialism. "Check out their house, and look," lamented Derek Walcott, "you bust your brain before you find a book." By 1980 social commentators were complaining, from their TT$500,000 homes, that the oil boom was the worst thing ever to have happened to Trinidad and Tobago.

All of this was not lost on the Doc, however. For although he was an arrogant man who turned off his hearing aid at the first sound of an opposing voice, he knew of his contribution to the mess. Intolerant of criticism, over the years he'd surrounded himself with mediocrities whom he despised. Black Power shook him and he'd thought to resign. The oil boom offered a solution to the underdevelopment which seemed so intractable. He brought more technocrats into the Government, hoping they could deal with the problems of near-paralytic inefficiency. They proved to be no more competent, and a lot less entertaining than the mediocrities. So by 1981 the economy was even more skewed, the society even more materialistic than before. In 1962 Williams had written: "The pronounced

materialism and disastrous individualism have spread to all parts of the fabric of the society." After 25 years in power he knew that the fabric had all but disintegrated, leaving only the materialism and the individualism. In March 1981, a month when sugarworkers, hospital workers, and (O, hard heart of History) teachers, demonstrated around Parliament, Williams ceased taking his diabetic medicines and dismissed his domestic servants. He slipped into a coma and, on March 29, quietly abandoned this world.

"We Must Do Better": Petro-dollars fed the worst aspects of the picaroon society. But they also allowed some positive developments. For one, it must be said that if there was much vulgarity in those years, Williams' Caribbean regionalism was something to be proud of.

Thus, for instance, Trinidad and Tobago lent more money to insolvent Caribbean governments than did any other country, including the United States with its well-publicized Caribbean Basin Initiative. Then there was the equalizing impact of wealth: blacks, browns, whites and Indians were no longer inevitably separated by disparities of income, occupation or residence. Consequently, race relations became more relaxed. Finally there was the rising status of women: increased secondary and higher education, and a job market which accepted everyone allowed women an independence never before tasted. Significantly, the nine women who contested elections in 1966 had increased to 26 ten years later.

The most visible development, however, was

Left, political slogans support Tobago's efforts at self-determination and recognition and, right, a downtown Port of Spain church overshadowed by the towering Financial Complex.

the creation of a new political party by one-time PNM Attorney-General Karl Hudson-Phillips. A catch-all for disillusioned PNMs, ambitious Indians, and dissatisfied businessmen, the new party called itself the Organisation for National Reconstruction (ONR): its symbol was a steel beam. With seemingly inexhaustible funds, the ONR launched a PR campaign modeled on U.S. practices, against corruption and inefficiency. "We must do better," was the ONR cry.

Meanwhile, leadership of the country and of the PNM had fallen to George Chambers, a former Minister of Finance. Chambers' low-key style and lack of Williams' brilliance left many people unimpressed. Others saw his informality as a step towards a regeneration of the party, however, and his campaign of heckling and insinuation set the tone for the fight.

From the media coverage, these two appeared to be the main contenders, but there were other important parties. NJAC had changed its mind about "conventional politics," and roamed the country holding meetings and painting ominous graffiti in red, green and black. They drew moderate crowds of curiosity seekers in the urban areas. Their message was a mild 'black' nationalism (stretched to include Indians), and a humanist 'philosophy of man.' "Let the people decide," was the NJAC cry.

And then there was the coalition National Alliance, comprised of the ULF, Tapia and the DAC. Lloyd Best called it the "party of parties," which represented the three "tribes" of Trinidad & Tobago: Indians, blacks and Tobagonians. The Alliance's program was, like NJAC's, a mild nationalism and, like the ONR's, a promise to be more efficient. So Best's response to the ONR slogan was: "You can't do better than Best."

The campaign resembled Carnival even more than ever with its *picong* ("stinging" from the French piquant, and referring usually to an absurd, boastful heckling). The ONR got the worst of it, however, and was successfully labeled a big business party of authoritarian bent. People hadn't forgotten Hudson-Phillips' Public Order Bill of 1970. The PNM told the public, "don't worry about the inefficiency and corruption, the bad roads and the electricity blackouts, because we guarantee your democratic freedoms."

The results were a foregone conclusion: the PNM won for the sixth time with 26 seats. There were some upsets, though. The ONR, which received the second highest number of votes, got not one seat. The ULF lost two seats to the PNM, and won eight. The DAC got the Tobago seats. Trinidad had decided to give Chambers a chance. That year the price of oil dipped, and the country's balance of trade showed a deficit for the first time since 1974.

Captain.... the Ship is Sinking! Since 1981 the price of oil has fallen lower and lower, and the Government's purse has likewise contracted. Immediately after his re-election Chambers began an austerity drive with the slogan, "Fête over, back to work." The timing was unfortunate, coming shortly before Carnival, and many people laughed, "the fête now start." The new stress on productivity temporarily brought many of the employer class back into the PNM fold, however, out of the ONR camp. But in next to no time it became clear that the Government was unable to discipline workers, and that corruption and inefficiency would continue.

Local government elections, hitherto ignored, in 1982 gave the opposition parties a chance to rally their forces. A tentative "accommodation" was arranged between the ULF-DAC-Tapia Alliance and the ONR, and they went in to do battle. Of 120 seats, the accommodation picked up 66, leaving 54 for the PNM, and none for NJAC. It was a shot in the arm for the opposition which got another fillip in 1984 when, despite a strenuous PNM effort, the DAC won 11 of 12 seats in the Tobago House of Assembly.

Since then, the opposition parties have been forced into unity by deteriorating social conditions. As state revenue fell with the price of oil, so did unemployment rise; as the trade unions retreated and wages shrank, so did inflation grow, especially since the TT dollar was devalued by 25 percent in 1985. Crime increased and the police seemed hardly able to check it. The expensive and ambitious education system failed to live up to its early promise.

Meanwhile, the ULF, DAC, Tapia and ONR have papered over their differences and, in September 1985, merged around a common "Platform For Democracy." Robinson is the political leader, and Hudson-Phillips and Panday are his deputies, in the National Alliance for Reconstruction. But a trade union-based ULF and a big business ONR must share an uncomfortable bed.

On Dec. 16, 1986, the National Alliance for Reconstruction won a landslide victory, taking 33 out of the 36 seats in Parliament. This is the first time since 1956 that the government of T&T have changed hands.

A.N.R. Robinson is the new prime minister and Chambers lost his seat as leader of the PNM to Patrick Manning. The victory of the NAR was greeted by spontaneous widespread celebration throughout T&T. At present the party is trying to make as much as possible of their great mandate. They have organized an environmental clean-up campaign mobilizing public support.

Right, President Noor Mohamed Hassanali.

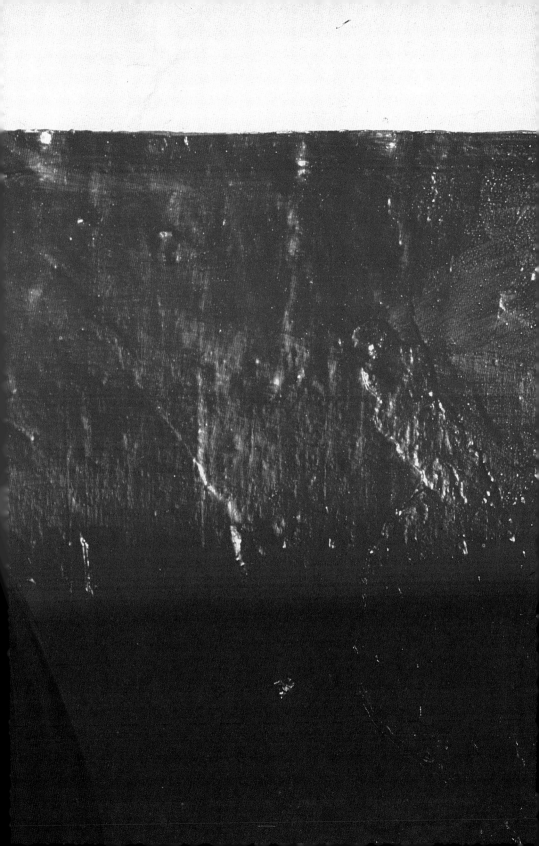

PEOPLE

Trinidadians may be the most heterogeneous people on Earth. For they are a people in a sense that other societies which harbor multiracial populations are not. The favorite national myth is that Trinidad and Tobago is a paradise of interracial harmony, and T&Ters view with self-righteous horror the ugly racial strife that seems endemic to other countries. Race is mentioned casually and openly in daily conversation, and Trinidadians appear unconcerned when racial stereotypes and differences are discussed. The truth, however, is infinitely more complex than either of these two extremes. Trinidadians do not, today, fight pitched battles, race against race but neither can the question of race be too glibly glossed over.

There is a nation of Trinidad and Tobago with a central core of culture in which all the races participate, and there is a significant percentage of the population which is of mixed race. But history has not succeeded in melting the peoples down entirely—either culturally or genetically—into one homogeneous block; and so, in Trinidad and Tobago, race is very much an issue, albeit an issue so subtle that it is not likely to assail the attention of the visitor.

Trinbagonians: Who are the Trinidadians and Tobagonians? The term "Trinidadian" will be used hereafter to refer to the combined peoples of the two islands, at the risk of causing offence to the Tobagonian sector of the population. The relationship between the two parts of the country is a thorny problem yet to be solved, and reflected in the clumsy name that they continue to tote around. Groups in Trinidad and Tobago have been agitating for the adoption of a composite name—proposed are "Trinago" and "Trinbago"—which would suggest integration and allow "Trinagonian" or "Trinbagonian." In the meantime "Trinidadian" tends to be used as the umbrella term.

The first people, of course, to inhabit the country were Amerindians, who migrated from the South American continent, discovering the Caribbean centuries before Christopher Columbus. As elsewhere in the region they were all but exterminated in the onslaught of European colonization. There is a tiny handful of people in Trinidad calling themselves "Caribs," and there are many among T&Ters whose physical

features suggest an Amerindian admixture in their ancestry. The Amerindian strain has fed into the pool, but is no longer a distinct racial presence.

Most territories of the Caribbean bear the mark of one European culture, at most two. The European element of Trinidad and Tobago hails from no less than three main sources. Spanish, French and British have all, at one time, ruled these islands, and in addition to these three major groups of European settlers there were minority groups of Portuguese, Italians and others.

But the bulk of the people of Trinidad and Tobago today are the descendants of Africans and Indians brought to work in the sugarcane and other plantations, the Africans transported by force and enslaved, the Indians arriving under a system of indentureship not too far removed from slavery. Together the Indians and Africans constitute upwards of 80 percent of the population. Within the last century Trinidad has received, and continues to receive, immigrants from China and the Middle East who come as traders.

The ethnic groups that make up the population of Trinidad and Tobago all arrived, then, under different circumstances. They came from different roots, thousands of miles apart; they came for different reasons, and they came to

Preceding pages: two faces of Trinidad; and an Asian Trinidadian in Scarborough. Left, "wining" at Carnival and, right, two spectators.

different roles. Inevitably they continue to be different from each other in many ways.

Plantation Legacy: Whites in Trinidad and Tobago remain a privileged minority, fairly aloof from the rest of the population. They live in affluent suburban settlements or on large inherited landholdings scattered around the country, and a few still earn an income from large estates passed on by their forebears — relics of the plantation system.

Whites are the traditional "aristocracy" of the society, who for centuries controlled the resources and reaped the benefits of all economic activity. Although today members of other groups have emerged to share the "commanding heights" of the economy with the old masters, whites remain the owners and managers of major business concerns — manufacturing, hotel

And it is whites who have kept alive in Trinidadian society European artistic traditions such as ballet and opera. The major national festival of Trinidad and Tobago — Carnival — has its origin in a European celebration (French, to be exact), and although it has been developed to its present state by the African population, white Trinidadians continue to participate in some measure in Carnival activities. Indeed, the most widely-acclaimed Carnival artist to emerge in recent times is a white man, Peter Minshall.

The diet of white Trinidadian families differs from that of the rest of the population for economic reasons, for example in terms of the balance of the various food groups. The poorer masses of the country consume a great deal of carbohydrate and fairly small amounts of the more expensive foods such as meat and dairy

industry, banking, the import and distribution trades.

Some whites work in education, in religious orders which function as the old "prestige" schools originally founded for white and mulatto children, and in the new private schools set up for the still predominantly light-skinned children of today's upper classes. All in all, the white Trinidadian is a white-collar worker. A white street cleaner, or chambermaid, or bus conductor would be a decided oddity.

The recreational activities of white society in Trinidad and Tobago are the traditionally upper-class pursuits of water sports (yachting, boat-racing, windsurfing, swimming), lawn tennis, golf, cocktail and dinner parties, or simply meeting at their exclusive clubs.

products. The diet of the people of Trinidad and Tobago is also greatly influenced, of late, by North American tastes, and this influence is more marked in households which can afford to buy the imported foods associated with American eating patterns.

But basic tastes in food preparation common to the bulk of the population are shared by whites, for a large element of what we see as the cuisine of Trinidad and Tobago emerged out of the kitchens of European settlers where African cooks with their own inherited ideas about food learned Spanish, French, Portuguese and British ways of cookery.

African Echoes: Next in order of arrival were the Africans. Alienated from the land by the experience of slavery, the African population has tended to gravitate towards urban centers, though the population of Tobago is almost entirely African. (Tobago was a separate entity and developed apart from Trinidad until less than a century ago when the two islands were unified. The smaller island does not have the same history of multiethnic immigration.)

Blacks engage in a wide variety of occupations, but shy away from agriculture. Black businessmen are also thin on the ground. The Afro-Trinidadian is a salaried worker—menial, semi-skilled and skilled. For years the Civil Service was monopolized by this ethnic group, which still occupies nearly the whole of its upper levels. There is also a class of black professionals: doctors, lawyers and other university-trained people. The means of social mobility for the African population has always been educa-

or sitting on a culvert watching the world go by. It means pointedly not doing anything too purposeful, or serious, or strenuous, whiling the time away in the company of cronies, talking or not talking, drinking or not drinking, playing all fours; going in a gang to the beach, to a party, to a cricket match...

The *joie-de-vivre* of the Afro-Trinidadian is proverbial, and the duty of enjoying all that is put on Earth for God's children to enjoy is taken very seriously indeed.

It is black Trinidadians who expound most readily upon the theme of how their "carnival mentality" is a barrier to the progress of their race, and how the other races are doing well because they are not given to spreading joy, etc... But the attitude of the Afro-Trinidadian to the life-styles of the other groups is am-

tion, rather than the route of entrepreneurship, the pattern for other ethnic groups.

It was the Africans who forged the calypso-steelband-carnival arts, and they remain the chief proponents of this aspect of Trinidad and Tobago culture.

It was they, too, who perfected the "lime," and this term has no translation because the concept belongs exclusively to this part of the world. To those who disapprove of the activity, liming means loitering, as in groups of aimless men standing around at street corners

Left, alluring legacy of European settlement and, right, scouting Trinidad style.

bivalent: it wavers between admiration and mild scorn for those who seem to spend so much time working and saving up that they miss out on living.

The staple of the black population is rice, a taste acquired from the Indians. Whereas in the rest of the Caribbean, African people make extensive use of root vegetables and green bananas, in Trinidad and Tobago these take second place to rice. Blacks retain a taste for the salted meat and fish which were an essential part of the food rations given out to their enslaved ancestors on the plantation. Today salted beef and pork and dried codfish are mainly used as flavoring for other dishes—rice-and-peas, stewed peas, *callaloo*.

The family patterns of Africans in Trinidad

and Tobago, as in the rest of the Caribbean, do not adhere too strictly to the official norms of marriage and the patriarchal family. Common-law unions are prevalent, and women have a great deal of authority in the context of the family. A large percentage of households are headed by women. Extended-family habits are still alive, mainly among the lower classes. Promotion into the growing middle class generally means adoption of the life-style beamed out from American television, which includes the restricted nuclear family pattern. The more affluent people become, the less use they have for the larger family.

New religions were developed by the African population on Caribbean soil. These religions combine elements of Christianity with African religious practices and beliefs. But Trinidad and

of African and European.

There are very many people of mixed blood in Trinidad and Tobago. But they do not, by and large, constitute a separate group. They are, culturally, back Trinidadians. Within a "black" family, complexions may range from black to palest brown, reflecting miscegenation somewhere along their ancestry. But there is a group of brown Trinidadians who have to be viewed as distinct from the mass. They are the heirs of the original "middle class" of the Caribbean — a privileged, carefully inbred social class.

This group has a very strong sense of being an elite. It jealously guards its racial "purity" — members choose only mates of the same color or lighter. There is not much to distinguish them in terms of life-style, from the whites. Indeed, in the popular mind, whites and upper-class

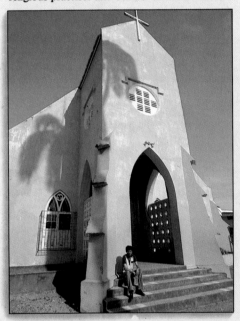

Tobago is officially a Christian country, with the Catholic Church being particularly powerful, so the syncretic sects are severely frowned upon. Practically every known sect of Christianity claims a portion of the black population: Roman Catholic, Church of England, Church of Scotland, Methodist, Moravian, Seventh-Day Adventist, Pentecostal, and more. A recent development in Trinidad and Tobago is the "Black Muslim" movement, that is Africans turning to Islam, but in their own Muslim organizations, not as part of the established Indian Muslim community already present.

An Indigenous Population: The mulatto did not come, of course, as an immigrant arriving from distant shores, but as a racial type produced on Caribbean soil, being the offspring

mulattoes are lumped together under the loose label of "French Creoles," although many families in this class bear Spanish, Portuguese, Scottish, or English names. The designation "French Creole" has to do with the fact that in the 18th Century whites and mulattoes were attracted to Trinidad from the French Caribbean by enticements such as grants of land, and soon became a powerful economic and political force in the country.

Eastern Elements: The East Indian presence in Trinidad and Tobago is one and a half centuries old, but is already the largest single group in the Republic, claiming over 40 percent of the population. The majority of Indians still live in rural communities, and farming remains their chief occupation. With increased access to secondary and tertiary education, however, Indians have entered the clerical and professional fields once occupied almost exclusively by Africans. Small and medium businesses are owned mainly by Indians, and a few Indian concerns have grown into major business enterprises.

Indians brought to Trinidad and Tobago a relatively intact and functional culture which adapted itself to the new environment and shaped the fabric of life in Indian communities for generations. Inevitably, the life-style of Indian Trinidadians has been and continues to be affected by the influences which prevail in the society, namely the culture of their African counterparts, as well as the essentially Western-oriented education system and mass media. But there remains a core of cultural traits which

not accorded them during the colonial period. Marriage ceremonies, for example, were not recognized. In Trinidad and Tobago major Hindu and Muslim festivals like Phagwa and Divali are now public holidays.

Indian family organization in Trinidad and Tobago has been eroded somewhat by Westernization. The traditional status of the Indian is challenged by near universal education to secondary level and by the influence of the media. But extended-family networks are stronger than in the African population. Many Indians live in large, multi-generation households, of the type made famous by V.S. Naipaul, although the patterns of authority which previously obtained in such households may not be operational today. But even where Indians split off into nuclear family house-

constitutes a distinctive Indian way of life.

A minority of Indians have been Christianized, notably by the Presbyterian Church. But the religions which the Indian immigrants brought with them, Hinduism and Islam, remain firmly in place. The majority religion is Hinduism, and both religions have very strong organizations which, like the Christian churches, set up their own schools. Eastern religions may be said to have gained, rather than lost ground, for today they enjoy an official recognition

From left to right: a black-German-Portuguese man outside a Portuguese church in Arouca; an Indian shopkeeper; an East Indian West Indian at the turn of the century; and today.

holds, there remains a strong bond of responsibility towards the larger family, which may include economic cooperation.

Indian food, of course, is quite distinctive. Among their standards are eggplant, a string bean known as *bodi*, tomatoes, green mangoes, potatoes, a variety of spinach known as *bhaji*, split peas, chick peas and pumpkin. A favorite seasoning is curry, in addition to other spices such as cumin seed, saffron and massala. Rice is basic to the Indian diet, and so is roti—a flat, supple bread that is eaten with vegetable or meat preparations.

Indian Trinidadians are as fond of the game of cricket as their African compatriots. A favorite form of recreation, too, is going to the cinema to watch movies from India. Indian music and dance are also greatly appreciated and there are highly accomplished Trinidadian Indian musicians, dancers and singers, some of whom are trained in the ancestral country.

Trading Places: The Chinese and Lebanese came as traders, and remain largely engaged in commercial activity—small trading and big business. The Lebanese are a tightly-knit urban community, whereas the Chinese are scattered all over the country: the "Chinee shop" is an institution in rural communities.

Both groups are relative newcomers and tend to keep active links with their countries of origin, so that items of their material culture are ever present. In the home of a Chinese family one is likely to be surrounded by Oriental decorations and kitchen utensils.

Because they are recent immigrants, Chinese and Lebanese cultures remain fairly closed—practiced "privately" while participating in the common culture of the country. But there is a greater level of integration on the part of the Chinese than the Lebanese and there has been some intermixture of Chinese blood with that of Africans and Indians; many people in Trinidad and Tobago bear no fewer than four different racial strains in their blood.

The mixing of races is part of the reality of Trinidad and Tobago, but what is the real nature of relations among the various peoples?

Status and Stereotypes: Race relations in Trinidad and Tobago are defined by the old hierarchy of white down to black, and by the newer and more volatile current of mistrust which runs between the two largest groups in the country: the Africans and Indians.

Europeans constitute a very small minority in Trinidad and Tobago—less than 1 percent—but they retain their economic supremacy and attendant prestige. Today, the traditional attitudes towards white people have been reinforced by the impact of the foreign (mainly American) media. Moreover, deep in the ethos of the Indian population of Trinidad and Tobago is the great esteem which their ancestral culture accorded the Aryan racial type of northern India.

Thus it is that the physical features of the Europeans are the yardstick against which Trinidadians evaluate beauty and worthiness in general. At the lower end of the scale of desirability lie dark skin and kinky hair; at the top, pale skin and straight hair. It stands to reason, then, that great approval also accrues to the physical features of the Chinese, the Lebanese, the light-skinned Indian, the mulatto (or "Spanish") and the "mixed" (provide one part of the mixture is light-skinned).

There are many manifestations of this race-and-color scale of assessment. For years a Trinidad and Tobago beauty queen was, by definition, a white or pale-skinned woman. The Black Power movement of the 1970s made some inroads into that tradition, and today it is more politic to choose a queen of the indeterminate khaki mix (not too pale, but not quite black, either) that is becoming the ideal physical type in Trinidad and Tobago.

When, for bureaucratic purposes, black Trinidadians are called upon to identify their race (e.g. in passport applications, I.D. documentation, census exercises), many choose to write "Mixed."

Black men on the rise up the social ladder acquire light-skinned, straight-haired wives as part of the trappings of promotion, and certain high-visibility "women's" jobs—bank teller, air hostess—until recently were filled only by light-skinned types.

Class Consciousness: Race relations are far from ideal. Trinidadians mix at school and at work, but not too much at play. "Integration" is involuntary—T&Ters interact when thrown together, not, generally, by choice.

Perhaps the maximum interaction among races is to be found at the top of the pile, where money and paleness of skin unite into one melange of whites, mulattoes, Lebanese and successful Chinese. The commercial giants who have emerged in the Indian population do not appear as yet to have been integrated socially into this set. This might be explained by one or all of a number of reasons. The Indian's base is rural, whereas the elite described above is urban. The Indian's cultural identification and sense of responsibility to family or clan do not predispose him to shift allegiance to another group.

Then there is what Trinidadians call their "middle class," which in their vocabulary may stretch from professionals to civil servants to well-paid skilled workers (especially in the wake of the oil boom). This group, like the mass of the working and peasant population, is largely African and Indian. There are practically no lines of communication between this block of the population (middle and lower classes) and the light-skinned upper class, and the current feeling between them is standard: the latter views the former with condescension and some apprehension, while the other views its superiors with a mixture of deference and resentment.

Racial stereotypes die hard, as do derogatory racial epithets. The African is a "Nigger," the Indian a "Coolie"; but these are the two

74

most extreme of racial insults. The names used for other music ethnic groups, are far milder in their import.

Chinese is abbreviated, almost affectionately, to "Chinee." Middle-Eastern people, who are mainly Lebanese, are casually lumped under the term "Syrian." Mulattoes are described as "red" which is not as flattering as "fair" or "fair-skinned." Curiously, there are no traditional insult-word for whites: in the 1970s, the era of Black Power, Trinidadians adopted from Black America the term "honky."

Education and Economy: Africans and Indians constitute the bulk of the population, and relations between them are uneasy. This fact does not preclude healthy relations at the personal level: firm friendships between individuals and families, communities in which the two races

not only live side by side but actively cooperate, and the miscegenation which has produced a whole new race, the "Dougla."

But there exists a fundamental mistrust between Indians and Africans in the mass, a rivalry that dates from the Indian's arrival to replace the African as plantation worker in the wake of Emancipation. Each has traditionally accused the other of wanting to "take over" the country, and the two races monitor each other's numbers with apprehension.

Since the beginning of party politics in Trinidad and Tobago in the era leading up to Independence, major political parties have been formed along lines of race (Indian and African) and elections clearly perceived as a struggle for African or Indian supremacy. For the whole of

this period – 30 years – it is the African-based party which has held sway. Partly because of this, but also because the Indians suffered a serious lag in access to education under the colonial regime, the Civil Service has until recently been an African preserve. Indians, then, seemed excluded from the running of the country.

On the other hand, Africans perceive Indians as taking over the economy of the country, because Indians are so visibly engaged in business activity, ranging from the selling of vegetables by the roadside to ownership of the sophisticated hardware store, whereas Africans have chosen a different route to success, the way of education.

What has perhaps exacerbated relations in the past few years is that the Indians has now caught up in education. With the increase in oil revenue, the incumbent government was able to dramatically increase educational facilities, notably at secondary level. This has given the Indians a new ubiquity which disturbs his African counterpart: the Indians who was once safely tucked away out of sight in the canefield, the rice patch or the family vegetable garden, is now turning up everywhere, in every kind of job. Africans feel upstaged, threatened, and Indians feel their resentment. The situation produces foolish muscle-flexing on both sides.

The juxtaposition of two different cultures has been an inevitable source of friction. The original encounter between African and Indian was the classic case of "host population" versus the immigrant with a foreign, therefore disturbing, culture of his own which (as is the case in such situations) he showed no inclination to relinquish in favor of the culture of the host.

But, in addition, in Trinidad and Tobago the host population had no strong sense of its own cultural identity. The circumstances under which the African had been brought from his ancestral land made cultural continuity very difficult. Africans from different cultures had been mixed together, languages forgotten, religions garbled – even the African's name was erased. Africans now practiced a new culture that was decidedly African-based, but the official, approved culture was European, and the way of life of the black population was not even seen as "culture." The attitude of the Afro-Trinidadian to his own culture was one of rejection, at best ambivalence. Salvation lay in being assimilated into the white man's culture.

The confidence of the Indian in his own culture, the strength and the cohesiveness which this culture gave to Indian communities, the Indian's refusal to be assimilated, tended to be interpreted by the African as arrogance. Africans take a dim view of the Indian population's continuing emotional relationship with their ancestral land—Trinidad and Tobago has been brought to the brink of war by the spectacle of Indian Trinidadians cheering on a cricket team from India playing in Trinidad against a Trinidadian team! And Indian music on the radio and Indian movies on national television were until recently a great affront to the rest of the population; but this is changing, and it is in the area of culture that the Republic is experiencing a shift from confrontation to interpenetration.

Racial Mosaic: The fact that the different ethnic groups of Trinidad and Tobago have some fairly distinct cultural traits does not pose any real threat to the concept of nationhood. "Cultural pluralism" is a term which has entered the vocabulary, and although race relations are not exemplary, Trinidadians set great

munication between themselves and the Europeans, as well as among the Africans themselves. Africans transported to Trinidad and Tobago took the vocabulary of their European overlords and poured it into the mold of a standard West African syntax, retaining some words from their own languages. As Africans lost their own languages, what would have started out as a pidgin for basic communication grew into a language capable of the whole range of expression.

The vocabulary of Trinidad and Tobago Creole is mainly English-derived but it also contains words which can be traced back to languages spoken in West Africa, among these Twi and Yoruba. But Trinidad spoke French (and its Creole counterpart) for about one hundred years of its history, so there is in the every-

store by their multiethnic image. At the heart of the mosaic, however, is a growing area of shared culture which makes it possible for T&Ters to coexist without major explosions of antagonism.

Creole Conversation: There is, on the one hand, the shared language. In all the Caribbean territories Creole (or hybrid) languages have developed out of the meeting of European and African. They are the achievement, in the first instance, of Africans, who in each society developed a lingua franca which allowed communication.

Left, at a traveling fair in Arima and, right, an offering is made on a small Hindu altar in the Ramgoolie Temple, Trinidad.

day language a large stock of French vocabulary and French constructions using English words.

Trinidadians will say "It making hot," as the French say "Il fait chaud"; and the expression "It have ," meaning "There is or are" is from the French "Il y a." T&Ters retain many French names for the vegetation of the country—*balisier* (wild banana), *pomme cythere* (golden apple), *pomme rac* (otaheite apple), *cerise* (a cherry-like fruit). Damaging gossip is *mauvais-langue;* a female crony is a *macommère;* a term of endearment is *doo-doo,* from the French *doux* meaning "sweet"; and the spirits who people Trinidadian mythology have French-derived names: *lajablesse, soucouyant, Papa Bois, lagahou.*

Traces of Spanish in the everyday language

are relatively sparse, given Trinidad's proximity to Latin America. Words for some of the dishes introduced by the Spaniards are derived from their language — *pelau, sancoche, pastelle*. And there is the terminology surrounding the activity known as *parang* (Christmas music) which is moving into the general vocabulary. Some fruits are called by their Spanish names — *sapodilla* and *granadilla*.

And today people in Trinidad and Tobago of every racial type use some Hindi words as part of their everyday speech. Non-Indians living in integrated rural communities have used Hindi expressions for a long time, and know a great many more of these expressions than the average Trinidadian. But today some Hindi vocabulary has become the common property of all.

Phagwa, Divali, Ramleela, puja, deya, Lakshmi; from Islam: Ramadan, Eid-ul-Fitr, Hussein. And Trinis know that the members of the Indian extended family (including grandparents and in-laws) are called by names such as *agee, bhowji* and *dulahin*.

The Amerindians have also made some mark on T&T language, again in the form of words for food — cassava, balata, roocoo, tatoo — but also in the wealth of place names they have left behind. Trinidadians use the language of their Amerindian predecessors daily in every part of the country when they speak of Tunapuna, Mucurapo, Guayaguayare, Naparima, Curepe, Tacarigua, Carapichaima, Maitagual and many others.

Indeed, all the place names bestowed by the various groups must be considered as part of

The Hindi has mainly provided words to do with food, cooking, clothes, religion and family. In the markets the Hindi *beigun* is steadily replacing "melongene" as the word Trinidadians use for eggplant. Indeed, the vegetables in Trinidad and Tobago are largely grown and marketed by Indians, so their Hindi names are passing into the vocabulary: *bhaji, bodi, aloo.* Some names of commonly-known Indian seasonings are *geera, massala* and *amchar,* and Trinidadians know that *roti* is baked on a *tawa,* and more and more people are becoming familiar with the cooking process known as *chungkay.* The orhni, the sari and the dhoti are articles of clothing familiar to all. Terms for the two major religions practiced by Indian Trinidadians are household words — from Hinduism:

the common language of the people of Trinidad and Tobago. English place names are not predominant — they are to be found in greatest concentration on the smaller island of Tobago: Scarborough, Roxborough, Plymouth. Spanish and French place names abound in Trinidad which is itself a Spanish name. Some of the Spanish place names are San Rafael, Las Cuevas, Sangre Grande, Sangre Chiquito, San Fernando, El Soccorro, Los Iros. Part of the legacy of French language are place names like Blanchisseuse, San Souci, Matelot, Champs Fleurs, Lopinot, Petit Bourg and L'Anse Mitan. These are some of the ingredients that go into the common language — basically a Caribbean Creole, but given its distinctive character by the special blending of peoples that took place only in Trinidad and Tobago.

Creole differs from Standard English in its syntax—the linguists have found a common syntax across Caribbean Creoles and have traced it back to the West African family of languages. The intonation of each Caribbean Creole is distinctive, and so is the pronunciation of individual sounds (specifically vowels) from Creole to Creole. So there is an unmistakable Trinidad and Tobago "accent" common to all people, of every ethnic classification, and they use this accent even when speaking Standard English. What is significant is that older Indians sound markedly different from the younger generation of Indian Trinidadians: the full acquisition of the common language was not an instant process but one which has taken generations.

that on both islands Africans constitute the majority of the population.

Rather than a separate, hermetic language, Creole can be seen as positioned at one end of a continuum which shades into Standard English at the other end. Where on the continuum Trinis pitch their language (i.e. whether they use pure Creole, pure English or some combination of the two) depends on situation, mood, topic, listener, level of education and class consciousness. And during the course of one conversation (or better still, one argument) speakers are liable to touch every part of the keyboard.

There is a certain amount of controversy over Creole, its validity, its propriety, whether it is a language or not, or just "bad English." But meanwhile everybody gets on with using it,

A most interesting indicator of the extent to which Trinidad and Tobago Creole (or, strictly speaking, Trinidadian Creole) has been shaped by its polyglot population is the fact that the Standard Creole of the smaller island, Tobago, is not quite the same as that of Trinidad, and has been found to have striking similarities with Jamaican Creole. Tobago is at the southern end of the Caribbean chain of islands and Jamaica is pretty near the top— the two are separated by over 1,000 miles of sea. But they are both different from Trinidad in

including many who think that they are talking English all the while. Since the vocabulary is mainly English, people can be vague about where Creole ends and Standard English begins.

Creole is used actively or passively by all the people of Trinidad and Tobago. It is safe to say that the great majority of people do not fully possess Standard English, and for many of those who do, it tends to remain a language written rather than spoken. But Creole is inevitably one of the media through which people *receive* communication. It is the language of calypso, for example, and the calypsonian is one of the most important communicators in the society.

Left, an elder of the Creole village of Blanchisseuse and, right, three schoolgirls.

The specific traits of a society tally exactly with the untranslatable expressions of its

language.
—Jean-Paul Sartre, *Black Orpheus*

To the extent that Trinidadians share a common code of communication not quite the same as any other, to the extent that they share their own set of untranslatables, they share a common culture, across race.

Food is another area where T&Ters share and share alike. There is a long-standing Creole cuisine which incorporates African and Amerindian elements with contributions from each of the European cultures (whose cooking is fairly different one from the other).

The Chinese influence has also gone into the standard diet: every self-respecting cook can make chow mein, and delicacies such as wontons have become part of the snacking habits.

The American fast-foods industry is a

areas in which a shared culture has developed — language, food and music. T&Ters, of course, share a great many other institutions which are not necessarily of their own making but which also constitute common ground — cricket, American soap-operas and the latest in Western fashion.

The subjective characteristics which the people share are, of course, harder to pinpoint. Are there any attitudes, values or behaviors which distinguish Trinidadians from other peoples? Is there a "Trini" personality that cuts across race? Here we have to rely, in part, on the image thrown back by other people's perceptions — how Trinidadians are seen, in particular by their sisters and brothers in the rest of the Caribbean.

There is, first of all, the perception of

feature of the landscape today, and has made all T&Ters (or the children, at any rate) eaters of chicken-and-chips, hot-dogs and hamburgers.

But what makes the diet of Trinidad and Tobago distinctive among Caribbean diets is the addition of the Indian influence. Already mentioned is the preference for rice over what is called the "ground provisions" or root crops. The Indian roti is a real rival to American-style fast-foods, and standard snack-foods are Indian: *channa, kurmah, polorie, bara* (served as "doubles"). Curry is taken very much for granted as one of the everyday options for food preparation and there is a very high level of tolerance for hot pepper. (For details on local cuisine, read "Roti on the Run" on p. 251-256.)

The Merrymakers: There are three tangible

Trinidadians as a people whose lives are a permanent "fête" (this being the word for T&Ters brand of partying), and the corollary of this assessment, that they are not terribly serious.

One cannot deny the element of hedonism in their make-up — T&Ters are not in the habit of apologizing for it. It has its source in the cultures of certain of the peoples who settled here, the Africans and the Latin peoples — Spanish, French and Portuguese — and it has been transmitted in the course of time to the whole population.

Trinidad and Tobago is the Caribbean country in which Carnival is the most highly developed. Indeed, there is nothing in the rest of the Caribbean with which to compare the Trinidad and Tobago Carnival. One has to go further afield, to Brazil, for example, another African-Latin culture, to find anything like its peer. Carnival in Trinidad and Tobago is a "season" which lasts for two to three months. It follows hard on the heels of the Christmas "season" which consists of a two-week run-up to Christmas Day peppered with *parang*, office Christmas parties, school Christmas parties and Christmas parties held by every self-respecting organization in Trinidad and Tobago, then a one-week binge stretching from Christmas Day to New Year's Day.

In addition, Trinidad and Tobago has a full calendar of public holidays which, along with weekends, give scope for serious fêting and liming throughout the year. There are no fewer than 15 public holidays in Trinidad and Tobago, mainly long-standing Christian holy-days to

which have been added Hindu and Muslim days of observance, and dates which commemorate events in the political evolution of the country.

It is perhaps more accurate to say that there are 13 public holidays, because the two days of Carnival on the road have never been declared official holidays. This is a curious carry-over from the colonial era, when the authorities and the upper classes viewed the street festival of the black mob with decided repugnance and would not dream of dignifying it with official recognition. In an 1833 newspapers Carnival

Left, a smile from Charlotteville, Tobago, and, right, jammin' during Parade of Bands.

was described as:

the shameful violation of the Sabbath by the lower order of the population, who are accustomed at this time of year to wear masks and create disturbances on a Sunday.

— Port-of-Spain Gazette, Jan. 22, 1833

Today, Carnival has active government approval and sponsorship, but Carnival Monday and Tuesday are still officially working days for government employees. Suffice it to say that on these two days the state of the nation is such that it is only the essential services which actually keep on working. Hence there are 15 holidays.

Trinidad and Tobago celebrates with a national stoppage of work on New Year's Day, Carnival Monday, Carnival Tuesday, Good Friday, Easter Monday, Whit Monday, Corpus Christi, Eid-ul-Fitr, Labour Day, Emancipation Day, Independence Day, Republic Day, Divali, Christmas Day and Boxing Day. And there is a movement afoot for the granting of a public holiday in commemoration of Double Ten, a Chinese observance.

Trinis earn the accusation of being unserious partly because they respond to hardship, repression and disaster with a determination to continue enjoying life. In 1970 Trinidad was the stage of a major popular upheaval, the Black Power movement. When the authorities imposed a dusk-to-dawn curfew for a period of time, Trinidadians gathered indoors before the mandatory hour and held all-night "Curfew fêtes." When the oil bubble burst and the economy crashed, bringing widespread retrenchment, unemployment, inflation, shortages, poverty— all the problems associated with a dire economic slump—a new kind of fête began to be advertised on the characteristic large posters that are always to be seen around the country proclaiming where the upcoming action is: people began to throw "Recession fêtes." Come hell or high water, Trinidad and Tobago will go down fêting. It is one way of coping with existence: who is to say that it is not a valid one?

This way of responding to life has nothing to do with the supposed behavior of mindless, grinning natives-in-the-sun whom the brochures are fond of describing as "happy-go-lucky." Mindless and happy-go-lucky Trinidadians are not. Theirs is a studied philosophy of life which rests upon a highly developed sense of humor.

For another feature of Trini personality which might contribute to a general impression of unseriousness is the decided irreverence of the Trinidadian, his refusal to be too impressed by anything or anybody, including himself. An important part of the tradition of calypso is what is known as *picong*, or sniping satire against individuals and institutions great or small. In the calypso tent, no personage, no office, no august creation of human beings is sacrosanct – there is no telling where the calypsonian will strike, and he strikes with exquisite humor, on behalf of all – Trinis cheer and egg him on.

This function of the calypsonian has spilled over into the phenomenon of the weekly newspaper. Weeklies proliferate in Trinidad and Tobago today and are read far more avidly than the traditional dailies. A major part of the attraction of the weeklies is their practice of punching holes in public figures.

This often cruel humor which levels all hierarchies and acknowledges no wonders of the world may be partly to do with the cynicism of One Who Has Seen It All. Not only is Trinidad and Tobago a fair approximation of the world in microcosm, but T&Ters also enjoy

(or suffer from) a relatively high level of exposure to the outer world. Trinidad and Tobago is not a tourist mecca, but it does harbor a sizable population of transient foreigners – people involved in the work of the multinationals, in trade, in diplomacy or in academic activity, for example.

Constantly exposed to the wider world through the multiple arms of the media, Trinidad and Tobago has the highest density of newspaper production in the English-speaking Caribbean. For a population of just over 1 million there are four dailies, a fluctuating number of weeklies, and innumerable periodicals put out by political and other organizations. Trinidad has two television channels and two radio stations. Practically no one is without access to a radio, and television sets are commonplace. In a large proportion of homes there is also the video. All the national media offer mainly foreign fare – canned material from the metropolitan countries.

Trinidadians have always done a fair amount of traveling to other countries, and during the oil boom years, foreign travel came within the reach of a large part of the population. Thus there is in the Trinidadians an almost metropolitan sophistication, with some of the negative attributes of metropolitan behavior. Trinidadians, for example, are more individualistic than their fellow West Indians and more competitive.

The 'Trickidadians': The experience of growing up in a multicultural setting, and the continuous exposure to international currents, make the Trinidadian an eminently flexible person, able to adapt to a variety of situations, able to continually absorb new experiences and learn new roles. Trinis sometimes are referred to as "Trickidadians" by other Caribbean people, for what may be perceived as chameleon behavior.

Their adaptive nature also reveals itself in a great capacity for imitation, and very successful imitation at that. A story that T&Ters hug to their hearts is the one about the visit of Chubby Checker, King of the Twist, in the 1950s. Towards the end of his performance, Chubby Checker committed the indiscretion of inviting anybody to come on stage and do the Twist with him. Chubby Checker was out-twisted, upstaged and thoroughly put to shame – any number of Trinidadians readily swarmed onto the stage and did the Twist better than the King of the Twist. Trinis adopt and master every new dance form that comes out of Black America, performing the pop songs of the world as though Trinis had composed them, wearing avant-garde fashions from international salons with more aplomb than the models who first launched them. An important aspect of what Carnival is about is the temporary borrowing of another persona – one may be, for two days, a king or queen, a devil, a commando.

It may be said that Trinidadians are entirely too eager to mimic, and that they are a nation of copycats. Amazingly, though, their flair for imitation does not rob them of their originality or creativity. It is almost as though the process of continually borrowing and discarding stimulates creative energies and serves in some way to affirm individuality. For Trinidadians remain a very distinctive people, and continue to fashion a new culture that is the hallmark of Trinidadians of every race.

Above, echoes of Asia at Icacos and, right, a Paramin boy.

CARIBBEAN CARNIVAL

Each year, two days before Ash Wednesday, the citizens of Trinidad and Tobago pay homage to the gods of antiquity and their ancestors, follow their muses and the promptings of the flesh, and celebrate life in an explosive and beautiful two-day bacchanal. The climax to a year-long build up of energy, creativity and ingenuity, Carnival is the ultimate expression of the spirit of Trinidad and Tobago. A kaleidoscopic display of musical and artistic creativity, of high-spirited camaraderie and hedonistic beauty, it opens the floodgates to unbridled self-expression, a spectacle of color, movement, music, sensuality and the lavish joy in life which seems a hallmark of Trinidad and Tobago.

In many ways the epitome of the country and certainly the primary attraction for most visitors, Carnival meshes all fibers of Trinidadian life—the histories of Europe, Africa, Asia and oppression, calypso and steel band, imaginative and applied artistry—into a dazzling parade. Every age, race, color and idea binds together without prejudice, united in the potent force of a truly universal festival. The brilliant sunshine of tropical winter highlights a riot of colorful costumes like a pot of gold at the end of the rainbow, while the music of the spheres was never so hypnotic, urgent and all-embracing. And though you can appreciate and even love calypso without having experienced Carnival, the two are inseparable in the minds of T&Ters.

A National Party: Carnival in Trinidad and Tobago, or more specifically in Port of Spain, is different and better than any other major pre-Lenten celebration. An integral part of both the black and the white communities for over 200 years, today Carnival knows no boundaries, as children and grandmothers, rich and poor, Indian, black, white and Creole merge in bands and at fêtes in a warm-hearted, exuberant national party.

Even a stranger is drawn in, if willing to soca and wine with the Trinis, and there is nothing that makes a Trinidadian prouder or more hospitable than a foreigner eager to immerse himself in Carnival. It's a feast for the eyes that can be thoroughly enjoyed as a spectator sport, but for an unforgettable cultural experience, you must "play mas'"—masquerade — with the locals.

Carnival is a highly organized festivity: you don't just take to the streets in last year's Halloween costume—except perhaps during Jour Ouvert, popularly known as "joovay." There are about 15 or 20 clubs whose sole purpose is to plan, execute and display Carnival costumes.

Called by the names of their main designers—Peter Minshall, Raoul Garib, Hart, Carvalho and Stephen Lee Heung are a few of the better-known—these clubs are open to all for a price, but contain a foundation of loyal members who every year wear the costumes of their band, marching together through the streets. Each band has a King and Queen representing that year's theme—Callaloo, Wonders of Buccoo Reef, Rat Race, Bright Africa and Ye Saga of Merrie England are a few—and each band of 500 to 2,000 people is divided into smaller groups dressed as variations on the theme.

The best way to join a band is to know a local who'll help you buy one of his band's costumes, which generally cost about US$100. If you don't know anyone in a band, check with your hotel or the Tourist Board: they often reserve costumes in certain bands. Wrongly condemned as an excuse for public drunkenness and sensuality, Carnival is, in fact, an exhibition and competition of the best in music and in design. Its influence is felt in the country throughout the coming year.

Months in the Making: Preparation for Carnival commences on Ash Wednesday, right after Shrove Tuesday, the last day of the preceding year's Carnival. Even as band leaders relax from the physical and mental exhaustion of the months before, they engage in a post mortem of the recent past. What's done is done, but of vital importance is the theme for next year. Should they play on a historical, fantastical, social, natural, traditional, or cultural theme?

Subject decided, research begins. Historical and ethnic themes require authenticity, and every idea needs multiple inspiration. Libraries and encyclopedias provide impetus, and pictorials are consulted for period and regional costumes. Some leaders explore the structures of the society to be portrayed, and elements of their customs and life-style are selected after careful consideration.

There are brainstorming meetings, supplemented by liberal supplies of food and drink, and quiet moments of introspection and imagination, yielding fantastic ideas for the drawing board. The designers then start to produce the enticing drawings displayed as advertisement and blueprint later on. Starting in January, the drawings are hung outside the clubhouses of each band, to be ogled and discussed by potential masqueraders.

Raw materials must be decided upon, trips are made abroad for bulk purchases of brilliant lamés, velvets, satins, imitation fabrics of animal prints, plastic materials, beads, feathers and the multifarious components of elaborate costume making. Several band organizers and designers choose to use local materials like wood, seeds, leaves, straw, shells and locally manufactured cottons, wire, foam, steel, fiberglass and the other articles of construction.

perience is necessary to construct a costume light, mobile and effective from a theatrical standpoint. Some could indeed be called floats, except they are carried by one individual and are not permitted to be pushed, pulled, or motorized. Devices such as small wheels and ball bearings placed to take the peripheral weight are used to facilitate easy carriage.

Numerous man-hours are dedicated to the production of these masterpieces. The end result is fussed over, admired and considered a birth experience by those who labored. During the first appearance on stage during the week preceding Carnival, when the costumes are judged in their categories, thousands crowd the Savannah to get a preview of the splendor of the mas'.

As the Kings and Queens prepare to cross

Years ago, before the advent of mechanical devices now commonplace — plastic molding machines and the numerous ready-made articles of decoration — there was the laborious task of making clay molds for papier mâché forms. Today this has given way to mass production of lightweight forms for head pieces and props, as well as molded parts for the bases of large costumes. The costume making commences many months before Carnival, and each step employs ingenuity and meticulousness, as the final result can be a complete failure if there is a lack of engineering and construction skill to make ideas practical reality.

For the large and often cumbersome costumes of the Kings, Queens and principal characters in the bands, a great deal of ex-

the open stage in front of the grandstands crammed with party-goers, members of rival bands — aficionados not content to sit in the stands and await the presentations and the direct supporters of the contestants — crowd the holding bay where all the real-life drama takes place. Excitement mounts as they line up and speculation as to the finalists and eventual winners runs rampant. Light-hearted banter is exchanged, some comments building confidence while others even in jest make for uncertainty.

The determination to win and the excitement of living the fantasy inspires each character to take to the stage with zest and flourish. The sight of these magnificent structures animated by their human motivators glittering under the lights as their movements synchronize with the calpyso or soca is overwhelming.

On the night of Dimanche Gras, the Sunday before the actual days of Carnival, the finals are held and the King and Queen of Carnival chosen amidst fanfare and boisterous applause. They will lead their respective bands with great pride and prestige.

Saturnalia and Slaves: Carnival traces its origin into ancient times, to the Phoenician celebrations of Dionysus, god of wine, vegetation, new growth and survival, and to the Roman Saturnalias honoring the god of birth and renewal. The Latin *carne levare*, to take away flesh, is said to be the root of the word carnival, which is an orgy of the senses preceding the Lenten period in Christianity when the things of the flesh are prohibited.

During the Roman conquest of Europe, in other Caribbean islands, especially the French-speaking lands of Martinique, Guadeloupe and Haiti. The slaves brought the Christian custom of celebrating Christmas on into Ash Wednesday, with an admixture of African rites and traditions.

At first the slaves' festivals were of a modest nature, and although there was much fragmentation among the slaves due to the variety of African "nations," the commonality of their belief systems, secret societies and rites of passage allowed for the shared celebration of ancestral dramas.

The slaves' fervor in music and dancing made up for the rusticity and makeshift quality of their disguises, and they ventured outside their areas grouped in bands carrying sections of *batonniers*— stick men, ritual protectors and

these pagan rituals underwent several changes in order to survive, and ended by being the exclusive province of the aristocracy. In this way the pantheistic customs survived the rigid decrees of the Middle Ages, when all celebrations that could be termed Bacchanalian or Saturnalian were licentious abominatons akin to devilry. By 1783, when Trinidad and Tobago experienced an influx of French settlers, Carnival was well established among the French as an aristocratic celebration.

With the French settlers came slaves acquired

Left, throngs in downtown Port of Spain and, right, time-out from the "Sombrero" band.

champions of their bands. In 18th- and 19th-Century Trinidad and Tobago, Carnival masquerade became a means for the slaves to relieve frustration with their lot, as within the confines of Carnival they could mimic and buffoon the styles and habits of their masters.

Meantime, the grand balls of masquing (dressing up) and revelry were reenacted on a more sumptuous scale in the plantation houses. By the early 19th Century the elite had taken their masquing into the streets in their own fashion, traveling in carriages from estate party to estate party.

After Emancipation, the days of Carnival became days of protest as ex-slave revelers threatened the ruling class and their towns in a number of ways. The lit torches of the Can-

boulay procession (from the French *cannes brulees*, burning canes) endangered the wooden buildings of Port of Spain as much as the lascivious playacting compromised the morality of the aristocracy, and the government feared the violence of the *batonniers* who accompanied every band. Attempts were made to outlaw Carnival (see History p. 36) but the French aristocracy, also at odds with the now-British government, intervened to protect their own right to revelry.

In the years since, each new group of immigrants has added to the festival, and old traditions—that of jamette, or the "underworld" carnival, of throwing powder and streamers, of Canboulay and *kalenda*—have faded. The nightly parties at friends' homes have given way to enormous public fêtes, and the steel band and calypso competitions are as much a focus of attention as the masquing. Carnival is now a thoroughly modern event, but one with a deep underpinning of history and old ritual.

Fêtes and Finals: Carnival officially begins at about 4 a.m. Monday morning, and the Sunday night before, Dimanche Gras, is one of great anticipation and revelry. Fêtes are held everywhere in Port of Spain: in private homes, hotels, bars, clubs and restaurants. The city scene is one of constant motion and music from five in the afternoon through five the next morning.

Most parties are huge, with hundreds of people dancing en masse. Though Jour Ouvert is the official start to Carnival, it is by no means the beginning of the fun. Excitement has been building for days prior, as various calypso and steel band competitions are held nightly for the preceding couple of weeks, particularly at the Spektakula Forum. The new calypsos for that year have been introduced at shows and on the radio, and by Carnival all are thoroughly familiar, and music lovers have chosen their personal favorites for "Road March."

Starting the Friday before Carnival, there are nightly finals for King and Queen titles, steel bands and calypsonians at the Queen's Park grandstands. Huge fêtes with live and taped music are held at the big hotels and are open to all for a small entrance fee. They're as full of locals as they are of foreign guests. The pounding music begins around five each night and plays without let-up until three in the morning both Friday and Saturday nights, and with the exuberant fun of Kiddie's Carnival on Saturday, by Sunday evening the mood is already one of joyful exhaustion.

Left, playing Ole Mas' and, right, West Indian Hiawatha.

But there's something about rum punch, beer and the rhythmic soca that lends a second wind, and by midnight Sunday the city is ready to explode. As the great countdown begins, players gather in costume at special band headquarters.

Joovay Jump-up: Around 4 a.m., strong coffee and tea, coconut sweet bread, sandwiches and other goodies are produced to counteract the liquor heads and provide sustenance for the next few hours. The cocks crow to herald the break of the day—Jour Ouvert—but thousands won't hear for the din of music and the shouts of laughter as players spill out into the streets, thronging behind their favorite steel band, or more traditional brass bands and drums accompanied by folk instruments.

The costumes of *joovay* are at once less

elaborate and more satirical than the colorful masquerades of Monday and Tuesday. For joovay morning, revelers don homemade costumes satirizing the political and social scene, or illustrating grotesque historical figures who have been a part of Carnival since its beginnings. The music makers are more rhythmical and more primitive than the amplified, electrified groups who lead mainstream Carnival, beating tin cans, brake pans and glass bottles with spoons and knives. Human rivers move slowly through the crepuscular light, jumping, gyrating and shuffling along in varying states of consciousness, all driven by the relentless drumming.

Traditionally called "Ole Mas," short for Old Masquerade, in this parade anything goes, as costumes are personal statements ranging from the horrendous and bizarre to the lewd and jocular. There are grown men in oversized diapers sucking on a baby's bottle full of rum, male politicians with a penchant for their aunt's underwear, caricatures of prominent figures and, most popular, those who have smeared their bodies with mud and axle grease from head to toe. These last delight in hugging onlookers, especially those dressed in white.

Today the traditional costumes of sweepers, tailors, doctors, pierrot grenades and *pai banan* (banana straw) characters are rarely seen in the city. These were the familiar figures of days gone by who used to rouse sleeping families with their falsetto speeches as they rushed into open yards offering their services for a small fee. The traditional players have given way to organized bands similar to the fancy dress bands, with well-thought-out themes and more colorful costumes than players of yore. The masqueraders and observers dance through the streets until morning, when it's time to get ready for the first Road March "jump up." Do try to get some sleep between 7 a.m. and 11 a.m., because the Road March is seven or eight hours of feverish dancing and singing.

Around 10 or 11 a.m. the larger bands begin to converge in costume at their clubhouses to prepare for the Road March — the heart of modern Carnival. There are four judging stands throughout the city, including Independence Square and the main and final one at the Savannah, and each of the bands must pass by each judging area. Routes have been set long in advance to prevent, as far as possible, traffic jams, but the main streets are packed from noon until dusk with parading bands. The bands are simply enormous parties led and inspired by the ear-splitting calypsos coming from accompanying flatbed trucks full of musicians and huge speakers.

When bands cross paths there are calypso battles, with each group of musicians trying to drown the other out with its favorite tune. Eventually one or two songs win out and one is chosen Road March, People's Choice. Until then a variety of songs inspires the revelers to dance for hours on end in the blistering sun.

Though Port of Spain is the center of Carnival activity and the locus for all the big competitions, San Fernando, Scarborough and other smaller towns have their own parades and fêtes, often preferred by veterans who can no longer stomach the incessant music, activity and crowds of Port of Spain.

Right, all that glitters is Carnival.

FESTIVALS

Hosay: To the casual onlooker at a Trinidadian Hosay (or Hussein) festival, it may seem incredible that what is being celebrated is a procession of deep mourning observed by Shiite Muslims in places such as Iran, Iraq, Lebanon and India. To those Muslims of the Eastern hemisphere, Hosay in Trinidad would seem a travesty of what in essence should reflect the grief, pain and martyrdom of Hussein and his brother Hassan, grandsons of the prophet Mohammed, during the famous Jihad (Holy War) at Kerbela in long-ago Persia. But in the one hundred years since Indian Muslims first arrived on these islands, there has been much intermingling of the European, African and Indian cultures.

What the hundreds of participants and onlookers in the present-day procession see, then, is the effect of a century of indigenization. Since 1884, when the Hussein Festival was first observed in Trinidad, there has been a painstaking attempt to keep the tradition alive, and until about forty years ago, Hosay retained its aura of mourning, with austere rituals brought over intact from the subcontinent.

Now the holy men who used to walk on beds of fire (some Hindus and Africans among them) no longer perform their daring feats, and gone also are the old women who sang the *Maseehahs*, wailing dirges, behind the *Tadjahs* (Ta'ziyeh), the elaborate and beautiful replicas of Hussein's tomb. But fire-eating is still seen on occasion, as is *Banaithi*, the dance where whirling sticks of fire make eerie patterns against the night sky.

The massacre of Hussein and his party was said to have taken place on Ashura, the 10th day of the Muharram month, in 680 A.D. The modern celebration takes place around the month of Muharram, and could occur twice within the Roman year, with different areas observing each occasion. The most popular processions are between February and March in towns such as St. James, Curepe, Tunapuna, Couva and Cedros.

After forty days of fasting, abstinence and prayers, devotees begin the festival with *Flag Night*. Flags of various colors are taken through the streets as a symbolic beginning of the battle of Kerbela, and are then placed on a mud

and wattle dais amidst burning incense.

The following night, two small Tadjahs, minaretted tombs made of bamboo with colored tissue, tinfoil, crepe paper, mirrors and coconut leis, are carried on the heads of dancers through the streets, accompanied by drums. At midnight there is symbolic contact, with dancers gently touching Tadjahs with their heads and against each other.

The highlight, however, is on the third night, when the large Tadjahs are produced to gasps of delight. These incredible works of art have borrowed from the Carnival tradition over the

years, with a lavish flair blending Eastern designs with local innovations. Six or so feet tall, and covered with glitter and color, the Tadjahs emerge from different yards to pass through streets bearing great significance for the descendants of those who brought the tradition. In the area of St. James, for example, in close proximity are Lucknow, Hyderabad and Delhi Streets, named after main centers of Muslim observance in India.

In addition to the Tadjahs, the two moons representing Hussein and Hassan are carried by specially trained dancers. These large crescent-shaped structures six feet across and three feet at their highest point are usually red, to represent the decapitation of Hussein, and green or blue, for the poisoning of Hassan. Sharp blades

Preceding pages: Phagwa procession. Left, Hosay 1904 and, right, Hosay today, with tassa drummers.

are inserted between the thickly ruched material, projecting upward for a spiked effect that gives the sign of battle.

The dancers whirl in a stately dance of the brothers' triumph over death as they move with one foot raised onto the ball and the other flat. The moons are placed over one shoulder with the pole end stuck in the *Shamotee* at the waist. The dancers appear mesmerized, and they enthrall the crowd.

At midnight, there is a ritual kissing of the two moons as the dancers come together with great ceremony and allow the moons to meet as if in brotherly embrace. This brings cheers of delight from the onlookers and perhaps twinges of pain for devotees.

The excitement of the festival is further motivated by the pulsating drums of the *Tassa*

The climax of Hosay comes as the Tadjahs and moons are wheeled into the streets the following day for their last procession to the sea. There they are ceremoniously cast after prayers and offerings have been made.

Phagwa: Spring is not known as a season in Trinidad and Tobago, but the vernal equinox doesn't go unnoticed among people whose traditions are based in lands far away. The Hindu festival of Phagwa celebrates this event as it does in India each year, heralding the Hindu New Year with gay abandonment.

Around the full moon in March, elaborate rituals celebrate the triumph of light over darkness and good over evil. As with other religious festivals in Trinidad, a Carnival spirit has gradually pervaded the festivities as a wider population becomes involved. Phagwa is not

players. These drummers are quite famous and attract great crowds who follow behind them dancing. Among the drummers, some are of African descent, drawn to tassa as they are to the African tamboo bamboo or indigenous steel drum. The younger generation of this Carnival-oriented society see this later part of the procession as a time to jump up and make merry. The West African attitude of jovial celebration at funeral rites surely influences their actions.

Another attraction is the dancing of the *Ghadka*. A stick fight/dance done by two men, each holds in one hand a stick about three feet long and a small leather pouch as a shield in the other. They perform in a circle drawn around them in the street, and go through their symbolic battle with observers egging them on.

confined to Hindus, but includes anyone wishing to participate.

Bonfires are lit to symbolize the destruction of Holika, the evil sister of King Hiranya Kashipu, and before the actual day of Phagwa, there are Chowtal singing competitions. Chowtal is a mixture of the religious and the secular, and the competitions display the skills of singers who perform both devotional songs and local compositions. The latter are more and more influenced by calypso, borrowing from its extemporaneous artistry. Special instruments such as the *Dholak* (a small skin drum), *Kartals*, *Mageeras* and *Janjs* (cymbals) accompany the Hindi singing and dancing.

One of the more popular rituals is the spraying of the *Abeer* powder, a red vegetable dye made into a bright fuchsia liquid and sprayed over observer and devotee alike. It creates a messy but colorful scene as clothes take on a tie-dyed effect and skin and hair are drenched. Recently other colors have been introduced as the festival becomes more secular, including the innovations of other ethnic and religious groups.

Dancing is a central part of Phagwa, and varies in style, tending toward the suggestive dances of Carnival but with a good admixture of East Indian movements.

There are reenactments of the legend of Holika during the day as bands similar to those of Carnival participate in competitions set up at several locations throughout the island. All manner of oriental costumes, many of them white, are worn with crowns, garlands, jewelry and flowers, and various characters from the

and across buildings, wherever a light can be affixed. The festival of Deepa Divali (pronounced "Duwali") is a national religious holiday celebrated by the hundreds of thousands of Hindus. This they do to honor Lakshmi, goddess of light, beauty, riches and love, she who was the wife of Vishnu and who was born out of the churning of the great ocean. For her they make elaborate advance preparations, offering pujas—sacrifices and prayers—in her name.

Weeks before the actual event, men cut long bamboo poles to build structures in village parks, school and *mandir* (temple) grounds, and their own yards. On these structures are placed tiny clay pots called *deyas*, filled with coconut oil and a cotton wick. The deyas are also placed along the walls of verandahs and fences,

epic drama are portrayed. The plays are more or less light-hearted, as befitting a celebration of rebirth.

A recent innovation has been the use of trucks as floats on which pretty girls are paraded as queens in fine vestments accompanied by drummers and dancing revelers who blend the African, calypso and East Indian rhythms and fashions.

Divali: On one November night Trinidad sparkles with the light of thousands of tiny flames and electric bulbs, strung through trees

Left, Phagwa celebrants covered with abeer powder. Above left, Phagwa dancers and, right, *deyas* lit for Divali.

on the ground and all possible vantage points.

On the evening of Divali the deyas are lit and tended during the night. They illuminate the way for the visitation of Lakshmi and must not be allowed to go out before the appointed hour. Modern embellishments have also made their mark on this festival as, more and more, electricity is used to augment the lights of the deyas. Strings of colored bulbs are used in the manner of Christmas lights, and, needless to say, this phenomenon brings thousands of non-Hindus out to visit the various well-illuminated public places.

Prior to the night of lights there are shows and pageants where Divali Queens are chosen amidst oriental dancing and singing. Special song competitions highlight local composers and feature star Indian musicians. It is a joyous occasion, and everyone tries to emulate the qualities of Lakshmi, spreading peace and goodwill.

Greetings and gifts are exchanged, with food being the traditional gift, and there is the usual abundance of sustenance provided in private homes, shared liberally with non-Indian neighbors and friends and the less fortunate in the vicinity. There is a special sacrificial meal of *parsad*, a doughy concoction of flour, sugar, milk and raisins, provided as an offering to the gods.

The import of Divali, the triumph of good over evil, has meaning on a national scale and so public prayer services are held for thousands, with the celebrants including clergy from other denominations who come together with their Hindu brothers and sisters to celebrate a shared

All masjids and homes are spruced up for the occasion and everyone dresses in traditional wear, with the women in *shalwar* and *kameez* (long tapered trousers with matching long tunic tops). Delicate veils are worn, but faces are left uncovered.

Observers prepare sumptuous dinners and large gatherings of all ethnic groups are invited to celebrate the occasion with Muslim friends. The traditional dish of *Sawine* is a requisite on the menu. A rich concoction of fine vermicelli boiled in milk, it contains raisins, sugar and chopped almonds.

Throughout the country there is an air of spiritual renewal as Muslims and non-Muslims alike honor and respect Allah, wishing each other *Assalam O Alaikum*.

Emancipation Day: For those of African

ideal.

Eid-ul-Fitr: The new moon of Ramadan marks the observance of Eid-ul-Fitr, the Muslim New Year, occurring around the month of June. It is a national holiday, but cannot be predicted exactly, as the actual day depends on the sighting of the new moon by a holy Imam. Official announcement comes after this sighting, and what follows is an obligatory day of feasting to break the month-long daylight fast. The usual visit to the *masjids* (mosques) for prayers and thanksgiving is followed by almsgiving to the poor in the form of money and items of food and clothing.

In this relatively private and subdued celebration, visits are paid to relatives and friends, and greetings and gifts are exchanged.

descent—almost half of Trinidad and Tobago's population—the newly designated Emancipation Day on August 1 is of special significance. Started in 1985, it replaces Columbus' Discovery Day, coming one year after the 150th anniversary of the abolition of slavery.

The day commences with an all-night vigil and includes church services, street processions past historic landmarks, addresses by dignitaries and an evening of shows with a torchlight procession to the National Stadium.

The event marks the achievements of the sons and daughters of slavery as well as reflecting on sobering thoughts of man's inhumanity to man, and honors the multiple contributions of the black people to Trinidad and Tobago's rich culture.

Independence and Republic Days: In August and September, Trinidad and Tobago also celebrates two patriotic milestones. On Aug. 31, 1962 the country gained its independence from Great Britain, and on Sept. 24, 1976, moved on to Republic status. The fact that both these events were achieved in a peaceful and civilized manner is enough to warrant enthusiastic thanksgiving.

Throughout the country the various villages and towns celebrate with sporting events, dances, concerts, exhibitions and seaside activities. Among the highlights is the military parade at the Queen's Park Savannah on the morning of August 31.

The emphasis here is on pomp, tradition and ceremony, without the ominous overtones of military might. The Regiment, Coast Guard,

conia, Hummingbird, and the highest Trinity Cross are bestowed on recipients who have made outstanding contributions to the nation.

Before the secular observances take place, however, official and unofficial church services are arranged. A great achievement in this multi-ethnic, multireligious country is the meeting of the various denominations as a mark of national unity. In 1984, clergy from eleven denominations officiated at the Cathedral of the Immaculate Conception in Port of Spain, marking the first time since the coming to the west through slavery that the African man was able to have his traditional beliefs accepted as religion by the orthodox faiths. A priest — Mogba — of the Shango Belief System (the Yoruba Orisha faith) participated in the liturgy.

This gesture of unity included religious func-

Police and Fire Services lead a host of voluntary organizations in an impressive parade observed by thousands.

The Police and Regiment Bands arrange popular calypsos into military marches, and at the end of the parade, everyone traditionally follows the Band through the streets to the Barracks, like children behind the legendary Pied Piper of Hamelin, only this time in Carnival style.

That evening, the National Awards Ceremony is held, when local awards like the Cha-

tionaries from the Hindu, Muslim, Divine Light and Spiritual Baptist (Shouters) faiths, among others, and the result was overwhelming and memorable.

During the first week of September, the annual Folk Fair brings a big taste of rural life and customs to Port of Spain. Over a hundred booths are established to display and sell hand-crafted items, locally made works of art and clothing, and traditional cuisine, sweetmeats and beverages. Traditional music and dance performances encourage the air of festivity.

One week later, around September 15, the Family Fair opens for a ten-day run. The emphasis is on family participation in art and food displays, lectures and nightly shows. On the Sunday nearest the 24th, a parade of historical

Left, a Best Village dance performance and, right, traditional dances on the beach.

floats climaxes the weeks of celebration.

Best Village: The Prime Minister's Best Village Trophy Competition began in 1963 as a small handicrafts fair, and has since expanded to five categories involving numerous towns and villages and hundreds of participants.

An effort to encourage and record the folk arts and local pride, Best Village is a month-long series of small contests culminating in a feast of music, dance, drama and song. Under the guidance of elders, young Trinidad and Tobagonians create shows on various themes pertaining to life in the village, using traditional dances, music and song.

It is in this setting that the African-French *bele* and *pique* are seen alongside the Hispanic *parang* and the African-derived *bongo* and *saraka* dances. Stick fighters are in full cry as

they dance the *kalenda*, while others excite their audiences with the *limbo*.

Rich folk music is sung by choirs including grandparents, grandchildren and everyone in between. Whole families participate in some villages. Around thirty-two villages reach the finals, presenting their shows at the grandstand of the Queen's Park Savannah, where at other times Carnival Kings and Queens display their arts.

In addition to the theatrical presentations, in the fall there are also craft shows, concerts, and a beauty pageant called "La Reine Rivée," patois for "The Queen Arrives," where costumes approaching the elaborateness of Carnival are featured.

The Limbo: Along with steel drum music,

visitors to the Caribbean associate the limbo with the sexy abandon of a tropical island. But the limbo as we know it today—exhibitionistic, glittery, sensual—is not the limbo of a bygone era, when men (and women) symbolically passed below the bar of the underworld to rise toward light and deliverance, representing the path the soul of the deceased takes in its journey to the next world.

The limbo was a way of assisting, encouraging and guiding the soul into the world of the ancestors. With much singing, clapping, drumming and ribald taunts, each dancer shimmied his way below the length of wood, held by two supporters who allowed the dancers to go no lower than hip level.

Now, of course, expert limbo dancers can easily clear six inches with a soda pop bottle as the standard measure, and the limbo is more a display of athletic prowess than an acknowledgement of another world.

Easter Sports Events: The Tobago Easter Goat and Crab Races are amongst the more bizarre traditions in Trinidad and Tobago. During the long Easter weekend, Tobago is flooded with vacationers from abroad and from the bigger island, and when people aren't on the beaches, they go to the races.

The crab races are a riot of fun as the owners spur their animals on to the finish line. But crabs are wont to be wayward, and bettors take their losses seriously as the crabs make their usual sideways instead of forward movements.

The goat races, featuring large sanaan goats, used to be a popular event for competitors, but now attract only a few. Those who do come, though, are assured of a full crowd of spectators, especially children, who delight in the butting antics of some furious and rebellious goats.

Three Men in a Tub: A more daring and expensive sport is the newly introduced Bath Tub Derby, run in March on the Mayaro-Nariva River in southeastern Trinidad. All manner of floating craft are constructed, with the absurd most favored. These are made to travel in grand style down the river on its course to the sea, piloted by crews attired in the most outlandish costumes possible.

The racers are egged on with the sounds of drums, bottles and spoons, and even percussion from the sides of the boats. Spectators play calypsos and reggae from huge portable tape players, and bikini-clad women come out to back their favorite teams. It's a day-long celebration ending with a huge public beach party.

Left, a participant in the last Discovery Day celebration, now replaced by Emancipation Day and, right, the Independence Day parade.

PLACES

Trinidad and Tobago are like one of those married couples one sometimes meets who are different enough from one another as to be almost incompatible, but who in successfully joining so many opposing qualities create a union unusually dynamic and all-encompassing. Within this small country are the cosmopolitan enticements of one of the most fascinating and sophisticated cities in the Caribbean and the serenity of a pastoral tropical island; the exuberant bacchanalia of Carnival and the quiet of deserted beaches; the wildlife of a mainland jungle and the beauties of a Caribbean coral reef; East Indians and Africans, Europeans and Asians; a tumultuous past and a wealthy and literate present; the elegance of international hotels and the intimacy of seaside bungalows. In short, there are the worldliness, ethnicity and industry of Trinidad and the friendliness, languor and natural beauty beaches of Tobago.

The travel section that follows has been divided into three chapters: Port of Spain, Trinidad and Tobago. For the most rewarding visit it is hoped that one would be able to see a bit of each. Many visitors come to Port of Spain first, so our tour begins there, with a short history of Port of Spain and how she grew, as well as an introduction to her sites and excitements. The capital offers a bustling cross-section of the history, culture and population of the whole country.

Next is a series of short trips, starting from Port of Spain, to the multitudinous attractions of Trinidad. Her smaller cities and towns, industries and countryside provide a more in-depth look at a nation unique in its geography and combination of cultural influences. Indian towns of sugarcane farmers and Creole fishing villages, mangrove swamps and mountain savannahs, the heavy industries and the balmy beaches offer everything a visitor could want.

Tobago is a perfect foil for the complications of Trinidad. It is more typically Caribbean, or at least more what vacationers have come to expect: endless sun, clear blue sea and sparkling sands, and many Trinidadians holiday there after the exhaustion of Carnival. In Tobago you can do nothing or a little bit of something, but you can't help but relax.

Finally, one of the country's primary natural resources and attractions is her people. Outgoing and sincerely friendly, Trinidadians are notoriously talkative, and their eagerness to make friends turns a sightseeing trip into a cultural introduction. And once you've been introduced, you'll fall in love.

SITE OF
FORT GEORGE
1804

INTRODUCTION TO PORT OF SPAIN

In Port of Spain gingerbread houses and modern 10-story office buildings standing shoulder-to-shoulder with ramshackle curbside stalls and decaying clapboard storefronts tell the story of years of colonial existence recently overlaid with independence and new-found wealth. All the strands of Trinidad and Tobago's multicolored fabric are tangled in a knot in her capital city, providing constant interest, confusion and conflicting images.

This is a good city to walk in, with a compact downtown area, crowded sidewalk life and pleasant parks and gardens. In the heat of the day the Emperor Valley Zoo and Botanical Gardens are a nice place to stroll, and any time there is a roti stand nearby for a cheap, portable snack. Most of the architectural, cultural and shopping attractions are within a couple miles' radius of one another, and the more energetic might well enjoy walking in the hot, quiet streets of the closer residential suburbs, or (during the day) in the noisy, crowded and lively lanes of Laventille.

Calypso and steel band are a primary attraction of the city, and plenty of small clubs, hotel shows and practice yards provide forums where long-time favorites perform next to newer talents. Around Carnival, of course, Port of Spain is a veritable supermarket of music, with calypso tents, pan yards and huge organized calypso and steel band "play offs" offering musical events every night for weeks.

Spectators take only half the pleasure of calypso if they are unfamiliar with the economic and social conditions of the country, because calypso lyrics run a constant, wry commentary on current events and pre-occupations. Getting to know Port of Spain and her people during the day will enhance your appreciation of the night's entertainments.

Hotel accommodations run the gamut from the international luxury of the Hilton Hotel, perched on a hill overlooking the Savannah, to private guesthouses in the suburbs. In every locale, warm-hearted Trinis make everyone feel right at home.

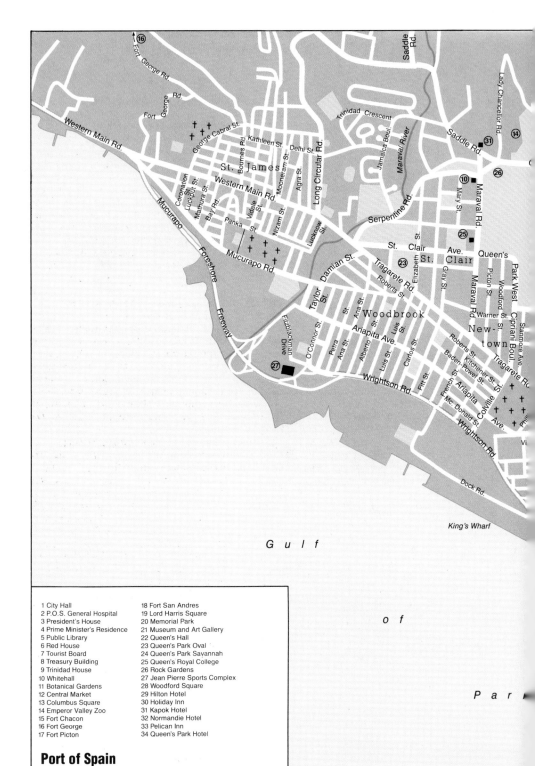

1 City Hall
2 P.O.S. General Hospital
3 President's House
4 Prime Minister's Residence
5 Public Library
6 Red House
7 Tourist Board
8 Treasury Building
9 Trinidad House
10 Whitehall
11 Botanical Gardens
12 Central Market
13 Columbus Square
14 Emperor Valley Zoo
15 Fort Chacon
16 Fort George
17 Fort Picton

18 Fort San Andres
19 Lord Harris Square
20 Memorial Park
21 Museum and Art Gallery
22 Queen's Hall
23 Queen's Park Oval
24 Queen's Park Savannah
25 Queen's Royal College
26 Rock Gardens
27 Jean Pierre Sports Complex
28 Woodford Square
29 Hilton Hotel
30 Holiday Inn
31 Kapok Hotel
32 Normandie Hotel
33 Pelican Inn
34 Queen's Park Hotel

Port of Spain

800 m/ 0,5 miles

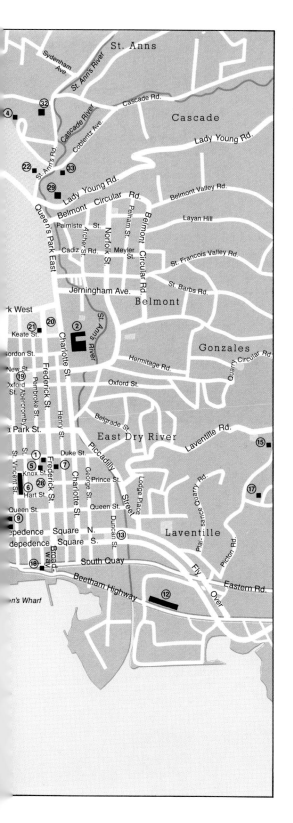

PORT OF SPAIN

Port of Spain sprawls eastward from the Gulf of Paria, and has for two centuries been spreading itself freely, today nestling in every curve of the Northern Range which rises up immediately behind it. In the rainy season the verdant foliage of these hills, stretching from east to west straight across the island, crowns the city with an emerald coronet that shows off the brilliant red of the flamboyant flower and the gold of the yellow poui tree. In the dry season, as the sun dazzles against galvanized roofs and concrete buildings, Port of Spain is as brown and as crisp as toast, its hills at times alive with brushfires that ignite and explode the bamboo and turn the undergrowth into black soot.

Nature, however, is on the side of the city. The rainy season lasts much longer than the dry and it takes only a few showers to effect a miraculous change from brown to green, so that Port of Spain is almost always green, its many parks, squares, gardens and open places living testimony of a tropical land on which nature has been pleased to bestow her bounty.

The lush and decaying confusion of the surrounding hills has a subtle correspondence in the nature of the city. The streets of Port of Spain are well laid out, but there the orderliness ends. The city is in many respects an unruly place, a characteristic deriving from its peculiar history. Port of Spain became the capital almost by accident, a fact that gave it a sort of frontier beginning, as people of different races and cultures flocked to the city willy-nilly, seeking new horizons.

In 1757, Puerto de los Hispanoles was a mere fishing village of mud huts and a few wooden thatched roof houses, surrounded by hills and swamps. Its residents then were mainly Amerindian and Spanish half breeds, most of whom earned their livelihood by fishing and occasional trade with the Venezuelan mainland. It was hardly an appropriate choice for a governor's residence, particularly a Spanish governor representing the grandee of his country. Since the 16th Century the capital had been **St. Joseph**, 12 miles inland. St. Joseph, surrounded by cocoa and sugar estates, was often affected by various tropical diseases and in the mid-18th Century by a serious shortage of workers. But as Trinidad had neither gold nor silver, she was of little interest to the authorities in Spain, and they permitted her capital to fall into disrepair. The situation was such that when in 1757 a new Governor, Don Pedro de la Moneda, arrived, he found his house to be uninhabitable and there was no money to effect repairs.

It was then that he decided to leave St. Joseph and set up residence elsewhere. Being a seaport, Port of Spain had a definite advantage.

The decision to remove the Governor's residence did not find favor with the Cabildo (Town Council), but Governor de la Moneda ignored them and rented a small house somewhere in the vicinity of present-day Piccadilly Street. The Cabildo eventually followed him to Port of Spain, which then had only two streets, **Nelson** and **Duncan**, surrounded by mangrove swamps, hills and high woods.

Around 1780 the arrival of the French in the colony started an agrarian revolution giving rise to commerce and trade, which in turn made expansion of the city inevitable and urgent. The surrounding mangrove swamps were filled in and land reclaimed from the sea. High woods were cut down to make room for more streets.

In addition, just before the British took over, the last Spanish governor, Don Maria José Chacon (after whom Trinidad and Tobago's national flower, the Chaconia, is named) had taken an unusual measure to facilitate the city's expansion.

The Rio Santa Ana then ran from the hills north of the city through the area now known as St. Ann's, and straight through the center of Port of Spain, its course being through what is now Woodford Square, down Chacon Street and Independence Square to the sea.

During the rainy season, the growing population suffered the effects of regular flooding, so in 1787 Chacon solved the problem by diverting the river to run along the foot of the Laventille Hills and thence to the sea. The area of the old river bed was filled in, enabling the city to grow as it has.

With the river harnessed, Port of Spain continued its development, and in the space of a few years the city had grown to eleven streets, seven running from south to north—Duncan, Nelson, George, Charlotte, Henry, Frederick and Chacon; and four from east to west—King, Queen, Prince and Duke. Around the same time, with the demands of a burgeoning popu-

Preceding pages: Port of Spain and the Gulf of Paria from Fort George; and Trinidad's modern highway system. Below, an old plan of Port of Spain and its suburbs.

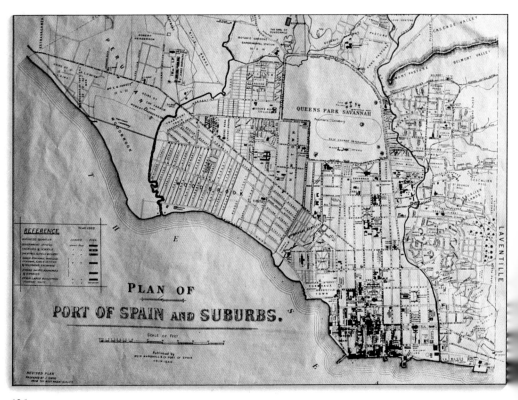

PLAN OF
PORT OF SPAIN AND SUBURBS.

lation, the city began to spread towards the valleys and slopes of what are now the suburbs of Belmont, Laventille, St. Ann's, St. James and Maraval.

The extent of Port of Spain's spread across the hills of the Northern Range is obvious today, particularly when darkness falls. Then the city is illuminated by twinkling lights from houses on the hills stretching from Laventille in the east, across Belmont, St. Ann's, Maraval, St. James and even beyond the boundaries of Port of Spain to the western districts of Carenage and Diego Martin. Many of these present-day hill residents are immigrants who came from neighboring Caribbean islands and started as squatters much as earlier inhabitants began. To a large extent, though, crudely constructed wooden huts have been replaced by more solid concrete buildings, and to the west of the city many hill dwellers are wealthy citizens who have built themselves mansions with a view.

And it is a breathtaking view of a city at once international, modern, provincial and seedy, both an old colonial town and the capital of one of the most prosperous republics in the Caribbean.

Today Port of Spain is a city of modern skyscrapers, of old fashioned gingerbread houses, of Gothic cathedrals, Hindu temples and Muslim mosques, all existing happily side by side. It is a city of modern apartment flats, department stores, high-fashion boutiques, oriental bazaars, cinemas, nightspots, Indian, Creole and Chinese restaurants. It is a city of informal malls and sidewalk stalls blaring calypso and pop music from their stands. It is a city of vendors, weaving between traffic selling peanuts and cashew nuts, of motorized carts peddling coconut water, chicken and chips, Chinese fried rice and Indian roti. It is a city of men with long Rasta locks encased in brightly colored woolen caps, burning incense on the sidewalks and selling homemade jewelry. It is a city with makeshift malls crudely constructed from boxwood. It is a city of stray dogs and vagrants, of missing street signs or signs hidden by overhanging vines.

The latest population figures show that half of the country's population of 1.2 million live in what is known as the east-west corridor, which stretches straight across the foothills of the Northern Range from Chaguaramas in the west to Arima in the east. A great percentage of this half is centered in Port of Spain itself and its

Left, strollers in Woodford Square and, right, view down Duke Street toward Laventille Chapel.

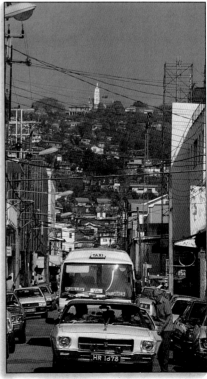

surrounding districts of Diego Martin, Morvant, Barataria and San Juan.

The formal boundaries of the city extend from Wrightson Road near the port, east along South Quay to the southern extremity of Laventille, across the northern end of Belmont, along Belmont Circular Road, then westward along Long Circular Road, St. Clair and the Maraval River, down George Cabral Street in St. James and to Mucurapo Road in the west, which leads directly back to Wrightson Road.

The majority who live in Port of Spain are to be found in the suburbs, as the inner city is more and more becoming a business and administrative center. The population focus of Port of Spain has shifted to suburbs such as Laventille, Belmont, Woodbrook, Newtown, St. Clair, St. James, Cascade, St. Ann's and Ellerslie Park.

But downtown Port of Spain is usually crowded during the day, with office workers, shoppers, limers and traffic. And the rapid development of the city, particularly since the oil boom, has meant that the streets of Port of Spain are almost always being dug up. If it isn't the Telephone Company (Telco) laying lines, it's the Water and Sewerage Authority (WASA) putting down water mains. The arguments rage as to who is responsible for the repairs, citizens complaining constantly about the dust or mud and the inconvenience. But the constant inconvenience is the price of progress, for almost every building, whether commercial or private, is served by running water and electricity.

And cosmopolitan Port of Spain residents are also accustomed to a wide choice of up-to-date goods, particularly in automobiles, appliances and clothing. Port of Spain is a fashion-conscious city and the oil boom of the 1970s and early '80s allowed indulgence in this regard.

Weekend shopping trips to Miami, Curacao and Caracas were commonplace then, as were holidays to New York, Toronto and London. There developed what is known as the "suitcase trade," with individuals buying at cheap prices abroad and selling at highly inflated prices in Port of Spain. The December 1985 devaluation of the TT dollar has affected this pattern but has not lessened the eye for fashion in the many boutiques stocked with clothes by local designers.

A great inspiration to style is the Port of Spain pastime of "liming"; standing and

The hills of Laventille.

talking at street corners, outside cinemas, bars and department stores, appreciating the minutiae of daily life. Attractive girls must virtually run the gauntlet everytime they pass a lime, and POS women easily pass muster.

More than anywhere else in the islands, Port of Spain shows evidence of the great and unusual variety of races, religions and cultures that make up the country. In a lunch hour lime downtown, one can easily see a panorama of race: people from west, central and eastern Europe, from Africa and India, Asia and the Middle East. Intermarriage has brought variations on the theme, and this blending of races is endemic to Port of Spain, more so than any other part of Trinidad and Tobago. A serendipitous side effect are some of the loveliest women (and men) in the Caribbean.

For a panorama that challenges the beauty of the population, the nearby hills of the Northern Range offer an excellent vantage point from which to get a sense of the sweep and size of the city. Four forts define the original boundaries of Port of Spain, and two, Fort George and Fort Picton, afford particularly good views.

Fort George is situated in the hills overlooking St. James, northwest of the city. To visit Fort George, take Tragarete Road onto the Western Main Road, and at the Cocorite Junction take the right turn for Fort George Road. The winding, hilly road climbs uphill steadily for about two miles.

It was built by Governor Sir Thomas Hislop in 1805, eight years after the island had been conquered by the English. Fears continued that the Spaniards would try to retake the island, and war had just broken out between England and her arch-enemy, France. Hislop knew that the French fleet was in the Caribbean and built the Fort in shooting distance of the Gulf. The Fort has been well renovated, and one can see the original dungeons, cannon balls and implements used by the soldiers who manned this fort. Above all it offers a breathtaking view of Port of Spain and far out to sea. Also at the Fort is a Signal Station designed by Prince Kofi Nti, son of King Kofi Calcali of Ashanti, West Africa.

Fort Picton, in the hills of Laventille, is one of the oldest fortifications in Trinidad. Take the Eastern Main Road to Picton Hill Road up to the Fort. Picton was a member of Sir Ralph Abercromby's victorious expedition in 1797 in which

Roxy roundabout at sunset.

Trinidad passed from Spanish rule to British rule. Abercromby left Picton in charge as governor and the latter built the Fort to protect shipping in the harbor as well as to protect the small settlement of Port of Spain.

The two other forts date back to Spanish times: **Fort St. Andres**, built in 1887 and now housing the Traffic Police; and **Fort Chacon**, built in 1770 in Laventille, opposite the Roman Catholic church.

The other classic way to view the city is from the sea, or at least from the seaside, down along the docks of the port. From this vantage, the twin towers of the Financial Complex, the revolving sky restaurant of the Holiday Inn and the slim chimneys of the T&T Electric Company and the hood-shaped roofs of the National Stadium stand out from an ocean of red and green roofs of smaller businesses and homes, punctuated by treetops and the mountains of the Northern Range.

Until the mid-1930s, **King's Wharf** had no facilities for the docking of deep draught ships. Cargo and passengers were off-loaded as they lay at anchor and were brought by launches to the docks. In 1935 work began on a deepwater harbor with an expanded quay frontage created by filling almost 400 acres with the earth excavated from the dredged harbor.

Today the harbor handles an annual average of 1.5 million tons of cargo. Several cruise ships dock at King's Wharf on their journeys through the Caribbean, and the ferry for Tobago also leaves from here, but overall the port is industrial and not picturesque.

Leaving the port, one crosses **Wrightson Road** to Independence Square, the latter stretching from west to east in a straight line. But a word about Wrightson Road, a section of which was known during World War II as the infamous "Gaza Strip."

Numerous and notorious nightclubs were located on Wrightson Road, frequented by U.S. servicemen stationed at various naval and other bases in Trinidad at the time. Part of the evening's entertainment usually included a raid by the vice squads and the arrest of striptease dancers. Now the nightclubs are gone and the Gaza Strip is a respectable part of Wrightson Road, scene of commercial and other strictly business activities.

Independence Square was laid out on reclaimed swampland in 1816 by Baron Shack, who planted it with trees imported from Venezuela. Really an avenue of trees with double traffic lanes on either side, it was first known as King Street, later changed to Marine Square, and became Independence in 1962, when Trinidad and Tobago ended colonial rule. From one end to the other, the dusty concrete Square is the very hub of business life in the city. Along the southern side are some of the most important building in the country, notably the **Financial Complex** and the **Textel** building, with its radio antennae proclaiming its function, as well as the offices of the Express and many shops.

The Financial Complex appears on the newer Trinidad and Tobago currency notes, appropriately enough, as the complex houses the Central Bank of Trinidad and Tobago, and the Ministry of Finance. Designed by a Trinidad architectural firm at a cost of TT$400 million, it was opened in March of 1985. Its two 22-story towers are clad in solar insulated glass strong enough to withstand earthquakes and inside, the walls are decorated with works of local artists and sculptors. During site excavation, the diggings revealed many remains of old Port of Spain, including the old sea wall, ships' anchors, cannon balls and items of Amerindian pottery.

On the north side of Independence Square are the large **Treasury Building**, which formerly housed the Central Bank, and the head office of **Customs and Excise**, as well as more banks and other business places.

The Roman Catholic Cathedral of the Immaculate Conception lies squarely in the center of the eastern end of Independence Square, and is one of two imposing cathedrals due to the enterprise of a British Governor, Sir Ralph Woodford.

From the time of his arrival in 1813, Governor Woodford began to make improvements in the city, which had been almost completely destroyed in the great fire of 1808. A man of foresight, he recognized that a city was not only a collection of large buildings, streets and commercial and residential houses, but a place that needed open spaces where people could enjoy leisure and physical activity. The heart of Port of Spain, the Queen's Park Savannah, was developed as a result of Woodford's initiative, as were a number of other parks and squares.

Woodford was an Anglican, but for historical reasons dating back to the time of Spanish rule, many state occasions were marked by church services in the Catholic church, at the time a small and unremarkable structure. Woodford considered that

Port of Spain should have cathedrals in keeping with the status of a growing town, and so in March 1816, he laid the foundation stone for the Roman Catholic Cathedral of the Immaculate Conception. Designed in the shape of a Latin cross, it is built of blue metal stone from the Laventille quarries. It is 210 feet long, 120 feet wide and its nave is 80 feet wide and long.

It took 16 years to build due to a shortage of funds as well as to delays with ships bringing material from abroad, such as the iron framework from England and the Florentine marble used for the high altar and the communion rail. The new cathedral was able to accommodate 1200 and the first service was held on April 1, 1832. At the time the sea came up to its eastern wall.

In 1984, the Cathedral underwent extensive renovations and 16 stained-glass windows from Ireland were added, as well as 14 Stations of the Cross made of Italian marble. Part of the renovation also included the adornment of the inner pillars with heraldic shields depicting the archdiocesan and national coat of arms, as well as the coat of arms of the city of Port of Spain, and the various religious orders of nuns and priests who have worked here. At the back of the High Altar is a magnificent stained-glass window depicting the apparition of the Blessed Virgin at Lourdes in France. The other windows depict the children of Trinidad and Tobago representing the various ethnic groups that comprise the population.

Immediately behind the Cathedral is **Columbus Square**, with a statue of Christopher Columbus. And beyond this square is **Piccadilly Street**, where Port of Spain began, and where today stands the imposing **Riverside Plaza**, with its government ministries and departments.

Back towards the more easterly end of Independence Square there are the mobile fast-food vans, coconut carts, and Chinese and Indian restaurants which cater to the thousands of people who work in the city.

Almost at the midway point is a section of Independence Square known as "**The Drag**." An informal craft market, its main products are leather shoes and sandals, knitted caps and afro combs. Many of the occupants of "The Drag" have, however, turned their stalls into makeshift homes, giving rise to problems of sanitation and considerable controversy among those who view "The Drag" as an eyesore, and suspect illegal activities.

Lunchtime lime, Port of Spain.

Independence Square is also a giant taxi stand for Trinidad's unique "pirate," or route, taxis and the more conventional hired cars. At Independence Square, travelers can get taxis going to any destination in Port of Spain and the rest of the country.

Pirate taxi drivers spend so many hours of the day on the road that they have made their cars as comfortable as possible. Many are air-conditioned or cooled by fans, sprayed with perfumed air fresheners, decorated with ornaments, lucky charms and religious objects, and of course all have stereo music. A trip in a pirate taxi introduces the visitor to the Trinidadian's love of argument, whether about politics, religion or sport, arguments that can often become heated and rowdy. Some taxi drivers have particular quirks, such as the famous one plying the route between Belmont and Port of Spain, who would never stop to pick up anyone, man or woman, considered by him to be "ugly."

"The Drag" extends from Chacon Street to **Frederick Street,** the main shopping boulevard in Port of Spain. At the latter intersection is a life-size statue of Captain Arthur Andrew Cipriani, the country's first national hero, Mayor of the City for many years, and a member of the Legislative Council, a forerunner of today's Parliament.

Cipriani campaigned as early as 1914 for unity in the West Indies, self-government, an end to child labor on the sugarcane fields and compulsory education. He died in Port of Spain in 1945 and is buried at Lapeyrouse cemetery.

This intersection of Frederick and Independence Square is a good point from which to move northwards on a tour of the city, keeping one's sight firmly fixed on the Northern Range as a point of reference.

Frederick Street is lined with department stores stocked with goods from all over the world, the largest being **Stephens & Johnsons** and **Kirpalanis**. There is also the **Colsort Mall**, with numerous small shops, shoe and fabrics stores, and two very large jewelry establishments, **Y. de Lima** and **Maraj**, where gold, silver, diamonds and precious stones are made into fashionable jewelry in the design of local motifs and where the visitor can purchase china, jewelry and other items duty free.

At the corner of Frederick and Queen streets, the first cross street as one moves north, is a large conglomeration of small, fragile wooden huts known as the **Fre-**

Roman Catholic Cathedral of the Immaculate Conception.

derick **Street Mall**. Here vendors sell clothing, costume jewelry, foodstuffs and leather goods, among other items. The site was originally a large variety store destroyed by fire some years ago, and individual vendors who previously sold in suitcases and box carts on the sidewalk around the city were relocated to this spot and built these huts, some as high as two stories, for themselves.

There are more stores all the way up Frederick Street until one comes to **Woodford Square**. More than any other British Governor, Sir Ralph Woodford left his mark on Port of Spain. He laid out the large square in the heart of the city named Brunswick Square, rechristened Woodford after his death. Woodford planted the park with many trees which continue to provide beauty and shade today. Its center is adorned by a fetchingly painted water fountain, a gift to the city from local merchant George Turnbull.

A focal point of life in Port of Spain, Woodford Square provides a thoroughfare between the east and west sections of the city, as well as a meeting place and forum for all sorts of people. There is day and night activity in the square: baptist preachers with lighted candles ring bells, would-be politicians get up on their soap-boxes, and at almost any hour small groups can be found vigorously arguing religion, politics and sports.

The Square has been the scene of much political activity, and in 1956, at the birth of the national independence movement, was unofficially renamed the University of Woodford Square, because of the lectures that were delivered there by the politicians of the era (see p. 50).

In 1808, after the great fire wiped out much of Port of Spain, tents were pitched in the Square to accommodate the homeless. Later that same year, following a slave uprising on one of the sugarcane estates, the rebellion leaders were hanged in the Square, their bodies exhibited as a warning to others.

In 1903, Woodford Square was the scene of a mammoth protest meeting against new water rates, following which the crowd surrounded the Red House, seat of Government, and burnt it down in a riot in which 17 people were killed.

In the 1970s, it was again a political focal point, this time of a Black Power uprising, when the Square was referred to as the People's Parliament. The largest funeral ever seen in the city took place in

Bananas being shipped out of the Port of Spain harbor.

the Square in 1970, to memorialize a member of the Black Power group shot by the police.

On the south side of Woodford Square is the **Trinity Cathedral**, main church of the Anglican faith. The original Trinity church was destroyed in the great fire of 1808 and rebuilding of the present one began in 1816, in the middle of Woodford Square.

But the residents of the city protested the construction of a church in their Square and won the support of Woodford, who ordered the construction stopped. He then laid the cornerstone at the present site. The roof of Trinity is copied from that of Westminister Hall, London, and it is supported by hammer beams of mahogany carved in England and shipped to Port of Spain in sections and fitted here. There are six stained-glass windows and a full-sized marble figure of Sir Ralph Woodford.

Looking west from Trinity is the **Red House**, the seat of Parliament. It got its colorful name in 1897 when the building was given a coat of red paint in preparation for the diamond jubilee of Queen Victoria and the public promptly referred to it thereafter as the Red House. The first Red House was burned down in water riots

of 1903. In 1904 rebuilding work began and the new House was opened in 1907.

The Chambers are open to the public, and the Wedgewood blue ceiling is its most striking feature. The columns and entablature are made of purpleheart wood, and under its great rotunda is a lovely water fountain.

The **Town Hall** or **City Hall** at the corner of Frederick and Knox streets is the administrative heart of the city. The present building was opened in 1961, replacing the original town hall destroyed by fire in the 1940s. The front is decorated with a mural entitled "Conquerabia," the Amerindian name for Port of Spain.

The Mayor, Aldermen, and the Councillors of Port of Spain have their offices in this building, and there is also a large auditorium for lectures, plays and other functions.

Next to the Town Hall is the **Trinidad Public Library**, and behind that, the small church of St. John the Baptist, built in 1854 by George Sherman Cowan, a missionary sent to Trinidad from England by the Lady Mico Charity to provide education for the children of former slaves.

He arrived here in 1840 shortly after Emancipation and a memorial of his work

The Woodford Square fountain.

is this small church with its flat triangular-shaped facade of natural stone and two small turrets. One of its walls is the last remaining relic of the old Spanish Cabildo building, forerunner of today's City Council. An outstanding feature of the building is a beautiful stained-glass window, a replica of Holman Hunt's "The Light of the World."

Opposite to the Library and St. John's Church, and standing on the entire block between Pembroke Street and Abercromby Street is the new **Hall of Justice**, opened in December 1985. To select its design a competition was held among local architects, but none of the submissions achieved the desired effect of a modern building that blended in with the Victorian architecture of the Red House and Trinity Cathedral.

In the end a design by the firm of Anthony Lewis Associates (who also designed the Financial Complex) was considered closest to the concept, and working in collaboration with a British firm of architects, they created the existing building.

Continuing northwards along Pembroke Street are several very old buildings of varying architecture standing side by side with modern buildings. Further up the street is the country's first secondary school, St. Joseph's Convent, which celebrated its 150th anniversary in 1986. The school is run by St. Joseph de Cluny nuns who came to Trinidad from France in 1836. The original French nuns were succeeded by Irish sisters and control has now passed to Trinidadians. The convent is today one of the leading girls' school.

Opposite to the convent is **St. Mary's College**, a leading boy's school established in 1863 by the Holy Ghost Fathers of Ireland. The school numbers among its alumni the first president of the Republic, Mr. Ellis Clarke.

Pembroke Street ends at Keate Street, where a right turn brings you to the corner of Frederick and Keate, the site of the **National Museum and Art Gallery**. The National Museum and Art Gallery was built as a Science and Art Museum in 1892 to commemorate the jubilee of Queen Victoria and was then called the Victoria Institute. Destroyed by fire in 1920, it was rebuilt in 1923. The National Museum houses a disparate collection of Amerindian artifacts, an exhibition of the petroleum industry in Trinidad, lithographs of old Port of Spain by Michel Cazabon and the work of contemporary Trinidad artists.

Shanty shops downtown, Independence Square.

Internationally known Carlisle Chang, Leroy Clarke, Dermot Lousion, Ralph and Vera Baney, Nina Squires and other contemporary artists are also represented here.

To the right of the museum is **Memorial Park** with its cenotaph in memory of Trinidad servicemen who died in World Wars I and II. The Memorial Park is planted with many beautiful flowering trees such as the red flamboyant and the yellow, pink, and purple poui.

But of all parks, the city's most beautiful is the **Queen's Park**, popularly known as the "**Savannah**," across the street at the north end of Memorial Park. The Queen's Park Savannah and its surroundings, which include the **Botanic Gardens** and the **Emperor Valley Zoo**, is in many ways the city's center.

North of early Port of Spain there used to be a sugarcane estate belonging to the Peschier family, known as St. Ann's Estate. In 1817 it was offered for sale to the Government and Governor Woodford made arrangements to acquire 232 acres for use by the city. A small family cemetery which had been used by the Peschiers was enclosed with a high wall with arrangements for the family to look after it, and even today, the walled cemetery in the middle of the Savannah is still in use by the Peschier descendants.

At the time of the sale, the Savannah was mainly used as a pasture for cows, but was also a place where the public could stroll and play games among the many beautiful samaan trees that offered shade.

In 1890 attempts were made to convert part of the Savannah into housing lots. This was vigorously protested by city residents, as have been all similar attempts over the years to reduce the size of the park for one reason or another.

The Savannah, Botanic Gardens and Zoo are all within walking distance of each other and can be reached from many avenues. From Port of Spain most route taxis pass around the Savannah or along streets very close to it.

Planted with many beautiful trees, the Savannah has a number of notable specimens. One interesting tree is immediately opposite to Chancery Lane on the southern side of the Savannah. The Cannon Ball tree is so called because of its fruit which is shaped just like a cannon ball. The dominating tree in the Savannah is the samaan, spreading out like a giant umbrella. There are also some beautiful yellow poui trees and flaming flamboyants around

The National Museum and Art Gallery.

the edges of the park.

The Savannah is home to the **Trinidad Turf Club**, whose grandstand is situated at the southern end of the Savannah. The club organizes horse racing, with its first recorded race in 1828.

Known as the big yard of horse racing, the Turf Club holds three different racing seasons each year. In June and July there is the Summer meeting; the Mid-Summer meeting falls in September and October, when the local equivalent of the Kentucky Derby for three-year-olds is run; and the Christmas meeting is held in January and February, when two-year-olds racing for the first time are introduced.

Horse racing is the most popular form of gambling in Trinidad and has spawned a fast-developing breeding industry and a growing punters community. It's amusing to see men who wouldn't give the time of day to their math at school armed with pen, paper and program, figuring odds as seriously as any stockbroker.

The grandstand's most popular use is in February, when all the various events and competitions of Carnival culminate in a week-long series of shows on its huge stage. At that time, the Savannah is ringed with makeshift food and beverage stalls and everyone in the city seems to be liming in the park or attending the show.

In summer, the Savannah is the scene of a favorite Trinidadian pastime — kite flying. The sky is then dotted with mad-bull kites — used for aerial fights — birds, fish, animals and more common kites.

The northern end of the Savannah forms a natural declivity, which has been converted into a rock garden known as the **Hollow**. Shrubs and flowers and fish ponds offer a pleasant scene.

Across the road from the Hollow is the Botanic Gardens, the oldest in the western hemisphere, having been laid out in 1820. The Botanic Gardens house the official residence of both the President of the Republic of Trinidad and Tobago and the Prime Minister. The former's residence, dating back to 1875, is clearly visible from the walkways in the Gardens and from the street, but the Prime Minister's residence, built in the 1960s, cannot be seen from the street. A good view can be obtained from the back side of the Hilton Hotel.

The Botanic Gardens was laid out by Governor Woodford and David Lockhart, the first curator, who is buried in the small cemetery in the gardens. This cemetery, called "God's Acre," is as old as the

Red House exterior (left) and interior (right).

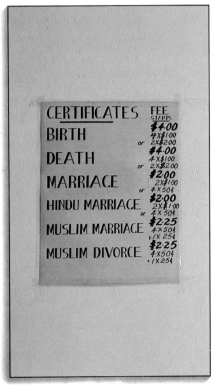

CERTIFICATES   FEE STAMPS

BIRTH $4.00
4 X $1.00
or 2 X $2.00

DEATH $4.00
4 X $1.00
or 2 X $2.00

MARRIAGE $2.00
2 X $1.00
or 4 X 50¢

HINDU MARRIAGE $2.00
2 X $1.00
or 4 X 50¢

MUSLIM MARRIAGE $2.25
4 X 50¢
. 1 X 25¢

MUSLIM DIVORCE $2.25
4 X 50¢
. 1 X 25¢

Gardens and many former governors are buried there, including the first Governor-General of an independent Trinidad and Tobago, Sir Solomon Hochoy.

The Gardens is laid out across undulating land, and its collection of native and imported trees is most impressive. Trinidadians, disregarding the botanical and scientific names of many of these trees, have created their own sobriquets. There is, for example, a tree known as "Raw Beef," because of a reddish sap that flows when the bark is cut. A fence had to be erected around the tree to protect it from visitors who wanted to see this strange phenomenon, and continued to cut the bark, seriously damaging the tree.

"There is also the "Hat Stand" tree, the branches of which are reminiscent of an old fashioned hat stand. The "Boat Lace" tree is so called because its flowers and fruit hang down from stems that are sometimes as long as two or three feet. There are beautiful specimens of palms and a tree called "Napoleon's Hat" because its flowers have three corner points.

In a grove of Palmiste palms, an Australian wallaby, which is not native to Trinidad, lies buried, a small plaque marking the spot. The wallaby was a pet of the Prince of Wales and died while he was a guest at Governor's House, during a visit to Trinidad.

The nearby **Zoo** was started in 1952 and is today the best in the Caribbean. It houses both native and foreign animals, birds, reptiles and fish. There are some beautiful wild deer, native to Trinidad, plus a good collection of tropical snakes. As far as possible many of the animals and birds live in a setting that closely resembles their natural habitat.

At night, mobile food vendors gather around the periphery of the Savannah, selling various snacks. There is corn on the cob, either roasted over an open charcoal grill or boiled in spicy stock with salted meat, and oysters in the shell are cracked open expertly and doused with peppery condiments for the waiting customer. Trucks laden with green coconuts, still on the bunch, do a good business selling delicious coconut water.

The buildings which surround the Savannah are most remarkable, their architectural variety ranging from a Scottish castle to a Moorish house, and offering a fascinating cross-section of cultural influences and prevailing fashions of the last century. On one stretch of its western side,

Playing soccer on the Savannah.

known as Maraval Road, seven of these truly amazing buildings can be seen. They are known as the **"Magnificent Seven"** or the **"Queens of the Bands."** Six were built in 1904 at a time when cocoa was king and there were many very wealthy estate owners of Trinidad, who competed with one another for stylish living. The seven are in various conditions of repair, though none is open for public visiting. For a look at the exteriors, a good starting point is the St. Clair Roundabout at the northwestern end of the Savannah.

Standing on the "Pitch," the walkway on the periphery, one looks right at **"Killarney,"** built in 1904. A copy of the design of Balmoral Castle in Scotland, it was built by the Scottish architect Robert Giles, for the Stollmeyer family, who were estate owners and whose home it was until the Trinidad and Tobago Government bought it in 1979.

Of imported brick, it is trimmed with local limestone. An Italian marble gallery surrounds the ground floor. The ceilings on the ground floor are of plaster of Paris, the gesso work of an Italian craftsman, while the woodwork and paneling are of various local woods. The floors are of Guyana purpleheart as is the beautiful

staircase with its harp-like design on the landing. There is a minstrel gallery with an elegant balustrade of purpleheart overlooking the staircase. A spiral staircase leads to a tower.

The second magnificent building is **"Whitehall,"** Venetian in style, now the office of the Prime Minister. In the early years of this century it was the residence of a wealthy cocoa estate owner, J.L. Agostini, who had Barbados coral brought here by sloop to be cut locally.

After Agostini's death, his widow sold the building to Robert Henderson, who was himself a wealthy businessman, and he took up residence there with his family. It was the Hendersons who gave it the name "Whitehall." At the beginning of the World War II, Whitehall was commandeered by the U.S. Armed Forces in Trinidad who occupied it from 1940 to 1944. It was purchased by the Trinidad Government in 1954.

Next comes **Archbishop's House**, the residence of the Roman Catholic Archbishop of Port of Spain. The architect was an Irishman, but the style has been described as Romanesque, reminiscent of a monastery. The marble and red granite were imported from Ireland and the roof

covered with copper sheeting and slates. The interior wood paneling, floors and the beautiful Y-shaped staircase are of native hardwood.

Flood Street, named after the Archbishop who built Archbishop's House, separates that house from the next queen, "**Roomor**." Roomor or Ambard House is a house of the French Baroque colonial style built by Lucien F. Ambard, an estate owner, using marble imported from Italy and tiles from France. Its attractions include Renaissance ironwork in its elongated columns. Of particular interest is its roof of towers, pinnacles, dormers, elaborate galleries and a cupola of unusual proportions. It was bought by Timothy Roodal in 1940, and is still the residence of that family.

"**Mille Fleurs**" is next, the home of one of the city's most distinguished Mayors, Dr. Henrique Prada. He was a very prominent medical practitioner before he entered politics, serving as Mayor of Port of Spain on three consecutive occasions from 1914 to 1917. The House is distinguished by its considerable fretwork. It was bought by the Government some years ago and is now the office of the National Security Council.

Next is "**Hayes Court**," the residence of the Anglican Bishop of Trinidad. A typical grand house, it has a pleasant mixture of French and English architectural style.

The last of the Magnificent Seven is "**Queen's Royal College**," a secondary school for boys. This is in German Renaissance style, built of concrete with facings of blue limestone and colored with reddish tint to contrast with the limestone. A clock was installed in the tower in 1913 and chimes on the quarter hour. This is where Trinidad and Tobgao's most famous novelist, V.S. Naipaul, went to school and where he won a scholarship to Oxford. It is also the alma mater of the country's first Prime Minister, Dr. Eric Williams, who was himself a distinguished academic, having also won a scholarship to Oxford from QRC.

Apart from the Magnificent Seven, the Savannah has other outstanding buildings dating back to the last century. There is **Queen's Park Hotel**, built in 1895, and **Knowsley**, now the Ministry of Foreign Affairs, the grounds of which take up an entire block. This building was constructed in 1904, and among its outstanding features is a marble gallery on the ground floor, a beautiful staircase of Guyana purpleheart wood and ceilings of plaster

Left, Victorian fretwork and right, "White Hall," the Prime Minister's house.

140

of Paris and gesso work done by Italian craftsmen. It was built as a home for William Gordon, a prominent city merchant, and purchased by the Trinidad and Tobago Government in 1956.

The oldest building around the Savannah is **All Saints Church**, which was built in 1846 and is also one of the oldest Anglican churches in the country. There are two important foreign missions around the Savannah as well; the United States Embassy and the Indian High Commission. Long lines outside the U.S. Embassy on weekday mornings are not to be mistaken for demonstrations. They are merely attempts by locals to get visas to the United States.

To some degree, the Savannah marks the northern end of the city proper and the beginning of the residential areas, called suburbs by locals though most are within walking distance of downtown.

One of the most fascinating is **Belmont**, which has the distinction of being the first suburb of the city. Situated to the northwest of Port of Spain, it rises on the slopes of the Northern Range and used to be a sugarcane estate until converted into a settlement for a number of African tribes. These Africans, because of the anti-

slave trade patrols along Africa's West Coast, had been able to escape being trapped into slavery. Brought to Trinidad, they were given land in various parts of Belmont. Their settlement stretched from Belmont Circular Road, near Observatory Street, to Belmont Valley Road. The names of some of these original inhabitants live on in place names such as Zampty Lane and Maycock Place, after leading members of the community.

Later on, other liberated slaves were brought to Trinidad from other islands and they also settled in Belmont. The early community was a well-organized one, complete with priests, chiefs, leaders and close-knit family units enabling the African cultural traditions to survive even to today. In Belmont one finds an African Rada Community, where religious ceremonial sacrifices are held according to African custom, accompanied by drumming, dancing, special food and the sacrifice of feathered animals.

Belmont was never laid out in the conventional sense of the word. Houses were built willy-nilly and it was only later that new streets were laid in a plan. The result is that Belmont is a labyrinth of narrow, winding lanes. The records show that it

has more lanes than anywhere else in the city, and it also has more people, more churches, more schools and has produced many leading citizens, including the President of the Republic of Trinidad and Tobago, Mr. Ellis Clarke, who was born in Myler Street.

Though many of the houses in Belmont today are still old wooden constructions, or a strange mixture of part wood, part concrete, the suburb has witnessed considerable progress over the years. Because originally the house lots were so small, expansion has largely been upwards. Today there are many narrow two- and three-story houses and commercial properties solidly built, some looking down on the tiniest of houses next door.

Standing at the top of the Lady Young Road, which runs outside the Hilton, one looks down on Belmont as a small fairyland of red- and green-roofed houses and striped awnings, a confusion of little lanes seemingly running in all directions. And in between are the fruit trees, their laden branches leaning heavily on roofs, with juicy mangoes, chenettes, guavas, plums and avocado pears clustered so closely together it seems a miracle of nature that cross pollination does not take place. Bel-

mont has its own library, an orphanage, a convent and legends galore. A well-quoted one concerns a green-faced donkey that roamed the lanes in the 1950s, frightening people because it could talk! It was from Belmont that the first pirate taxi took to the streets of Port of Spain.

Belmont has an exquisite Gothic church, **St. Francis of Assisi** on Belmont Circular Road, and a rumshop with the unusual name of the **Tiger Cat Bar**. The country's first "lunatic asylum" was here, until it was re-sited in St. Ann's and promptly took on the more respectable name of a mental hospital.

Belmont has the distinction of owning the only upside down hotel in the world: the **Trinidad Hilton**, set in the foothills of the Northern Range. From the lobby one descends to the other floors, as the hotel is built down the side of a hill. One's balcony hangs over extravangantly verdant surroundings, with a view of the Savannah, mountains and the Gulf of Paria.

Where Belmont's settlement was African in origin, in **St. James**, the city's most westerly suburb, the influence was decidedly East Indian. St. James too was a sugarcane estate, and the workers there were largely East Indians who arrived in **Beetham Market**.

Trinidad as indentured laborers. The streets of St. James bear witness to its earliest inhabitants with names such as Delhi, Bombay, Madras, Calcutta, Benares, Ganges and so on.

St. James is mecca for the annual Hosay Festival, when it is possible to hear classical tassa drumming, as small effigies of mosques parade through the streets. (See p. 105) There is a Muslim mosque on the Western Main Road in St. James and a Hindu temple on Panka Street.

At the entrance to the suburb is an important building, in fact the oldest government building still in use in Trinidad today. It was built in 1827 by Governor Woodford to provide a barrack for His Majesty's Forces in the Windward and Leeward Islands. Today it is used as the Police Training College, and is known as **St. James Barracks**.

Laventille, to the northeast, is a suburb second only to Belmont in interest and character. The Laventille hills are lined roof to roof with houses, some solidly constructed, others makeshift shanties, easily reduced to ashes in the frequent Laventille fires.

The two roads into the area are Duke Street Extension via Piccadilly Street, and Picton Road, a turning off the Eastern Main Road near the Central Market and the Beetham Highway Roundabout. Both roads are winding and narrow and require considerable driving skill, particularly when overtaking, an activity which taxi drivers have exalted to a fine art. The unwary, however, run the risk of crashing off the road and, as has often happened, straight onto the roof of someone's living room or bedroom, as many of the houses are built a foot or two *below* the level of the street, down the hill's incline.

Laventille is a highly depressed area, with much unemployment, and thousands of suspected illegal immigrants from the neighboring islands. There is a resulting lack of running water and sanitation, though there is no shortage of motorcars, television and video sets. Laventille has passed into history in the words of poet and playwright Derek Walcott, who wrote a poem on Laventille hills, and it was at Laventille that a Spanish navigator and astronomer, Don Cosmos Damien Churruca, set up an observatory where, for the first time in the New World, he fixed the meridian.

Present-day Laventille revolves around its steel band, the famous **"Desperadoes,"**

Fort Picton panorama.

whose leader Rudolph Charles was a legend even before he died in 1985. He was carried to his cremation site on a "shariot," a casket made of steel drums. The larger than life character of Charles was immortalized in the words of the 1986 Carnival calypso by David Rudder entitled "The Hammer," which won both the national calypso contest for the best song and the Carnival Road March, i.e. the song that is most popular with parading bands.

"The Hammer" eulogized Charles as he lived, always dressed in army fatigues and tall boots, marching across the hills of Laventille with a hammer in his hand, a hammer he used not only for tuning musical notes out of the steel drums, but for keeping wayward Laventillians and "badjohns" in check. The Desperadoes, as their name implies, were once noted for street fights and general rowdiness.

There are many accounts as to exactly where the steel band started in Port of Spain. Some say it was in a yard in East Dry River, when a man called "Fish Eye" experimented on an old oil drum and beat out the tune of "Mary Had a Little Lamb." Others state that the first sounds of the steel band emerged from a yard in Woodbrook, while others argue that it originated in Laventille.

What is not in dispute is that when World War II ended in Europe in 1945, VE Day was marked by an impromptu victorious carnival of celebration on the streets of Port of Spain, accompanied by the music of the steel band for the first time in the history of Carnival. Now every town and neighborhood in the Republic has its own band, and around Carnival, they are all out practicing at night in the pan yards. See the Appendix for a selected list of bands and their practice spaces.

Woodbrook, situated to the west of the city, was settled in 1911. Another sugar estate, it belonged to the Siegert family, creators of Trinidad's famous Angostura Bitters. The streets in Woodbrook bears the names of members of the Siegert family, namely, Petra Ann, Rosalino, Alberto, Luis, Alfredo and Carlos.

For decades Woodbrook was largely residential with comfortable medium-sized dwellings. But since the 1960s, commerce has crept into Woodbrook and several old homes have been converted into business places, resulting in warnings from the City Council, and Town and Country Planning. However, to the credit of the new occupants, efforts have been made to preserve much of the district. Of interest also is that

Woodbrook was the traditional suburb of the middle classes and this included all races, including Syrian/Lebanese families who came to Trinidad in the 1930s and 1940s.

Large numbers still live in Woodbrook, but those who have been successful and their descendants who are in the professions have moved to the more expensive areas such as St. Clair, Ellerslie Park, Federation Park and Fairways in Maraval.

The popular suburb of **Federation Park** is a reminder of the period from 1958 to 1962 when Port of Spain was the capital of the short-lived West Indies Federation (see p. 52). Here the curving roads bear the names of Caribbean islands — Barbados Road, Trinidad Crescent, Jamaica Boulevard, Antigua Drive, Montserrat Avenue — and spacious buildings that could have been ersatz embassies are now gracious private homes.

Newton and **St. Clair** are other nearby suburbs. St. Clair was laid out in very large lots at the turn of this century and today is still a highly prized neighborhood with many elegant houses and gardens, several occupied by foreign ambassadors. The "Magnificent Seven" were part of the early development of St. Clair on the Savannah side, which was most highly sought after by the wealthy planters of the era.

Further north of Port of Spain are the suburbs of **St. Ann's** and **Cascade**, the latter of which started off life as a very large sugarcane estate in 1794 owned by a French royalist from Martinique by the name of de Mallevault. At that time it comprised 1,395 acres and included the Fondes Amandes valley. Over the years sections of the estate were sold out, and while the great estate house known as **Coblentz** is still there, its days of lavish entertaining are long gone, today's residents being the occupants of the flats into which the house has been converted.

St. Ann's is the official address of both the President and the Prime Minister of Trinidad and Tobago. In St. Ann's there are also the high walls of the monastery of the cloistered nuns of the Order of St. Dominic. The monastery was founded here in the last century by nuns fleeing political troubles in neighboring Venezuela. The monastery is entirely self-sufficient, grows its own food, and supplies altar bread for religious ceremonies as well as artistic decorative work for statues and altar vestments. The monastery has its own chapel. The only time the nuns leave the cloisters is when they die.

Coconut trucks and food shacks line the Savannah's perimeter.

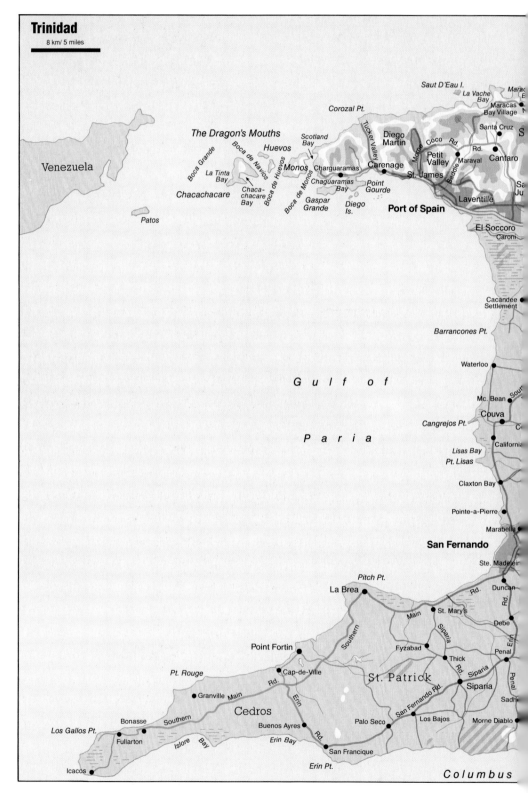

Trinidad

8 km/ 5 miles

Saut D'Eau I.
La Vache Bay
Mara
Maracas
Bay Village
Santa Cruz
S

Corozal Pt.

The Dragon's Mouths

Scotland Bay

Diego Martin

Coco Rd.

Rd.

Tucker Valley

Petit Valley
Maraval
Cantaro

Huevos

Boca Grande

Boca de Navios

La Tinta Bay

Monos

Charguaramas

Carenage

St. James

Ba

La
Ju

Chaguaramas Bay

Point Gourde

Chacachacare

Chaca-chacare Bay

Boca de Huevos

Boca de Monos

Gaspar Grande

Diego Is.

Port of Spain

Laventille

Venezuela

El Soccoro

Caroni

Patos

Cacandee Settlement

Barrancones Pt.

Waterloo

Gulf   o f

Mc. Bean

Sou

Couva

Cangrejos Pt.

C

P a r i a

California

Lisas Bay

Pt. Lisas

Claxton Bay

Pointe-a-Pierre

Marabella

San Fernando

Ste. Madelein

Pitch Pt.

Duncan

La Brea

Rd.

Rd.

Main

St. Mary's

Debe

Siparia

Fyzabad

Penal

Point Fortin

Southern

Thick

Pt. Rouge

Cap-de-Ville

Rd.

Siparia

St. Patrick

Rd.

Siparia

Penal

Granville Main

Erin

San Fernando Rd.

Sadh

Bonasse

Southern

Cedros

Buenos Ayres

Palo Seco

Los Bajos

Morne Diablo

Los Gallos Pt.

Fullarton

Islore Bay

Rd.

Erin Bay

San Francique

Icacos

Erin Pt.

Columbus

INTRODUCTION TO TRINIDAD

While Port of Spain is the administrative and tourist hub of Trinidad, much of the country's character and wealth emanate from her provincial towns, industries and countryside. It would be difficult to get a true picture of Trinidad without visiting some of the rest of the island: the sharp cliffs of the north coast and flat palm fringed beaches of the east, the Caroni Swamp and mountain rain forests, the Pitch Lake and oil and sugar industries of the south, are all as essential to Trinidad and Tobago as Carnival, calypso and steel band.

You can tour the island by driving yourself or hiring a car with driver, and taxi drivers who serve the major hotels are often glad to sign on for a day's tour, providing an insider's view of the sights. Even the furthest points are only three hours or so from Port of Spain, and a number of tours can be made in a half-day, if necessary. Primary roads are in excellent condition—though often crowded—and even secondary roads tend to be easily negotiable, if bumpy.

Since most visitors to Trinidad stay in Port of Spain, this section is organized as a series of day (or two- or three-day) trips starting in Port of Spain. All tours begin from Stollmeyer's Castle, west on the Queen's Park Savannah.

TOURING TRINIDAD

North Coast Beaches and Santa Cruz Valley: The beaches of the **North Coast** are a popular day trip with locals and visitors alike. The Saddle Road out of Port of Spain passes through some of the more popular suburbs of the city and its coastal continuation, the North Coast Road, provides lovely vistas of valley and sea. On weekends and holidays everyone goes to Maracas or Las Cuevas Bays, so be prepared for some traffic.

Leaving Stollmeyer Castle you will come to a small roundabout by the Ministry of Agriculture, Lands and Food Production, where you should turn left onto Long Circular Road. After the third gas station in Boissiere Village turn right onto the Saddle Road.

At the left corner is the **Trinidad Country Club**, first the estate of the de Gannes de la Chancellerie family and later the home of the de Boissieres, after whom Boissiere Village was named.

Made into a Club by the Canning family, the Club was used exclusively by whites until about a decade ago. Today membership policy is more liberal, and a visit there is a way to meet and mingle with a variety of residents.

Now owned by J.B. Fernandes, the distillers of the popular Vat 19 rum, it has tennis courts, swimming pool and other facilities and is popular for its Christmas and Carnival dances. Your hotel can arrange for you to attend.

In the residential area of **Maraval** the Saddle Road passes through a highly urbanized area. **St. Andrews** and **La Seiva** were sugar estates, now converted into residential areas — the case with many of Port of Spain's suburbs.

The Chaconia Inn, whose restaurant and club are a weekend haunt for the younger generation, is alongside the road on the right, its walls covered by vines. **Andalucia**, another residential area, is on the left, and immediately after is the Maraval Reservoir, built in 1854. Still in perfect condition, it supplies the area with water from the Maraval River — little more than a stream.

The Roman Catholic Church on high ground on the right is characteristic of most churches in Trinidad — a bit of history, an abundance of pride. This one was built in 1931 and dedicated to Our Lady of Lourdes. A grotto behind the church was built by Spanish missionaries of the Augustinian Order who were in Trinidad until 1950. The marble altar was donated in 1872 by J. A. Cipriani, father of Capt. Arthur Cipriani, wartime hero and trade unionist. Next to the church is an old tomb and on it is engraved *Et Sacerdot en aeter-nitum:* You are a priest for eternity.

Haleland Park, a former nutmeg plantation, is another residential area noted for its gracious homes and landscaped gardens. At Catalina Court apartments are signs to the **Moka Golf Course**, the best course on the island. The golf course is on the old Perseverance Estate which was originally owned by William Hardin Burnley, an Anglo-American who took up residence in 1802. Visitors can become temporary members through their hotel.

Further on, the Saddle continues into Santa Cruz Valley. On the left, large pillars signal the entrance to the North Coast Road. The vegetation here is abundantly tropical, with balisier palms, the flower of the People's National Movement party; bamboo; samaan — the enormous canopied trees; and every other imaginable tropical tree and plant.

In the dry season, March through May,

when the immortelles and poui are in bloom, the range is a carpet of red, pink and yellow. Drive up and around curve after curve, but take care: this mountainous trip is best made without the use of alcohol. The flora and fauna of the Northern Range are relics of the Venezuelan jungle, proving that Trinidad is a continental island, dissimilar to the oceanic islands further north in the Caribbean.

There are two official lookout stops on the Road, both breathtaking. The first looks down on La Vache Bay, and the second, Maracas. Between the two are freshwater springs, and at the first stop a fruit vendor sells silicon dioxide quartz, an inexpensive and pretty natural of this range.

Maracas is a wide, protected bay, a favorite with weekend picnickers and suntanners. On sunny weekend days, Trinidadians bring hampers of food, floats and games and make a day of it. The length of the beach lends itself to cricket and soccer and pick-up games abound.

Where the sea or shore is marked with a red flag, beware of strong currents. But usually the sea is warm and pleasant with gentle waves.

At the left end of the beach in a cove

is the sleepy fishing village of Maracas. Maracas residents are of Spanish-Amerindian descent and there are still a few who speak a Spanish patois. Seines dry on the beach next to overturned boats and pirogues drift at anchor in the bay. Late afternoon is the best time to buy fish, and carite and kingfish are plentiful in these waters. Ask the villagers for recipes.

In the village is a small chapel dedicated to St. Peter, and on his feast, a Sunday toward the end of June, townspeople hold small celebrations.

For those keen on fishing themselves, the fishermen here and at the village of La Filette further on might take you out. Make an evening tide on the Caribbean going out at around 5 p.m. and you'll return before dawn. A night out in the wind in a small boat with only a lantern and the moon for light is not everyone's idea of a good time, so consider well. If you do go, on your return you might see vultures, locally called corbeaux, standing on top of the posts in the cove like sentinels, waiting to catch the first rays of the sun. They prefer fish for food and so can be seen at most ports in Trinidad.

Las Cuevas, about fifteen minutes up and down the shore road, is more secluded

Farming in the Santa Cruz Valley.

and usually less crowded than Maracas, though the facilities are similar. The beach restaurant serves fish and wild meat such as lappe, agouti and quenk.

"Las Cuevas" is Spanish for caves, and into this long bay flows the Curagate River, creating sandy hollows in the low banks ideal for picnics and outdoor barbecues.

Past Las Cuevas the North Coast Road follows the shoreline past La Chupara Bay and La Filette, ending at the town of Blanchisseuse. Along the way are many small beaches, some quiet, some with heavy surf, and most accessible by footpaths down the rocky cliffs. Keep an eye out for a large rock offshore which serves as the local equivalent to Los Angeles' "Hollywood" sign: the rock is spray painted with an advertisement for one of this regions' chief industries. It says "HOLLYWEED."

Blanchisseuse is a quiet hamlet with little besides a church and an old bell for announcing masses, funerals, weddings and the like, a dry goods store, a bar and the school at the top of a hill. There are many families who live year-round in the village, leading, by and large, quiet rural existences, as well as city dwellers who own holiday homes. The coastal road beyond the village is impassable by vehicle, though the town can be approached from the mountains. (see p. 164)

Return the way you came to the pillars marking the entrance to the North Coast Road and make a sharp left over the Saddle, a narrow pass between two slabs of the hill. Santa Cruz is a green valley which used to be an enormous citrus plantations and now houses a stud farm which produces horses for weekend racing, and some small towns. Today the valley of Santa Cruz is highly urbanized, and although it can no longer be described as "the country," it has retained its calm aura.

The San Antonio nursery just off the roadside has an array of both fruiting and flowering plants, but if you buy, check with immigration before attempting to take live species out of the country.

You will come to the church dedicated to the Holy Cross, behind which lies the **La Pastora Estate** and estate house. Owned by Antonio Gomez, a senior judge when Sir Ralph Woodford was governor of Trinidad from 1813 to 1828, it later belonged to Hippolyte Borde, who wrote the first history of Trinidad, covering events on the island from the late 15th to the late 18th centuries.

On a small rise to the right stands

Las Cuevas Bay beach facilities.

the estate house of Dr. John Stollmeyer's family, the family who once owned Stollmeyer Castle. They came from America to make their fortune in citrus and cocoa plantations.

The many pools of the **La Canoa River** a little further down are good for swimming, with their clear, cool waters. The village of the valley is called Cantaro, consisting of the hamlets Petial, Gasparillo and La Pastora. The name La Pastora crops up again and again in Trinidad because of Trinidadians' devotion to the Virgin of shepherds, taught to them by Capuchin monks, the first missionaries to this new world.

Branch off from the Saddle, taking the old road on the left to look at Spanish ruins. There is also a monument to the Amerindians here, a statue replica of an Arawak wearing loin cloth and painted naturalistic colors. Legend says that wherever a treasure is buried an Indian was killed and buried next to it; hence this monument. However, digging is not suggested. There is also a consecrated chapel and an old cemetery whose tombstones carry part of Trinidad's history.

Backtrack to the Saddle and continue onward. **Croisette**, pronounced "Quasay"

Left, Maraval and, below, a Creole family goes a-strolling in Blanchisseuse.

by locals, is the heart of activity in **San Juan** (pronounced Sajua). Inhabitants of this area were noted for speaking a French patois, hence the corruption of certain words. Today the community is a mixture of descendants of Africans and East Indians, the patois tongue now almost non-existent.

In days gone by, San Juan was the first stop for the train, therefore market day is everyday and the town is highly commercialized. You are now on the Eastern Main Road, which will take you, to the right, past Barataria, a suburb of San Juan, onto the Beetham Highway and into downtown Port of Spain with the Laventille hill on your right.

The view of Laventille from here is of greenery, water tanks, high tension wires and large clusters of ramshackle homes. This is one of the more depressed areas of Port of Spain but has been home to some of its greatest musicians.

Should you prefer another route to town, at Barataria turn right at the traffic light onto Lady Young Road, named after the wife of the former Governor. Driving over the hill, Morvant, a lower class housing area, is on the left. After several turns and curves is Belmont, then the entrance to the Hilton Hotel on the right, and a few hundred yards down, the Queen's Park Savannah.

Eastern Main Road: The Eastern Main Road leads out of Port of Spain all the way to the Manzanilla coast, and along the way, particularly closer to the city, are a number of points of interest. Mount St. Benedict, the Asa Wright Nature Centre, the University of the West Indies and the Aripo Savannah, are all along the Eastern Main, as well as other places of interest, and it falls to the traveler to choose how many sites he'll stop by in one day.

The various sites have been grouped into day trips. Some will take an afternoon, while others will take a lot longer, particularly if you choose to linger for picnics, or hike into the woods.

An afternoon's tour is the drive to the St. Augustine Campus of the University of the West Indies followed by tea at the monastery of Mount St. Benedict.

Leave Stollmeyer Castle, taking the Lady Young Road to the Churchill Roosevelt Highway. Signs of industrialization are on the left, and parts of the Caroni Swamp on the right. The third traffic light is **Aranguez Junction**.

Aranguez was once called the food

basket of the country, but now it's just a collection of smallholdings, its farmers suffering from the effects of flooding and inadequate marketing outlets for their produce. Beautifully decorated fruit stalls stand at the junction, and just before rainy season begins in June there are piles and piles of watermelons lining the roadside.

The next traffic light leads onto the Uriah Butler Highway, on the left to the **Mount Hope Medical Complex** and on the right to San Fernando. Turn left and go for about a mile if you want to see the very modern medical complex. It's about a mile down the road to the left.

Straight ahead, the Churchill Roosevelt leads to the **University of the West Indies campus**. The campus is spread over more than 200 acres, and official tours can be arranged by contacting in advance the Public Relations Department of the University at 663-1359.

The University of the West Indies was first established in 1948 in Mona, Jamaica. In 1960, the Imperial College of Tropical Agriculture at St. Augustine, founded in 1923 as an agricultural college for the British Commonwealth, was incorporated as the Faculty of Agriculture of the UWI, heralding the opening of the St. Augustine

Campus. There is a third campus of the University in Barbados, and Extramural offices in several other Eastern Caribbean islands.

In 1963, the first Chancellor, Princess Alice, Countess of Athlone, opened the new buildings for the Faculty of Engineering and, later on, the John F. Kennedy College of Arts and Sciences and the Faculty of Agriculture building. In that same year the library, notable for its collection of West Indian references, was moved to new premises in the JFK complex. Nature lovers might want to look at the slide collection of flora and fauna of Trinidad housed at the library. It was compiled by Professor Julian Kenny in honor of UWI's 25th anniversary.

Faculties at the St. Augustine campus include agriculture, engineering, arts and sciences, natural sciences, social sciences, and, strange as it may seem to some, the first year of law and education and the final year of medicine.

At the northern end of the campus is the exit to the Eastern Main Road. Turn right and drive to St. John's Road, on the left, the well-paved entrance to the monastery. Eight hundred feet above sea level, Mount St. Benedict affords an excellent

A vista from the Northern Range.

158

view of the Caroni Plains and the Piarco Savannah.

The white-walled, red-roofed collection of buildings which comprise the monastery were first home to Benedictine monks in 1912, when civil unrest in Brazil forced them to flee temporarily. Later, communications with Brazil became difficult and the monks affiliated themselves with the Belgian Congregation.

Since then, Mount St. Benedict has expanded and now includes St. Bede's School for teenagers, the seminary where most Roman Catholic priests for the English-speaking Caribbean are trained.

There is a guesthouse used for retreats, where visitors can stay overnight or just for tea, awaiting the ringing of the bells for the Angelus. The vista over the plains is well worth the trip, both in bright sunshine or hazy weather, or perhaps at dusk when the variable light provides an entirely different scene.

Beyond the UWI, the Eastern Main Road passes Lopinot, a restored 19th-Century agricultural estate, and from thence leads into Arima, the turn-off to the Asa Wright Nature Centre high in the Northern Range. Around Arima are a number of other nature sites, including the Cleaver Woods, the Aripo Savannah and the Arena Forest.

Any one of these sites would provide a good day's trip, and ardent bird watchers might well choose to stay a few nights at Asa Wright.

Take the Eastern Main Road into the Quasay, passing the wide open green spaces of the Aranguez savannah. Between Port of Spain and Arima, the Road is highly populated, commercialized and busy, with one housing area succeeding the other in an unbroken chain.

St. Joseph, once St. Jose de Oruna, then St. Josef, and finally its present Anglicized name, was the first capital of Trinidad, during Spanish rule. Beyond that, there is little to remark.

At St. Joseph the Maracas Royal Road meets the Eastern Main, leading into the Maracas Valley. The Royal Road provides a delightful drive through thick green vegetation past small, privately owned estates.

You can bathe in the **Maracas River**, visit the modest **Maracas waterfalls**, or climb **El Tucuche**, at 3075 feet high, one of the higher peaks in the Northern Range. If you do choose to hike up the mountain, find an experienced guide before setting out, as trails can be precarious and poorly marked. For the falls, follow the Waterfall Road and then walk for twenty minutes through the forest. The falls are 312 feet high.

Back on the Eastern Main Road past Tunapuna and the UWI is the turn-off onto the **Caura Royal Road,** just after the El Dorado Consumer Cooperative. On the right, amidst spreading samaan trees, is the government-run Chest and Heart Hospital.

The Tacarigua River follows the Caura Road for miles, and presents a number of cool, breezy picnic areas. There are a number of dirt nature trails, including a beautiful one linking this valley to Maracas. Check at the Forest Division Recreation Centre five miles up the Caura Road for advice and directions.

In the '50s, a dam was partially built in Caura, and a Roman Catholic Church had to be torn down to accommodate it. Residents, Amerindian descendants, were resettled in Arouca and Lopinot. The dam couldn't be completed because of sandy soil and a scandal ensued. Village gossip has it that the Catholic priest's resistance to the whole idea doomed the project from its inception.

On the Eastern Main Road, continue

Mount St. Benedict Monastery.

east to the Tacarigua Orphanage. The sign to **Lopinot** is clearly marked. Charles Josef, Comte de Lopinot, left Haiti (then St. Domingue) after a slave uprising in the mid-18th Century. He went to Jamaica, heard about land grants in Trinidad, and came here in 1799 with his wife and 100 slaves. These land grants came as a result of Romme St. Laurent, a French Grenadian who visited Trinidad and was so impressed with the richness of the soil and flourishing crops that he advised the King of Spain to grant lands to French settlers.

In 1783 the Royal Cedula of Population was passed, the conditions for grants being that settlers observe allegiance to the King of Spain and be Roman Catholics. Lopinot's first land grant was in Tacarigua. This estate, however, was his second, deep in Arouca where he moved when his sugar crop in Tacarigua failed.

The road to the estate is narrow and winding, climbing gradually through the lush forest. There are a few houses as you enter, then a well-kept savannah, with tables for picnickers. Also a few vendors of lettuce and other greens as you travel on, and a bar near the car park.

Over the ravine is the restored portion of the original house. The few pieces of furniture within were said to belong to Colonel Thomas Picton, the first Governor of Trinidad under the British. In 1803, the Comte Lopinot completed the residence on the Estate he named La Reconnaisance. He died there in 1819. Both he and his wife are buried on the banks of the river named after him.

Although there is nothing spectacular about the site itself, the Comte de Lopinot played an important part in the history of Trinidad as an estate owner and eschater—a sort of tribunal head and judge. There are no Lopinots left in Trinidad today, but the elders of the village have been honored by a photographic exhibition on permanent display at the house.

On leaving the estate, drive back to the Main Road and into **Arouca**. The Spanish-style church on one side of the square is dedicated to San Rafael, and across from it is the building that used to be the Cabildo, or municipal building. Many Aroucans betray their heritage; they have the features and coloring of Amerindians.

Further on, the town of **D'Abadie** is an area of small crop and livestock farms. At the fir forest, look for Cleaver Trace, which leads to the **Cleaver Woods**.

The **Ajoupa Hut** here is a reproduction

Jinnah Mosque at St. Joseph.

of an Amerindian shelter, with clay utensils and copies of other artifacts used by Amerindians. Modified versions of the clay oven are still used in many parts of the Trinidadian countryside. Heated with wood or dry coconut shells, the baking pans are placed on long wooden pallets and thus inserted in the oven. They are usually housed in small outdoor sheds. The trace leads to a small ravine and clean stream, a pleasant short walk.

Arima was once the third largest town in Trinidad, but has now given way in importance to such towns as Chaguanas, nearer the heavy industries down south.

Arima began as a large Amerindian settlement and then became popular with French planters. Today the population is a mixture of African and Spanish blood, but those who claim to have descended from the Amerindians still celebrate their heritage during the month of August and crown a "Queen of the Caribs."

Arima has a certain old-world charm, and there is architectural evidence of the French and Spanish presences. The dial at the town center is a familiar traveler's landmark to many.

Past Arima is **Waller Field**, an old American base now a farming area. The

Cumuto Road connects the Eastern Main with the Field, across a broad, lovely savannah.

The **Aripo Savannah** and **Arena Forest** are prime bird-watching spots, with over 50 species to be seen. If you come to the savannah and forest to bird-watch or hike, plan on an all-day trip. If you follow the Cumuto Road over the river and past a small pump house, a dirt trail immediately after leads deep into this natural grasslands dotted with palms and other tropical trees.

Another alternative is to hike up the **Aripo Valley** into the mountain forest. Three high-level species, the Blue-capped Tanager, the Orange-billed Nightingale-Thrush and the Yellow-legged Thrush inhabit the upper heights of the range.

Just outside of Arima is the Blanchisseuse Road, leading to the Asa Wright Nature Centre and thence to the shore. The Blanchisseuse Road is near a government estate called Mount Pleasant which once bore cocoa and coffee but is now mostly abandoned. The road winds up through deserted areas, paralleling the Arima River through stands of all sorts of jungle vegetation. Look for nutmeg trees with their brown and red nuts. There are also mahogany, cedar, samaan, poui, immortelle,

Farming at St. Joseph, left, and poui blooms litter cattle grazing grounds at Aripo Heights, right.

corote and the odd teak.

The balisier can also be seen, but is noted for having snakes hidden in its palm. Keep in mind while hiking that there are many species of snake in the Range and a number are venomous. In the last century, the English brought the mongoose from India to eat them, but instead the mongoose is near extinct and the snakes are thriving.

Much of this area of the Northern Range was used for cocoa and coffee farming, and you might notice the sliding-roof drying houses across the hills. The panoramic views of rain-forested peaks and valleys, with enormous bamboo plants and exotic wild flowers is a pleasure not found elsewhere in the Caribbean islands.

Asa Wright is an ideal starting point for nature hikes, not least because they will provide expert guides. Go early in the morning and have lunch at the Centre, or else spend the night and take night and dawn bird-watching hikes.

Do not return to Port of Spain through Arima but continue to Blanchisseuse. The forest drive is awe-inspiring, as it climbs up and then descends gently to the sea. Again, the roundtrip tour to Asa Wright via Arima and back by the North Coast Road is a good day's journey.

Caroni Swamp: The huge flocks of brilliant red Scarlet Ibises coming home to roost at dusk across the flat deep green vistas of the **Caroni Swamp** is perhaps one of the most unforgettable sights in Trinidad. A visit to the Bird Sanctuary is an afternoon's tour, one best taken on the weekends when traffic on the Uriah Butler Highway is lighter.

You can book a boat in advance by calling Nanan at 645-1305 or Ramsahai at 663-2207, or set off without a reservation and make arrangements upon arrival. Binoculars, mosquito repellent and a sweater are recommended.

Start as usual from Stollmeyer Castle taking the Lady Young Road to the Churchill Roosevelt past Aranguez where you turn right onto the Butler Highway which connects Port of Spain with San Fernando and the south. The drive from Port of Spain takes a little over an hour.

The highway was named after Princess Margaret when it first opened in 1955 but was renamed in honor of Uriah "Buzz" Butler, an oilfield worker who led labor uprisings in 1937. (see History p. 44)

As you drive past the National Brewery

Balandra Bay.

you will find yourself in County Caroni. The Caroni River can be seen on both sides of the road, with the swamps to the right. Take the first turn left onto the flyover bridge and turn sharp right into the swamp, where you will see the jetty from which boats depart. It is best to arrive around 4:30 p.m.

Flat-bottomed outboard motorboats ply narrow mangrove waterways where the trees are entangled with branches and undergrowth and thick roots show above the water level. There are 157 species of birds to be found here, spread out over 15,000 acres of protected land.

Tell the boatman that you wish to await the arrival of the egrets and the Scarlet Ibises or he will only tour you through the waterways. The birds travel in squadron formation, transforming the drab landscape with movement and color, just as the sunset lends its own brilliance to the scene.

It is said that the Ibis feeds on the Venezuelan coast and flies to the Swamp for the night, a distance of about 40 miles across the Dragon's Mouth. No one seems to see them during the day.

At dusk, between six and seven, you will be in need of refreshment. Where the Butler Highway meets the Churchill Roosevelt, turn right and head for **Valsayn**, a built-up area by-passed on the way to the UWI.

It was at Valsayn on the present site of the Government Stock Farm that on Feb. 18, 1787 the Articles of Capitulation were signed by José Maria Chacon, the Spanish Governor of Trinidad, handing over the island to the British.

Valsayn is now a middle-class residential area of both sides of the highway. On the right enter the **Valpark Plaza**, and there you'll find a number of restaurants, including the popular JBs, named after Johnny Boos, the scion of a wealthy business and landowning family, who died in 1984. Afterwards, take the highway back to the Lady Young Road and down into town.

Northeast to Toco: The county of St. David on the Northeast Coast is Trinidad's closest point to the sister isle of Tobago. Take the Lady Young Road to the Churchill Roosevelt Highway, and pass Valsayn. Near the end of the Highway, there is a left turn onto the Eastern Main Road. This takes you straight onto the Valencia Road, through the Valencia Forest and past the Valencia River.

Typical scenes at Salybia Beach near Toco.

Trinidadians often light a wood fire and cook on the banks of the river. Up the Camaca Road are hiking trails which lead to the Oropouche Caves, housing colonies of the nocturnal oilbird. The **Oropouche River**, which crosses the Camaca Road about 11 or 12 miles up, is excellent for fishing and swimming.

Drive straight through fir and pine forest on the Valencia Road to a sign which gives directions to Toco and Sangre Grande. Turn left to Toco.

The side roads are traces and trails, the main road curving past estates in Matura on the left. You will go over the Oropouche River, and come to a beach further on where the famous leatherback turtles come to lay their eggs.

The leatherbacks are an oceanic species weighing up to 500 lbs which live out at sea but come to the temperate countries to lay their eggs. Between the months of March and June they come to an open or exposed beach where there is heavy surf and coarse sand like Matura or Turtle Beach on Tobago. They lay an average of a hundred eggs each of the four to six times during a ten-day interval that they lay and seem unperturbed by the interested eyes of naturalists.

Go on to **Balandra Bay**, good for swimming and body surfing. There are many holiday homes in Balandra, some of which can be rented for a weekend. A visit to this part of the island should ideally be not less than a weekend. Check the newspaper columns to see if there is a house for rent and having arranged for a house, take linen and towels, food and drink. Avoid parking your car dead under a coconut tree. There is no prize for guessing correctly what would happen.

Although Blanchisseuse is not that far from Matelot, the North Coast Road is not accessible by car. If it were, getting to Matelot would certainly have been easier by avoiding the Churchill Roosevelt Highway and traveling the beautiful terrain of the North Coast. Many Matelot villagers travel the coast by boat, however, and many of them have found marriage partners in Las Cuevas.

After Balandra you are on the **Toco Coast**. This entire coast is far more awe-inspiring than the East Coast, with sharp, sheer cliffs and protected bays and coves. Breakfast River with its lovely bay is good for swimming.

From Port of Spain to Breakfast River is about an hour and three quarters, but

A sylvan sunset in Toco.

to the village of Toco it will be a further half hour for it is on the other side of Point Galera. There is a marvelous bay between Toco proper and Point Galera called Salybia. Off the beach are large trees, providing shade for snack vendors.

In Toco you are back on the North Coast in the county of St. David. There is a spot between Toco Bay and San Souci Bay good for surfing, and at San Souci the road takes you inland to high ground to a place known as Monte Video. As you go down again towards the sea cross the Grand Riviere, another beautiful swimming spot. This river flows on both sides of the road and is lined by huge trees. From there go on to Paria and Shark River (also good for swimming) where in days gone by there used to be a tub race. This bay goes on further after Paria than Matelot and is ideal territory for hunters, swimmers, fishermen and artists.

Matelot is a small coastal fishing village on a bay good for swimming. At what appears to be the very end of the road is the Roman Catholic Church and Presbytery. A left turn just at the church leads through the village to the river. You will have to walk part of the way. Cross the bridge some 30 feet above the river and walk to the playground from where you can walk to the river's bay. This is a very quiet area and is worth an hour's stay in good weather.

You will return as you came, back to Valencia and Waller Field onto the Churchill Roosevelt Highway and straight into Port of Spain.

Down the Islands: Because the network of roads in Trinidad is built for getting into Port of Spain, touring the island means using the same route time and again. Break the monotony by going across the sea "down the islands," or "down the main" to the small archipelago that reaches across the Dragon's Mouth toward Venezuela. **Chacachacare**, **Huevos**, **Monos** and the others provide resorts, prisons, beaches and good fishing waters for Port of Spain residents, and can be seen on day trips or weekend jaunts. Monos, Huevos and Chacachacare are the links to the mainland, while **Gasparee** and **Patos** are outside the chain.

In 1791, Don Gaspar Antonio de la Guardia, Procurator Syndic, in charge of state lands in Port of Spain, presented Governor Don José Maria Chacon with a petition that these islands be ceded to the Cabildo of Port of Spain to increase revenue. The petition was passed on to the first commissary of population, Don Pedro Ybarrate, who replied that the King of Spain had no occasion for the islands of Monos, Huevos and Patos and was pleased to cede them to the Cabildo.

Chacachacare had already been given to Gerald Fitzpatrick Carry, an Irishman, for services rendered to the King of Spain, though it had to be returned if the King needed it. He grew cotton and sugar apples there for awhile, and later there were whaling stations located on Chaca, as it is fondly called by Trinidadians. Chaca is now a solid part of "down the islands," though Patos has remained outside of Trinidadian ownership.

Patos was leased in 1876 to one L. Dennis O'Connor for 30 years, to raise stock and catch fish for salting. Patos soon grew too lonely for Mr. O'Connor. The land reverted to Spain, and in 1940 was ceded to Venezuela in connection with establishing boundaries. When you are near Patos you are in Venezuelan territorial waters, so do not visit it as travel between the two lands is not entirely free.

There are several routes to "down the islands." You may take a boat from the Port of Spain harbor and your hotel can

assist you in doing so. You can leave from the **Yacht Club**, privately owned but with facilities for visiting yachts, from the **Yachting Association** or the **Island Owners' Association**.

For the first, call in advance and see what facilities they have to offer. There are members who are prepared to make tours. The Yachting Association will also provide information on what arrangements can be made.

At Island Owners', Mr. Daniels owns a well supplied shop. You can call him through the Chaguaramas Naval station and arrange to rent a boat.

To go to the Yacht Club, turn sharp left at the Castle on the Serpentine Road and get on to the Western Main Road, driving through St. James. Keep on the highway at the end of the highly commercialized area, and go past Cocorite, once the port for the old sea planes.

Straight ahead there will be several roads on your left but keep on the highway with two lanes. There is a fork in the road, the right going to the suburb of Diego Martin and the left, which you will take, going towards West Mall. The highway becomes a single lane and on the right is the entrance to Goodwood Park and on the left Bayshore, two housing areas with expensive homes. At about the Glencoe Supermarket on your right you will see the entrance to the Yacht Club.

For the Yachting Association, drive through **Carenage**, a sizable village and hometown of one of Trinidad's former leading cricketers, Bernard Julien. Julien played professional cricket with Kent County in England and then joined the blacklist of sportsmen when he toured South Africa with a rebel team of West Indian cricketers.

The sea is always on your left. St. Peter's church, which holds its festivities in grander style than that in the tiny village of Maracas, is nearby.

Chaguaramas is a long stretch of beach, very popular with people employed in Port of Spain who use it during their lunch break or on evenings. When Chaguaramas was leased to the U.S. Armed Forces during the Second World War everyone had to show a pass to enter. This is no more, but you still cannot get past the sentinels of the Trinidad and Tobago Defence Force at what appears to be the very end of the road.

Before you reach there, however, you will come to the Convention Centre with

Calypso Beach Resort on Gasparee.

flags of all nations flying. On your left is the helicopter port of the National Security services. Shortly after are the tall masts of yachts in the natural marina. It is a beautiful spot, with even blue waters, and colorful sails atop the boat. Below them as they reflect in the water are the hills of the bay in the background, the trees under which you may be standing and the even greener Northern Range behind you with its scattered buildings.

On the far side of the marina is **Hart's Cut**. Fifteen feet wide and four feet deep it cuts across the isthmus of Chaguaramas. The proposal for the scheme came from a police superintendent named Hart and the cut was opened in 1856. It proved to be a great service to both fishermen and residents for it allowed them to avoid the long, difficult pull around Pointe Gourde.

Your first tour of the islands is to Monos. Cruising and boating along the mainland, you will pass **Staubles Bay**. Today the Trinidad and Tobago Naval Station, it was from Staubles that the Northern Range was shelled by government forces during the Black Power uprising of 1970.

For years Staubles was the point of departure for Island Owners', before then

a very fashionable club. You will see many derelict homes which were once holiday resorts and later, during the war, homes of senior officers of the U.S. Armed Forces. The house on the very point belonged to the Canning family, and later the U.S. Armed Forces turned it into a club called Crow's Nest. Even later still Prime Minister Dr. Eric Williams turned it into a resort home for himself and his daughter Erica when she was a young girl.

The open channel of water is the first Boca, or mouth, and the small rock next to Monos is called "Dent Ma Tetron." There is a special current here called Raymoo (phonetically spelt) which inspired the old Trinidadian caution, "Don't row your boat if Raymoo is running." It is a strong and tricky current, and if you are fishing you will feel Raymoo pulling your line.

All the bays or points on Monos have names. The first one, **Marie Elba**, is owned today by the Gatcliffe family. Tommy Gatcliffe is said to be one of the two people alive who know the secret formula for the world-famous Angostura Bitters. There is a large house sitting on a projecting rock and a good bank for fishing 'Jacks' not far off this point.

Left, fishing dinghies and, right, the relaxed attitude of down the islands.

The second point is known as **Gittens**, the third is **Copperhole**, and was originally a whaling station. You can see the copper cauldrons in which the whale blubber was boiled partly submerged in the shallow waters at this point. The bay is called **Turtle's Bay**.

Your boatman will be able to tell you the owners of the homes which face the mainland or the Gulf of Paria. To the back of Monos is a sharp drop of sheer rocks into the sea — a spectacular sight. This channel divides Monos from Huevos, which is owned by the Boos family who also own JBs, a local restaurant. This is the second Boca and most beaches here are open to the public. The deep sea fishing "down the islands" is famous. Franklin Delano Roosevelt came here to fish during the war. If you are keen on this sport then you would either have taken along your tackle or the man on the boat may have brought his. Don't press your luck, however, and there are good grouper banks behind Monos and Huevos.

It is through the huge swells and choppy waters of these Bocas that speedboats are tested every year during the Great Race. This race is held around Columbus' Discovery Day, the Saturday before the first Monday in August. All boats leave the Yacht Club, pass through the Bocas, around the North Coast and finish at Store Bay in Tobago.

Scotland Bay on the mainland near Teteron is a good point for a swim. This is a white sandy beach where you can anchor in the shallow waters.

Gasparee: Another tour is to Gasparee, which originally belonged to Don Gaspar de Percin. When the Spaniards capitulated in 1779, there were lengthy litigations as to whom and to which country these islands belonged. Prior to capitulating, Chacon built additional forts on Gasparee, hoping to defend the island, but the Spanish fleets did not give sufficient assistance for his plan to work.

Later there were two whaling stations at Point Baleine or Whale Point. Cotton was grown on this island, and there is a fort on Bombshell Hill facing the mainland. There was a well-run guesthouse at Point Baleine where Noel Coward stayed and wrote a novel called *Point Valeine*. There is also a Roman Catholic Chapel where boats can be seen heading about 7 o'clock on Sunday mornings.

Today the **Calypso Beach Resort** is at

The rich fishing waters offshore gave Point Baleine its name.

1. Île de la Trinité. — Baleines.
1. Isla de la Trinidad. — Ballenas.

Bombshell Bay. Highly built up, it has hundreds of cabanas clustered together. This development was to be a part of a time-share arrangement with an international chain, but plans collapsed for undisclosed reasons. One businessman was known to have lost more than seven million (TT) dollars in the deal. The point of departure is after the power boats jetty and the sign "Calypso Beach Resort" is clearly marked. If you are a guest for the day, the Calypso Beach rate is $15TT to go across and $10TT for the use of the beach. There is a small beachmobile for transporting your baskets to the top of the hill.

Apart from this built-up part of the island, there are many lovely homes and there are those who live on the island year round. Gaspar Grande, as the island is alternatively known, also has some underground caves popular with visitors. The entrance is at Point Baleine. You go down steps now and not a rope ladder as children did long ago. There are the usual stalactites, stalagmites and bats. At high tide the caves can be filled with sea water.

On your return to the mainland you pass a small island inhabited by centipedes. The five smaller islands to the east of Gaspar Grande were originally the Diego Martin islands. They are **Caledonia**, **Lenegan's** and **Neilson**, granted to a Dr. Neilson and later called Belair. Here the East Indians who arrived as indentured laborers were kept until they were assigned to estates. **Pelican** and **Rock** were quarantine stations. There are also two larger islands: **Creteau**, sometimes known as Begorrat; and **Carrera**, at one time called Long Island, were first holiday resorts. Creteau is now a stone quarry and Carrera became a prison in 1877. Today prisoners are sent there for hard labor.

Chaca: The adventurous visit **Chacachacare**, the largest island of the link. Chacachacare is supposedly a word resembling the chattering of monkeys, but in Venezuela it is called the island of the deer, and when the Spanish first arrived they called it El Caracol. Whatever, it has been Chaca as far back as most Trinis can recall.

The third Boca separates the islands of Huevos and Chacachacare, and between Chacachacare and the Venezuelan mainland is the Dragon's Mouth. Those of the Spanish fleet prayed and offered masses to their favorite virgins and saints to go through the Dragon's Mouth safely. There

Yachts at anchor in a natural marina.

are months when it is like a lake and others when it is deserving of its name.

On the island is a lagoon of saltwater and an attempt to extract salt was once made. Chaca is as if neatly divided into two separate landmasses, with a narrow strip of land joining them. The island slopes towards the inside of the bay, and the west sides of the hills descend sharply to the Caribbean Sea. The bay on the west side has black sand and is called **La Tinta**, meaning ink. The smugglers from the mainland, and there were many, brought their boats from the Venezuelan side, into Trinidad territorial waters via the island.

In 1877 the British established a leper colony here, building some extraordinary red brick Victorian houses: the doctors' residence, the home for the nuns who cared for the lepers, a hospital and a chapel. The lepers lived all over the island, but the sanatorium is now closed. Swimming and fishing are excellent.

A boat larger than a pirogue should be used for a visit to Chaca. Call the Yacht Club and a member would be prepared to rent his boat and provide company for the journey.

Choose one of the afternoons of those tours when you have returned early, say

around 4:30, to go back to Port of Spain by another road.

Leave Chaguaramas, passing Carenage. On your left you will come to Glencoe and Newbury Hill, both residential areas. Bayshore is on the waterfront on your right. The view from Windy Ridge, one of the housing areas, is terrific. On a clear day look all around you from here, down on the sea, across the Northern Range and the city.

At the traffic light, turn left for **Westmoorings**. This was a swamp where it was customary to catch crabs in the moonlight to be used in the local callaloo dish, until the swamp was filled in the '40s and developed for housing.

You will come to St. Finbar's Roman Catholic Church and St. Anthony's school, where you turn right onto the Morne Coco Road for a scenic drive which takes you all the way to the church in Maraval on a hill dedicated to the Virgin of Lourdes. Make a right turn and you are on the Saddle Road. You may wish to stop at Chaconia Inn for a drink.

On another day, you might take the road to your left before the Seventh Day Adventist Community Hospital. The sign reads Mucurapo. This will take you to the

The modern equivalent of the donkey cart, near Gran Couva.

foreshore named after Audrey Jeffers, a prominent social worker. It gives another view of Port of Spain, from the lay-by where it is customary to see many cars parked in the night — a sort of lovers lane.

On your right is the **Jean Pierre Complex** for indoor sports. Jean Pierre was captain of the national netball team which in 1979 won the world championship jointly with New Zealand. The competition was held in this very stadium. The highway takes you straight onto Wrightson Road.

On another day visit Blue Basin, the River Estate where a small falls and old estate provide an attraction for local children. Just after West Mall take the turning for Diego Martin.

Victoria Gardens is a new housing development on your left. Ridgewood Tower apartments are also on your left. At the sign saying Crystal Stream turn right and bear left again. At Majuba Crossing head for the residential area of Blue Range.

At the junction of Diego Martin Main Road and Petit Valley, turn right, then left and you will come to the River Estate, bought by the Government in 1897. A cocoa, coffee and citrus estate, it is now urbanized. The old water wheel has been restored and there is a shed with historical information about the area.

The Blue Basin River and Falls are cool and invigorating, and are a nice stop on a hot day.

San Fernando and the South: The southern part of Trinidad — which to Trinidadians seems to be anything below the latitude of Port of Spain — comprises everything from the oil and other heavy industries to East Indian cane farming villages to the pitch lake at La Brea.

Though the sights of the south are not always amongst Trinidad's most picturesque, to know the country one must see the lower two-thirds of the island. San Fernando is only about an hour's drive from Port of Spain, and there are many people who commute daily between the two cities.

The southeastern coastline presents another kind of marine beauty from that of the rocky northern coast, as beaches here lie beside low flat wide coconut groves which stretch miles to the sea. The first tour goes to a part of the deep south including Chaguanas, Couva, San Fernando and Pointe-à-Pierre.

Go to the Butler Highway and take the first flyover as if going to the Swamp, but this time make a left into Charlieville along the Caroni Savannah Road. The Charlieville Road leads into the highly commercialized city of **Chaguanas**. People here are mainly of East Indian descent, children of indentured laborers, many of whom left the declining sugar industry to become professionals. Chaguanas is a growing area, and what was a depressed collection of small villages ten years ago has mushroomed into a town with nice middle-class homes, now the third most important city in Trinidad.

The town is built around a one-way main road with a market and branches of the big chain stores and commercial banks. The many malls — Mid-Centre, Ramsaran Park, Centre City, Medford Plaza — are an indication of Chaguanas' prosperity.

On Chaguanas Main Road can be found the **Lion House**, former home of V.S. Naipaul, the Trinidad-born novelist now living in London. In the tragicomic *A House for Mr. Biswas*, Naipaul described the house as the home of the Biswas family. A two-storied building painted white with stone figures of lions against the pillars of the top floor, this modest dwelling was the crowning achievement of Biswas' life, in a novel that describes with exquisite detail and humor the pathos of a man whose intelligence and sophistica-

Chemical factory, Point Lisas.

tion are sufficient only to make him realize his limitations.

From Chaguanas take the Old Southern Main Road to **Edinburgh Gardens**, another housing area. Edinburgh was the site of a U.S. Armed Forces Airbase during the War and Chaguanas is synonymous in many Trinidadian minds with the Yankee base. The soil here has a degree of clay and is therefore unsuitable for cane, but there is some beef herd and vegetable farming and several potters in the area. It is from here that every year millions of *deyas* (small earthen bowls) are made for use by Hindus to celebrate the Festival of Lights, Divali (see Festivals, p. 107).

Further along you come to **Brechin Castle**, the beautifully kept main factory area of Caroni Limited, the state-owned sugar company purchased from the British firm of Tate and Lyle in 1977. **Sevilla House**, occupied by senior management of the company, is perched on a hill. The road leading to this former estate house is lined by royal palms and the grounds take the form of an 18-hole golf course used by senior management. Caroni Limited owns another factory at Usine Ste. Madeleine near San Fernando.

The town of **Couva** is inert compared to Chaguanas. Though the vendors have been provided with a market, it suits them financially to sell their wares on the sidewalks. The old railway station is still the heart of activity here.

Not far away is the convent of the Holy Faith, a school in the grounds of the house of a former overseer of a plantation. The old house is beautiful, though the school is merely a collection of new buildings spread across large areas of land. Visitors to Couva always look for the popular Chorro's Restaurant, well known for its roti.

Keep on the old road past **California by the sea** where there is a sugar warehouse. California is mainly a sugar housing settlement, where many residents were granted small loans by the Sugar Welfare Association to build houses. It is from Point Lisas Bay next door that Caroni Ltd. sends its sugar abroad.

Point Lisas is a massive industrial complex built at the cost of almost $3 billion (TT). The Iron and Steel Company, Fertilizers of Trinidad and Tobago, National Gas Company, National Energy Corporation, a power station of the electricity company and other heavy industries are all stationed here. Tours of these areas are

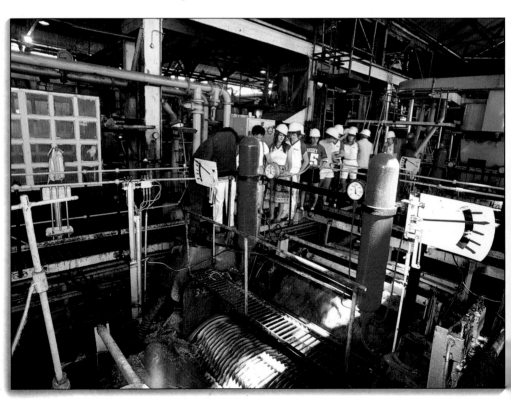

A sugar mill in Couva.

172

available for those having a special interest in industry, or for potential investors interested in downstream industries.

Just after is **Claxton Bay**, a small village made dirty by the dust from the state-owned Cement Factory. Further down is Farrell House, a hotel up on a hill on the right with a beautiful view of the Gulf of Paria. The sunset is beautiful from here. Farrell House is a good hotel used mainly by businessmen visiting the oil and industrial sector. Conference facilities are available. You can have an excellent lunch on your stop here or you may decide to stay overnight.

When you leave Claxton Bay, you enter Victoria County. The entrance to the city of **Pointe-à-Pierre** was heavily guarded during the War, close as it was to strategic industries. You will come to the large Pointe-à-Pierre refinery, formerly owned by Texaco but acquired by the Trinidad and Tobago Government in 1984. Almost everything in this area is government-owned, an indication of the massive nationalization and industrialization program embarked on during the oil boom.

This is a beautifully hilly area and the natural scenery provides a stark contrast to the abundant man-made. In driving through you will see the Augustus Long Hospital and Club House. The bungalows and the bachelors' quarters are on high ground looking down on the rigs and tanks.

Pointe-à-Pierre's lake is in the hands of the Wild Fowl Trust because of the hundreds of species of birds that alight here, and the special lily which grows in this lake. A small wooden building, like an enlarged version of a bird house, provides literature on the various species. Birdwatchers and nature lovers should contact members of the committee or Molly Gaskin, who heads the Trust, if they wish to visit this nature center. She can be reached at 637-5145.

Pointe-à-Pierre has the sulfurous smell of any refinery area. The **Guaracara Park**, owned by the oil company, is a good sporting center. Formerly the scene of the popular Southern Games, with leading international track and field stars, the ground's use has been expanded to include football games, territorial cricket matches and night cricket under floodlights.

The next town is **Marabella**, urbanized, commercialized and with a daily roadside market. You will by-pass San Fernando by skirting St. Joseph Village, a middle-class housing area in San Fernando.

Making earthenware pottery in Chaguanas.

The sugar crop begins in January and ends in June, so in these months buffalo-drawn carts traverse the southern outskirts of San Fernando. The sign on the right saying Siparia is the one you will take.

Enter the **Phillipines Estate**, once owned by Sir Norman Lamont, a Scotsman who was gored by a bull on his own plantation. Part of the estate has been developed into Bryan's Gate, a residential area.

The Phillipines Estate was left to the government for agricultural development, but they turned it down. Then it was offered to the Imperial College of Tropical Agriculture and they too turned it down. Thirdly it was to go to a distant relative of Sir Norman's soldiering in Africa. He had no interest in an estate in Trinidad and instructed it to be sold. And so it landed in the hands of property developers. The old estate residence surrounded by samaan trees is now used as site offices.

Pass by **Penal**, mainly an East Indian town with its power plant serving the entire southwestern peninsula. At Siparia there is a well-known statue of La Divina Pastora at the main Catholic Church called the Black Virgin of Siparia.

This devotion to Mary, the divine

Shepherdess, was brought from the sheep-rearing community of Andalucia in southern Spain. The Capuchin monks were the first missionaries to come from Spain to convert the Amerindians, and they instilled their traditional devotion to La Divina Pastora. In 1759, the last mission was formed in Siparia. According to legend the statue was brought by the Capuchins from Venezuela when fleeing an Amerindian revolt.

The statue is rather small, of brown complexion with pink cheeks and black hair. She is dressed in blue voile, her hair adorned with artificial lilies. Around her neck are many necklaces, offerings from devotees. There are perpetual lights illuminating the statue.

Over the years, Hindus and other non-Catholic groups have been attracted to La Divina Pastora. When the railway line reached Siparia, making the south accessible to the Indians, they became devotees and developed their own name for her, Soparee Kay Mai, meaning Mother Kali.

The feast of La Divina Pastora is on the second Sunday after Easter, when the statue is carried in procession; a big day in the life of Siparians. The locals adorn themselves with new clothes, and feasting and celebrating are the order of the day.

After Siparia is Santa Flora and then Palo Seco, meaning dry wood. This is now oil territory. Just past is Rancho Quemado, meaning burning hut, the name no doubt connected with an Amerindian occurrence.

You should make a side trip to **Fyzabad** to see the statue of Uriah Butler, prominently placed where the oil workers' riots of June 1937 took place. With top hat, he is dressed in black as was Butler's wont. June 19 is celebrated as Labour Day with rallies and fiery speeches on this spot.

Leave Butler in Fyzabad and go onto the Siparia Erin Road, heading straight for the sea. **Erin** is a fishing village with liming fishermen and a generally slow pace.

Here the sea is a bit muddy, but you can clearly see Venezuela, seven or eight miles away. You can buy Venezuela parrots or pretty hammocks in town, and occasionally whales are washed up on this shore.

Go back to San Fernando, by-passing Fyzabad, onto the Mosquito Creek. You will pass the mouth of the Oropouche River and on a tributary further on is a crematorium called the Shore of Peace. The Oropouche River goes inland through La Fortune and Woodland, where there is

A buffalo-drawn cart near San Fernando.

a mixture of both sugar and rice.

Nearer to San Fernando is the Godineau River. It is said that a Dr. Singh killed his wife and threw her body into the Godineau but the tide brought in her body and he was discovered.

During spring tide in the month of October, the water from the Gulf of Paria covers Mosquito Creek creating traffic problems. To the right is the swamp.

On your way to San Fernando you will pass La Romain, a residential district, a new middle-class development called Gulf City, and the Cactus Inn. Take Lady Hailes Avenue with San Fernando main thoroughfare on your right. Turn off on the Rienzi Kirton Highway. This short link road was named after Mrs. Gertrude Kirton, a former Mayor of San Fernando, and Adrian Cola Rienzi, a former member of the Legislative Council and the founder of two trade unions—the Oilfield Workers Trade Union and the All Trinidad Sugar Estates and Factory Workers Trade Union.

Worshipers of the Black Virgin of Siparia, left and right. You will enter San Fernando, passing Naparima College, a prestigious boys school.

You come to **Harris Promenade**, commemorating Lord Harris, Governor of Trinidad from 1846 to 1854. The Roman Catholic Church, Our Lady of Perpetual Help, was consecrated on May 29, 1849. The Town Hall and Council were established in 1846 and the wharf opened in 1842. It was then that San Fernando began assuming some importance. Now it is second only to Port of Spain.

On this promenade there are several churches of other denominations, Methodist and Anglican, and a statue of Mahatma Ghandi is prominent. There is also the engine of the last train which left Port of Spain for San Fernando, marking the end of railway service in Trinidad. An old calypso, "Last Train to San Fernando" said if you don't get this one, you'll never get another one, so on its last journey, people were crammed into the carriages, heads sticking out and some even managed to get onto the roof of the train, just to be on that last ride.

Take High Street, the main business street, and ask for "Ali's Doubles." This is an Indian delicacy, a bite in the taste. Try it with a cold drink.

High Street and Harris Promenade join at the Library Corner, a popular meeting point in San Fernando with its non-functioning clock. "Meet me at the Library

Corner," is what most people say about an appointment in San Fernando. The library is a well-appointed red brick building recently restored. Just on the left of the Library Corner is the Naparima Girls' School, and off on the right on Harris Promenade is the Catholic-run St. Joseph's Convent, another girls' school.

On Circular Road is the headquarters of one of the country's most powerful trade unions, the Oilfield Workers Trade Union, formed in 1937 just after the Butler riots. Its president is George Weekes, who will celebrate his 25th year as president in 1987.

San Fernando is built around a hill, the lower portions of which were privately owned and provided house builders with a high grade gravel. So for years, landowners operated successful quarries before they were stopped by the government. There used to be steps leading all the way to the top where there was a plateau with what seemed like a small peak at the very edge. Today the hill is just an ugly mark on the town, as the quarrying destroyed most of the vegetation and the steps are covered with overgrowth. It is a sore point with many residents.

Return to Port of Spain by driving back through Marabella past the Union Park Race Course and onto the Solomon Hochoy Highway. Sir Solomon was the first Trinidad and Tobago citizen to be made a governor of Trinidad and Tobago.

The Union Park Race Course is built on Tarouba Estate, an old sugar farm. A large part of it is converted to a sugar housing settlement. On an afternoon, if attending a race meeting, take time if you can a little after five to see squadrons of Scarlet Ibis and egrets heading for the Caroni Swamp to spend the night.

Stay on the Solomon Hochoy Highway, and at Claxton Bay's turn-off, on the second hill after the bridge there is a statue of a headless woman. Countless stories surround this statue, the most popular being that the daughter of an overseer had been seeing a laborer on the estate. One day the father tried to keep his daughter at home and placed a snake at the meeting point to scare away her lover. The girl ran away to meet her boyfriend and was herself bitten by the snake. The father built this statue for her.

Motorists swear that on nights they see the young girl walking on the highway, standing before their cars. There certainly have been many accidents in the immediate

Intricate fretwork of an old estate house, Siparia.

area. Others say that the statue is just one of the Virgin Mary.

Continue onto the Butler Highway turning left onto the Churchill Roosevelt. You will find your way easily to the Queen's Park Savannah.

To Icacos Point and La Brea: The deep south is the peninsula of land stretching out from the southwest corner of Trinidad toward the west and South America like a bigger shadow of the northern peninsula which contains part of Port of Spain and her suburbs. The La Brea tar pits are located there, as are a number of fishing villages, lookout points and beaches.

It is about a three hours' drive to the furthest point on this tour, so if you plan to see a number of sights and return to Port of Spain the same evening, begin your journey early. Also keep in mind that in Trinidad on a weekday there can be traffic jams as early as 7 a.m. on the major highways.

Take the now-familiar Butler Highway onto the Solomon Hochoy Highway, which intersects Butler at about Chaguanas. Bypass San Fernando and go into Mosquito Creek. Gulf City is on the right and La Romain on the left.

You will pass through a heavily-wooded area, past the Chatham Youth Camp to Chatham Junction. The ward of Cedros begins here. There are small villages and some forested areas until Bonasse, way out towards the furthest point.

There is a good place to swim near Manmohansingh Park. Turn left onto Perseverance Road, driving through fields of coconut trees, into the village of **Fullarton**.

This is a "ribbon line village," as are most of the towns in Cedros, where the road is in the middle and houses strung out along the side. People from Fullarton often use the beach in preference to the road, walking along the sand that connects Fullarton with Bonasse when returning from the movies in the latter town.

The two main means of livelihood in this area are fishing and coconuts. Today the coconuts are being affected by red ring disease, which dries the palm.

Ask for Kelman, who owns the village inn and has a lot of ideas on how to spend time usefully. He'll tell you how to make good fish broth in the open and regale you with stories of the village in the old days, though he himself may only be in his mid-thirties.

Hills of San Fernando.

Leaving Fullarton bear right at a fork in the road to **Columbus Bay**, again driving through a private coconut estate, and through the village of Los Gallos.

It is believed that Columbus dropped anchor here on his third voyage to the West Indies. Columbus Bay is a crowded beach on holidays and most weekends, but if the tide is low you can drive another two miles along the secluded beach or walk all the way to **Icacos Point**.

Icacos is another fishing village, the furthest point on the southwestern peninsula, and seven miles across the Serpent's Mouth from Venezuela.

An old lighthouse for fishermen is fast receding into the sea from erosion. From Columbus Bay or anywhere along that beach you can see **Soldado Rock** and three other small rocks. The negotiations over Patos concerning the boundaries landed Trinidad with Soldado. That was all the importance attached to the very small rock, until about 12 years ago when the zealous coastguard from Venezuela (La Guardia Nacionale) began patrolling the waters around Soldado and roping in fishermen for the Venezuelan jails near the Orinoco. If any fisherman offers you a boat ride, as they are wont to do, insist that he doesn't go past Soldado or pray that your Spanish is adequate.

On the way back, turn sharp left at the gas station at **Cap-de-Ville Junction**. Cap-de-Ville is a growing town on the outskirts of Point Fortin, a small fishing port and a town which is said to breathe: its wide streets permit sea breezes to blow freely. This town was built around the oil industry, its growth closely related to the Shell refinery, nationalized in the mid-'70s and renamed Trintoc. There is an old section of the town called Teschier Village, occupied by the semi-skilled workers of the refinery who live in nearby semi-detached houses.

The playground at Mahaica saw the birth of some fine national footballers and one of the country's leading football teams, Point Fortin Civic Centre, has its home ground here. There are special housing quarters for Trintoc's senior staff at Clifton Hill, as usual beautifully landscaped and with a golf course.

You will leave Point Fortin and come to **Vessigny Beach Camp**. This small beach with changing facilities is in a calm area but in rainy season, the water is quite dirty.

Five minutes north is **La Brea** and the pitch lake. This is one of the three pitch lakes in the world, the others being in Los Angeles (Rancho La Brea) and Venezuela (Guanaco). Go to the restaurant near the lake or the newly-open visitors facilities and ask for an official guide. Ignore those who pester you on the road.

A good guide and perhaps a witty one will tell you where on the lake you can find a cure for your ailments, most probably your sinus or aching joints. He might even explain how you can bathe in this lake but not how you might sail on it as one popular publisher of British romance stories once printed. The lake is big and black and you can walk on it and at times feel yourself sinking. Don't wear high heeled shoes.

In the late 16th Century Sir Walter Raleigh came to the south of Trinidad, mentioning in his notes that he used some pitch from the lake to caulk his ships. He claimed it was better than anything else he had reason to use. José Maria Chacon tried to encourage the pitch industry at La Brea, opening a factory and to prepare pitch for export at a rate of 700 barrels a year. The first shipment went to the Royal Arsenal in Spain. Today pitch is sent to European countries and most of the Caribbean, and paves roads in New York City and Paris, amongst other places.

Left, "black gold" at La Brea Pitch Lake and, right, a roadside shop in Princes Town.

The village—which is how it should be described—the court house and post office seem to relate closely to the surrounding pitch. When the sun is very hot, the street and the houses move. Romme St. Laurent refers to two pitch lakes in La Brea and perhaps the village was built on one of the two. A drive through La Brea calls for a cushioned bottom. Though roads are leveled and repaired with pitch, for the roads of La Brea there is no hope.

Brighton, the local port, has a long jetty for tankers to come alongside and receive buckets of asphalt, or oil from Trintoc. People say that "You pass me like a Brighton bucket." In other words, as if you didn't see me, you went by so quickly.

Pass the town of Rousillac and on reaching Silver Stream River, you come to the end of the swamp. There are lots of mosquitoes and sandflies in this area, as well as Otaheite, a fishing village.

There are several ghost towns in the south, but to spot them you will need an oil expert or a southerner in the know to be your guide. There are pumps just pumping away or you may see an oil rig covered with vines. Oil wells that once produced but have been capped are called ghosts.

The Atlantic Coast: Our next tour will be to Central Trinidad, and will take the form of a round trip to the East Coast, passing through sugarcane farms to the flat beaches of the East. The County of Caroni is synonymous with sugarcane and the rolling greenery of the Caroni Plains.

The cane arrows (flowers) are a beautiful sight just before harvest. A cane field then looks like a green wall with a sweep of white tops going on for miles.

Turn right at the Uriah Butler Highway. Time and again you will come across French family names like de Gannes, de Verteuil, Lange, Rostant and Melizan, families who received land grants from the crown in the 18th Century.

There is an interesting book written by Anthony de Verteuil about his family between 1800 and 1900, giving an excellent insight into this family which intermarried with the other French families that came to the island after the Royal Cedula of Population. If you find there are not as many Spanish names, they headed "Down the Main" to South America in search of the legendary El Dorado, never finding their gold.

Turn off at Chaguanas, left through Montrose, past Longdenville, named after

Nariva River and Cocos Bay.

a governor from 1870–1874. The people of these areas are mainly East Indian descendants of indentured laborers, now small sugarcane farmers or employees in the sugar industry. They were brought here after the abolition of slavery, first arriving on the *Fatel Rozack*, a passenger boat in 1845. To date their children have maintained most of their customs, cooking, dress, music, religion and some form of speech which is why Indian movies are so popular in Trinidad today.

The **Caroni Plains** mean miles and miles of sugar. These plantations too were once held by the British company Tate and Lyle but were bought by government in the mid-'70s. You will skirt the Montserrat Hill, surrounded by huge cocoa estates. You can ask to visit the San Salvador Estate, owned by Robert Montano, a businessman who has decided to explore the agricultural potential of the Central Range. Montserrat soil is said to be one of the very best for planting.

It is a delightful drive through Central Trinidad, with clean air, the smell of orange blossoms and beautiful scenery between the Caroni and Naparima Plains. From the town of Todd's Road, originally a railway station, the scenery is ever changing. At moments the forests seem to close in on you, creating an arbor. Note Hindu temples, mosques and an occasional Catholic or Anglican church. The Hindu homes are identifiable by flags planted on bamboo poles in the yards. These flags are up whenever there is a *puja* (prayer meeting) at the home. If you hear the sound of a conch shell it means one is in progress.

Turn right at the sign reading Tabaquite. On the hill is a luxurious round house, with two smaller houses next to it. This is the Lakeside Farm for cattle farming, with a lake at the back.

To visit the **Navet Reservoir** take the Carry-Nariva Road on your left into Brasso Venado (Arm of a Deer). The Reservoir is in the heart of Tabaquite, and supplies water to most of South Trinidad. To visit the waterworks itself you will have to make arrangements through your hotel with the Water and Sewerage Authority. On the outside of the secured area, however, is a mini-dam in cool surroundings where you can picnic.

About ten years ago, when the mini-dam burst, throwing 2 million gallons of water all around it, people came from all over Trinidad to camp on its banks, catch-

Activities at Mayaro Beach.

ing and cooking cascadura, a freshwater fish with a hard arrowed shell back. There is an old tale about the cascadura which has been written into poetry. Those who eat the cascadura will, the native legend says, wheresover they may wander, end their days in Trinidad. In the Brasso Venado forest there is a hunter's trail for the adventurous. The wild meat is said to be good here, but you need a license from the Game Warden to hunt.

You will drive through a teak forest said to be the largest in the Western Hemisphere, an awesome sight in an area where habitation is at a minimum. Teak is a durable timber which doesn't warp or shrink and so is used for shipbuilding, furniture and houses.

At Brasso Caparo River there are the remnants of a cocoa estate, and men with cutlasses and donkey carts walk the roads looking much the way they did 100 years ago.

Turn right for **Rio Claro**, a town that could be called the capital of Nariva County, as it is the seat of the Nariva Mayaro County Council. The town has a heavy Spanish influence and boasts a good parang group. It is a busy town, about 50 miles from the city. Big banks and stores have branches here.

The words of the songs by the Paranderos concern the Virgin, St. Joseph and the birth of Christ. The Amerindians were taught to make and play Spanish string instruments, to sing and venerate important Catholic feasts. The Capuchins were all for this and today there are good parang bands from Arima, Santa Cruz and the Palo Seco, Santa Flora area. The music is gay, and the singers wear pretty flowered clothing.

Leave Rio Claro on the Mayaro Road and soon you will see wide expanses of coconut trees, indicating that you are approaching the sea. Before the seaside town of Plaisance you will go over two wooden bridges over the Ortoire River. Turning left will take you north and eventually to Manzanilla.

Long ago, to get to Mayaro from Manzanilla there were two car ferries. There was a shop at the first ferry owned by a Chinaman, for there was not much to be had in these out-of-the-way places. Then the shops in what were known as outposts were owned and run by Chinese. Chinese immigrants were also brought as laborers, mainly from Canton, the first batch arriving on the *Clarendon* in the 1850s.

Coconut trees at Cocos Bay, below, and at Mayaro, right.

The ferries were soon replaced by the wooden bridges known as Bailey bridges, built by the U.S. Armed Forces to facilitate movement in that part of the island.

The trade winds keep this coast refreshed year round. Across the East Coast, as the crow flies, will take you straight to Africa, and according to Romme St. Laurent, coconuts arrived here when an African ship transporting the nuts ran aground.

The Sunday before Easter there is a tub race from the first Bailey bridge to the mouth of the river after Point Radix about a mile and a half away, even though the Ortoire is noted for alligators and water snakes called anacondas. These species have been washed into the river from the Orinoco in Venezuela when it overflows its banks. The tubs are made with plastic buckets, old bath tubs or any old containers, and are filled with drinks. To qualify the racers must have consumed all by the end. You may want to attend this outlandish event. For information go to Veni Mange, a restaurant on Lucknow Street in St. James.

Manzanilla is divided into two coconut estates, or cocals as they are called. The first as you are driving south to north belongs to the Bovell family. You will see many buffalypsoes (a buffalo used for beef herd) grazing on the estate. The second cocal is owned by the Huggins family, one of the big landowners.

Swimming along this coast is pleasant and a late afternoon at sunset is delightful. On moonlit nights the beach is a silvery white. If taking a tour strictly to swim in Manzanilla, bring along your hamper, or you might find the villagers are great at whipping up at short notice, sandwich and drink or some will even make a cook-up of pigeon peas and rice with some morsels of chicken thrown in with pumpkin.

On one of these swimming tours take time to stop at the Sou-Sou Land La Mariquita Estate. On the Manzanilla Road, about four miles from the beach you will see the Cocoa Village townhouses on one side and across the street the sign saying "La Mariquita."

It was until recently a cocoa estate owned by the same family which built the cocoa houses. However, with high land taxes and low prices for cocoa, many owners were willing to dispose of their land.

One of the big purchasers over the last two years has been Sou-Sou Land Limited,

a company which has been buying land and developing on behalf of the landless for housing. Sou-Sou is a patois word meaning penny by penny, and is a traditional form of banking among low income groups in Trinidad. Participants in these projects contribute any surpluses in income to purchasing their land.

The La Mariquita Estate is spread over 148 acres, of which 120 plots, each of 10,000 square feet, are allocated to housing. The estate is a mixture of cocoa, citrus, bananas and some pineapple, and is one of the few estates in the country open to visitors. The estate house was built in the mid-'70s but is old-fashioned with wooden floors and a rolling roof patterned after the cocoa drying houses. The founder of Sou-Sou Land, John Humphrey, hopes one day to make this estate into a showpiece for Trinidadians, Tobagonians and tourists alike. Anyone wishing to visit the estate can contact Dr. Allen Sammy at 623-8115.

Moruga and Guayaguayare: The last tour will take you to two distant points on the island, Moruga in the county of Victoria and Guayaguayare in the county of Mayaro. Prepare yourself for an entire day.

The route is the usual one down the Uriah Butler and Solomon Hochoy Highways to the San Fernando by-pass. Turn left at the Furness Watson Building midway on the by-pass, into Cocoyea. About five miles out you will see the sugar refinery, **Usine Ste. Madeleine**, a part of Caroni Limited, its beauty surpassing that of the rolling fields of Brechin Castle in Caroni. The road to the refinery is lined with royal palms as at Brechin Castle.

Ste. Madeleine is one of those areas in Trinidad where the class contrast is quite apparent. On the one hand there are the company homes of senior staff at the refinery overlooking the Ste. Madeleine pond, the sprawling yards, and the well-maintained golf course.

On the other, there are the simple, sometimes ramshackle homes of the estate laborers, whose children play their Sunday cricket on the unkempt roadside playgrounds. There are the railway lines on which the carriages roll in with company cane, but you will also see long lines of buffalo-drawn carts, the animals drooping in the midday heat waiting for the farmers' cane to be weighed.

More information on the sugar industry can be obtained from the Public Relations department of Caroni Limited who will

A colorful home of a sugar worker in Guayaguayare.

organize a tour of their operations for you. This includes a distillery in the north which produces Caravel Rum for export. Molasses is one by-product of the refining process whose production a visitor can observe.

Continue along the Manahambre Road past other sugar villages—Jordan Hill, Cedar Hill and Manahambre—into **Princes Town**. As you enter you will see the Anglican Church where two poui trees were planted by Prince Albert and Prince George, who later became King George VI. They visited Trinidad in 1880, arriving on the *HMS Bacchante* and were guests of Governor Sir Henry Turner Irving. When they visited the south, what was known as "the Mission" was renamed Princes Town, in their honor.

On the left past the church is the police station and court house which from its ferret work is known to be of French influence. Leave Princes Town and take the Moruga Road past villages called First, Third, Fourth, Fifth and Sixth Company.

These villages housed disbanded Anglican soldiers from the American Civil War who were sent to Trinidad to make their fortunes. The Second Company was lost at sea, hence no mention of its name.

Each company village has its own cemetery and church.

In this part of Trinidad there are typical old houses and rolling savannahs. You are going through flat lands and the area is called precisely that in French, Basse Terre. The road goes straight into the fishing village of **Moruga** with its one main street.

Today, the name Moruga is linked with members of the Baptist faith and a cult called obeah. People from all over Trinidad descend on the small villages around Moruga to visit the obeah men and women. Obeah is a folk practice which uses the "bush bath" to wash out the evil. or light, using candles to do evil. For the bush bath herbs are selected and boiled according to the problem, but it is difficult to say what these selections are.

Like magicians, obeah men never tell. You can go to the obeah man if you want to get a job, if you want to persuade your young man to marry you, if you want to keep a delinquent husband at home or even to heal you of some kinds of sickness. Almost every house on the Indian Walk Road is a Baptist shrine.

The beach in Moruga is extraordinary at low tide. You have to walk at least a mile

Blue skies over Moruga.

and a half on the seabed of sand before you reach the water. If you walk a considerable way out you will appreciate a delightful scene of the fishing boats stuck in the sea bed, waiting to rise again when the tide comes in with sheer cliffs behind you.

You will also see the church, the old plantation house on high ground and this seabed of sand extending for miles on your left and right. To swim means a long walk to the water unless the tide is high. This is where Christopher Columbus spotted the three hills (those of the southern range) which led him to call the island Trinidad. To see the three hills you have to be out on a boat like Columbus, closer to the Guayaguayare area.

Though Discovery Day (first Monday in August) has been renamed Emancipation Day, villagers continue to celebrate the grand occasion, complete with the arrival of Christopher Columbus in 15th Century garb who moves onto land, kissing the sand and lying flat as Roman Catholic priests do on ordination, claiming it in the name of the King and Queen of Spain. He is usually accompanied by his fleet. If you are near on this day, don't miss the opportunity to take part in the festivities.

Look at Moruga on your map. It is on the southern coast about one-third distance from the southeastern tip and as the crow flies north you will come to Arima, the center of the county of St. George, at the foot of the Northern Range.

Return by way of the road leading into New Grant, Tableland and Fonrose, into Rio Claro and onto the Mayaro Road.

Mayaro is in the county with the same name and on the Mayaro beach road you will see the built-up residential area where employees of Amoco (American Oil Company) live. A number of local families have beach houses here and there are two coconut plantations owned by the de Meillacs, another of the French families.

You can stop anywhere along this beach for a good refreshing swim. Two major currents meet here, creating a crisscross effect in the waves. With no premium on time you may stay here quite a while, taking in the fresh sea breeze from the Atlantic.

The beaches here are strewn with chip-chip shells and during chip-chip gathering season many a delicious dish can be made of the shell fish. But be prepared to wash them over and over to be rid of the sand.

Drive south to **Guayaguayare**, an Indian-sounding name like Chacachacare. In the same manner, people fondly refer to it as "Guaya."

At Galeota Point on the very tip of the coast, you will see the oil rigs, way out at sea. It was from here in the mid-'70s that most of the country's oil wealth came, taking Trinidad from an impoverished third world country to something resembling a sheikdom with a wealthy select few, and then to a country with a growing middle-class.

From Upper Manzanilla to Rushville in Guaya is about 44 miles of flat sandy beach lined by endless, tall straight coconut trees.

Return to Port of Spain along the Mayaro Road into Manzanilla over the Ortoire River. From Manzanilla drive on to Sangre Chiquito, Sangre Grande and Valencia. Then take the turn-off for the Churchill Roosevelt Highway which will bring you straight into the Beetham Highway and Port of Spain.

You have covered the length and breadth of Trinidad, you have traveled to the four points. Time and again you have taken into the Northern Range which is the most beautiful, because it is the heart of the Trinidad rain forest and a special paradise for nature lovers.

Left, a basket case (or "straw man") and, right, the circular at Sangre Grande.

Tobago

1300 m/ 0,8 miles

Tourist attractions:

1 Kariwak Hotel
2 Sandy Point
  Beach Club
3 Tropikist Hotel
4 Crown Reef Hotel
5 Mt. Irvine Hotel
6 Back Bay
7 Turtle Beach Hotel
8 Arnos Vale Hotel
9 Blue Waters Inn
10 King's Bay Waterfall
11 Richmond Great House

C a r i b b e a n

Castara

Castara Bay

Mount Dillon

King Peter's Bay

Woodlands

Runnemede

Culloden

Moriah

Mount Thomas

Golden Lane

Indian Walk

St. David

Nutmeg Grove

Vale Rd.

Les Coteaux

Easterfield

Arnos Vale

Plymouth

⑧

Arnos

Les Coteaux

Courland Pt.

Adventure

Franklyn's

Concordia

Mason Hall

Belmont

Great Courland Bay

⑦

Plymouth Rd.

Providence Rd.

St. George

Northside Rd.

Adelphi

Courland

The Whim

⑥

Black Rock

Lower Quarter or Roselle

Mary's Hill

Providence

Mesopotamia

Mt. Irvine or Little Courland Bay

⑤

Grange

Orange

Hill

Orange Hill

Rd.

Calder Hall

Friendsfield

Mou St. Geor

Booby Pt.

Buccoo

Bethel

Patience Hill

Lower Town

Morne Quiton

Hillsbor. Bay

Buccoo Coral Reef

Buccoo Bay

Buccoo Rd.

Prospect

St. Andrew

Bacolet

Scarborough

Minister Bay

Minister Pt.

Bon Accord Lagoon

Golden Grove

Carnbee Village

Lambeau

Rockly Bay

Bacolet Pt.

St. Patrick

Diamond

Milford or Sandy Bay

④

Bon Accord Village

Canaan

Shirvan

Mt. Pleasant

Auchenskloch

Little Rockly Bay

Tyson Hall

Kilgwyn

③
✈
①

②

Friendship

Brown's or Crown's Pt.

Robinson Crusoe's Cave

Canoe Bay

Cove

Columbus or Kennedy's Pt.

190

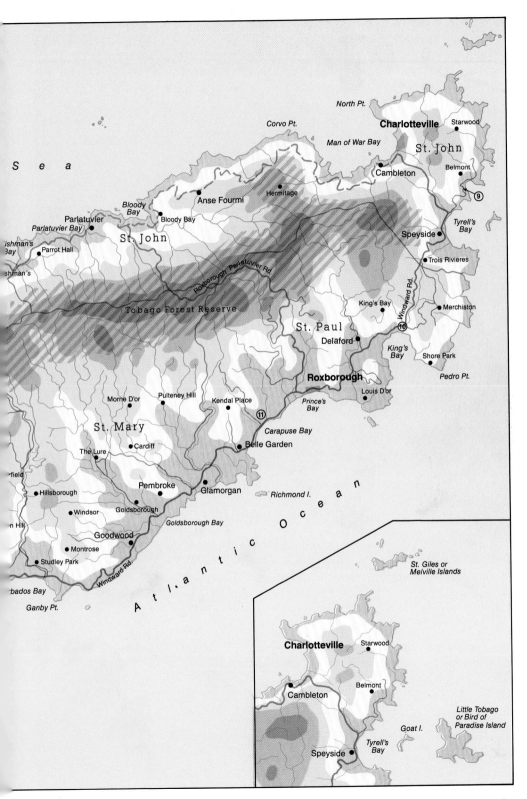

S e a

North Pt.

Corvo Pt.

Charlotteville Starwood

Man of War Bay

St. John

Cambleton Belmont

Hermitage S 9

Bloody
Bay Anse Fourmi

Parlatuvier Tyrell's
Parlatuvier Bay Bloody Bay Bay

ishman's St. John Speyside

Bay Parrot Hall Trois Rivieres

shman's Roxborough Parlatuvier Rd.

Windward Rd.

Tobago Forest Reserve King's Bay Merchiston

St. Paul 10

Delaford King's
Bay Shore Park

Roxborough Pedro Pt.

Morne D'or Pulteney Hill Louis D'or

Kendal Place 11

Prince's
Bay

St. Mary Carapuse Bay

Cardiff Belle Garden

The Lure

field O c e a n

Hillsborough Pembroke Glamorgan Richmond I.

Windsor Goldsborough

Goodwood Goldsborough Bay

n Hill A t l a n t i c

Montrose

Studley Park St. Giles or
Melville Islands

bados Bay Windward Rd.

Ganby Pt. A t l a n t i c

Charlotteville Starwood

Belmont

Cambleton

Little Tobago
or Bird of
Paradise Island

Goat I.

Speyside Tyrell's
Bay

191

INTRODUCTION TO TOBAGO

Like a Caribbean island of fifty years ago, Tobago stands relatively unmarked by international tourism. Numerous unspoiled beaches, largely deserted save the occasional fisherman or group of local children, picturesque bumpy roads winding past palm groves, tiny hamlets and locals waiting for a "drop," small hotels frequented by Trinidadian vacationers, a place where an outsider can still be an interesting anomaly and not simply an oppressive necessity: this is Tobago.

From the cosmopolitan snap of Port of Spain to the rural languor of Tobago seems a far longer distance than the mere 20-minutes' ride on a BWIA Airbridge flight. Though they are indeed united in more than just economic and political ways, there are subtle (and not so subtle) differences between Trinidad and Tobago. Where Trinidad presents a surprising mixture of African, East Indian, Oriental and European culture and people, almost 90 percent of Tobagonians are of black African descent. And while Trinis tend to be a cosmopolitan bunch, even Scarborough, Tobago's largest town, is more of an enlarged market village than a real city.

But Trinidad and Tobago were of the same piece of South American land, and so Tobago offers the same diverse geography and plant and animal life. Twenty-six miles long but only three miles wide, Tobago is a constant feast for the eyes, as even interior roads are usually only fifteen or so minutes from glimpses of the sea, and a route through the mountainous interior passes stands of enormous creaking bamboo and dense jungly growth before suddenly giving way to vistas of a sparkling white palm fringed beach, or open pastures grazed by placid cattle and scruffy goats.

The fish-shaped island is circumnavigated by two main coastal roads. However, the "head" and "tail" are beyond the reach of this circle, and north of Charlotteville there are only paths. Any point on the island is reachable in a few hours' drive at most, and most drives are a good day trip, with as much to see along the way as there is at the final destination – if you have one!

TOBAGO, TROPIC OF DELIGHT

From the air, Tobago appears like a travel brochure picture, with bright blue water sparkling around a rolling green land, stretches of pale beach and frothy waves defining the perimeter. The mountains of the interior loom deep green and dusky purple.

Tobago is rumored to be Robinson Crusoe's island, and some guides would happily show you his exact cave, though the caves of the southeast tip could have been formed by wave action or man. More important than the verifiability of this claim, though, is the truth that Crusoe could have subsisted happily here. Tobago is a self-contained paradise, a verdant island where the visitor could well imagine himself housed in a palm-frond cottage, sustained on the fruits of land and ocean, eternally entertained by the mutable beauty of the landscape of sand, sea, sky and mountain. And the island remains largely untouched by international tourism, though 400-plus years of European occupation have considerably shaped geography as well as population.

Most place names reflect the recent European history of the island—Studley Park, Les Coteaux, Roxborough, Aukenskeoch, Courland—and the ubiquitous bright orange immortelle, imported as shade for cocoa trees, is as much a reminder of the colonial past as are the crumbling sugar mills hidden here and there in the forests. This is still an agricultural place where almost everyone makes at least a part of his living from farming or fishing.

Top-notch international hotels, droves of European and American tourists in search of a Disneyland ideal of Caribbean sand-and-sea, obsequious hotel employees are all happily nonexistent on Tobago. Accommodations are suited stylistically and economically to Trinidadian needs and tastes, and each beach has its own personality, with fishermen's nets drying on one and goats grazing the edges of another but only the rare non-hotel beach inhabited by vacationers. Since the country is not yet 100 percent behind—or dependent on—tourism as a source of national income, the way many other Caribbean islands are, the foreign visitor tends to be of a more adventurous and adaptable type.

Preceding pages: Tobagonians take a lime near the Windward Road; and, rhapsody in blue at Arnos Vale Hotel. Below, aerial view of an island paradise.

Traditionally, visitors to Tobago want to get away from the hustle and bustle, and Tobago generally shuts down at about 9 each night. But for those who want to hear a little music or have an after-dinner drink, the various hotels offer the best opportunity. Even if you aren't staying at a particular resort, you're welcome to visit, and you're as likely to meet a Tobagonian as a tourist from the States.

Crown Point and Crusoe: Most visitors to Tobago fly into **Crown Point Airport**, at the southwestern tip of the island, though some still take the ferry from Port of Spain to Scarborough. The airport, renovated in late 1985, is a comfortable blend of the modern, the tropical and the touristy, a warm gusty wind blows scents of the sea through the hangar-like building. There are no baggage carousels, so travelers wait on the tarmac for the luggage truck, and then rummage for their own things.

Out front, taxi drivers jostle for passengers, but don't choose one until you've investigated the options. A number of hotels provide minibus transport to and from the airport, and if you're staying at one of the nearby hotels like Sandy Point or Kariwak, you can pretty much walk there. Car rentals are also available at the airport. Taxis are expensive, particularly for the further ends of the island (see Appendix at the back of this guide), and a taxi driver can be your best guide. Agree on the charge before you begin.

Right next to Crown Point are a number of modern hotels. Air traffic noise doesn't seem to be a major problem, and the hotels are convenient to the major tourist attraction of **Buccoo Reef**, but this corner of the island is basically flatlands, so don't miss the rest of the island even if you do stay here.

The **Sandy Point Beach Club** and **Crown Point Condominiums** offer apartment-type accommodations in modern, air-conditioned buildings, as does the **Tropikist Beach Hotel**. Also nearby is **Kariwak Village**, worth a trip for dinner and drinks just to see what owner/manager Allan Clovis is up to.

One of the most knowledgeable and helpful hoteliers on Tobago, he presents art and photography shows of local artists, can find you a good taxi driver/guide, or point you toward a secluded beach where pre-Columbian arrowheads and potsherds can still be found. He is a storehouse of local intelligence and tourist advice.

Though the **Bon Accord Road** to the

airport is little used past the airport turn-off, it does lead to some quiet shallow bays. This is the area Robinson Crusoe is said to have inhabited. Continue around the runway, past Sandy Point Beach Club all the way to the end of the road. You'll have described a horseshoe. Through the low-growing sea grapes is a lovely half-mile double curve of sand, a flat, narrow and deserted beach only occasionally disturbed by landing planes. **Canoe Bay's** waters are shallow and calm, and seldom visited by more than the infrequent local fisherman or runner. Poke around in the clay banks for remnants of earlier inhabitants.

Buccoo Boat Ride: Return along the airport road to reach **Store Bay**, whose name is an Anglicization of its first Dutch settler, Stoer. This is a jump-off point for trips to the Buccoo Reef. The Bay can be approached by the Pigeon Point Road further on, or more quickly from a small side road across from the airport.

The beach itself is merely pleasant, a protected cove nestling against low rocky ledges. On the right is the modern **Crown Reef Hotel**, much favored by vacationing Trinidadians: clean, characterless, modern. The bathing facilities are extensive here, with changing rooms, showers and toilets, and a number of red-roofed cement pagodas with picnic tables and benches. Throughout the island, the T&T Tourist Board has built extensive beach facilities, which can be used for a small charge (US 30¢ or TT$1).

An outdoor pavilion has a bar and food, but some of the best food shacks on the island have taken advantage of the tourist trade here, and delicious crab curry, turtle and conch roti, and fresh fruit are all for sale at little stands, many adorned with colorful paintings and slogans.

The trip to the reef is the closest thing to a tourist attraction Tobago can boast, and is worth the TT$20 just to satisfy your curiosity. Its success depends on the quality of the boat you get. Unfortunately, it's hard to know beforehand what a boat will be like, since tickets are bought on shore and boats rest offshore until the moment they must pick up passengers. Most of the "glass" consists of a central plexiglass panel in varying stages of cloudiness, so check with friends or your hotel about the best boatmen when you go.

Also keep in mind that you'll be in and out of the water, even for boarding, so wear a bathing suit. The boatmen provide snorkels, masks and rubber shoes for the **Wild Orchid.**

reef. However, a good fit cannot be guaranteed so bring your own mask if possible. Since the currents out at the reef can be quite strong at times, it is advisable to go on a calm day to get the most out of the trip.

It's a twenty-minute boat ride to Buccoo Reef, but ten minutes out is the equally renowned **Nylon Pool**, basically an offshore sandbar whose thigh-high pale turquoise waters and soft clean sand provide a sybaritic bath. Floating in the still lagoon with the deep ocean on one side and palm-fringed beaches on the other is an entrancing experience.

Out beyond the pool lies the reef, a coral fringe much destroyed by pollution, boats and thoughtless tourists and locals. (See Above and Below the Water, p. 222) Boats remain about half an hour before returning to shore.

The boat may stop at **Pigeon Point** to let off passengers. This is the beach used in almost all of Trinidad and Tobago's travel ads for its intense aqua waters, graceful palms and picturesque thatch-roofed dock. But don't get off here unless you want to pay for a taxi back, because it's a long (half-hour) walk back to Store Bay.

Owned by Gordon Grant, Pigeon Point is the only private beach on Tobago, lying surprisingly enough, at the end of Pigeon Point Road. When driving, keep to the left at the major fork and at the end of the pavement continue down the dirt road to the guard. The entrance fee in 1986 was a reasonable TT$5, about US$1.50.

The beach is a long idyllic stretch, the vacationer's Platonic ideal of a Caribbean seashore. Food shacks and picnic tables are shaded by royal palms, while beyond, cattle graze the soft green grass of a coconut grove, like something out of a Rousseau painting.

All over the island there are areas reserved for grazing cattle. Until the 1960s these were generally coconut estates, when labor became expensive and scarce. The beach curves around into the **Bon Accord Lagoon**, a fisherman's harbor perfect for strolling and beachcombing.

This is probably the best place on the island for shells, lying as it does off the reef. The classic conch shells with their sunny pink and apricot insides are scattered here and there where fishermen have left them after removing the meat. At mid-morning or late afternoon a fisherman might return with his catch of yellow and

Windsurfing at Pigeon Point.

pink snapper, hog fish, or conch. Not as perfectly groomed as Pigeon Point, this beach is scattered with palm fronds, coconut hulls and the more mundane rubbish of bottles and cans, but it is often uncrowded even when Pigeon Point is overrun.

Like Buccoo Reef, Pigeon Point is a tourist's necessity, it is advisable to avoid it during weekends, when it is likely to be crowded with visitors from a cruise ship offshore, getting their two hours' taste of Tobago.

Good Surfing and Golf: Along the Bon Accord Road are the towns of **Canaan** and **Moriah**, small settlements named after the religious missions which originally occupied these sites. There are small shops and a couple of roti stands serving the concrete block homes. Further along, near the **Shirvan Road**, are government-funded housing areas of neatly similar concrete block houses.

Continue down the **Milford Road** to the Shirvan Road toward the northeast. You'll pass signs for **Buccoo Beach**, a rocky, littered and sometimes polluted public beach not worth a stop. The Shirvan Road is quietly pretty, and runs near the water through pale green groves of tall palm and squat banana.

Shirvan turns into the Grafton Road, with the **Mount Irvine Bay Hotel** marked by the pink, orange and purple bougainvillea that fringes its cottages and by the neatly clipped greens and towering palms of its famed golf course. The most American-fancy of the Tobago hotels, Mount Irvine is built on the site of an old sugar plantation owned by Charles Irvine in the latter half of the 18th Century. The golf course is open to anyone for a fee, and there is a restaurant built around the old stone sugar mill.

The **Museum of Tobago History** is also on the hotel grounds. A one-room display area is tended by Edward Hernandez, passionate and learned when it comes to the history of his island. There are shells, pre-Columbian and European tools, buttons and tableware from pirate ships and colonials, potsherds and a host of other archaeological finds from all eras of Tobago's history.

The public beach just northeast of the hotel has some of the nicest and most complete facilities. A favored spot for surfers, there are good waves breaking about a quarter mile offshore. The changing room building is built next to the old site of

Fishing boats at rest at Plymouth.

198

the Mount Irvine Estate sugar depot, where ships from all over deposited their ballast of slate and bricks in exchange for sugar and, later, cocoa cultivated on the estate.

Now there are the usual locker rooms and showers, as well as a small bar where you can sit at a concrete table and drink Carib with a bake 'n' shark. Local parties are sometimes held here at night, featuring wild game and wild music.

The deep, clean beach is dotted with sea grape trees whose leafy canopy has been trained into sun umbrellas. The sea floor is rocky in places, and at low tide there are wonderful little pools caught in the declivities, swarming with sea roaches, crabs and tiny fish. Safest bathing spots are delineated by yellow and red flags.

Secluded Sun Spots: For a really secluded beach, walk a short way down the main highway to a rusted, rickety gate leading into a palm grove. Walk across the grove to the sea, past benign cattle to the cliff, and it should be easy to find a spot to climb down to deserted **Back Bay**. This is a favored beach for nude sunbathing but is usually deserted and the waves can be quite good for body surfing.

Continuing along the road toward Black Rock and Plymouth, keep to the high main road to the right, or take a turn a bit beyond the Back Bay entrance and take the shore road along **Grafton Beach**. This long, wide, usually empty stretch of beach is easily accessible from places along the road. It might be totally deserted, or there could be a couple of people running dogs and fishing for sea roaches, the tiny sand colored crustaceans which look exactly like their nickname and are used for bait for offshore fishing. It's a nice place for a swim as well, as there are often gentle waves, but there can be strong currents at times.

Also off the Grafton Road between Mount Irvine and Black Rock is a dirt driveway leading to the old **Grafton Estate**. Once owned by the Smith family, who have had a long history in Tobago, it has been preserved as a bird sanctuary for many years. Since the death of Mrs. Smith the future of the estate has been in question, but even though the house was in disrepair in 1986, there were lovely views of Grafton Bay and many cocricos, motmots and other birds swarming around. The nature walk may still be penetrable.

Just outside the small village of Black Rock is the unassuming **Mon Cheri Café**,

Left, archaeological finds at the Museum of Tobago History and, right, a modern monument to Tobago's first European settlers.

which often appears closed. Try it anyway, for their wonderful kingfish pelau and other inexpensive Creole dishes.

Of Turtles and Kings: Northeast of Black Rock is the **Turtle Beach Hotel** on **Great Courland Bay**, once the site of an early settlement and now famous for the immense sea turtles which come up on the beach at night to lay their eggs. Courlanders, more commonly known as Latvians, were some of the first Europeans to settle on Tobago, Lutherans looking for a place to emigrate after the Thirty Years' War.

The settlement was begun around 1659 by Duke Jekabs, a godson of James I of England. Eventually the Courlanders sent to Tobago by Jekabs were absorbed into other colonies on the island, some at Mount Irvine, or Little Courland, Bay.

The bar at Turtle Beach is popular on the nights the hotel hosts its weekly steel band show. During egg-laying season in April and May, groups meet at night to observe the turtles on the beach, who seem unperturbed by the presence of humans.

Beyond Black Rock is Plymouth, the biggest town on the north side, but don't go looking for a town center. Plymouth is mostly a small residential village on a promontory overlooking Great Courland Bay, with small shops for local needs, a gas station and one tourist attraction: **Fort James**.

The fort was built by the British in 1768 as a barrack, and named after King James II. Now all that remains is a neatly kept low stone edifice, set amid clipped lawns and a few botanical plantings. Peering in through the window reveals the fort's present usage — as a tool shed. The view from the escarpment is nice, with vistas of curving Turtle Beach to the left and fishing boats at rest closer by.

The approach road to the fort passes a small concrete block School for the Deaf, the local grandstand and field, and another Tourist Board attraction mentioned in every guidebook. In the courtyard of a small stone church is the **mysterious tombstone**, whose inscription reads, *"She was a mother without knowing it and a wife without letting her husband know it except by her kind indulgences to him.— Betty Stiven 1783."* One can just imagine Betty's domestic situation.

Take Jager Road to the ocean, and if you can get around the fence you might find Carib and Arawak tear-drop axes in the freshwater rivers where they meet

Baby turtles on Turtle Beach.

200

the sea.

In Plymouth is the modest **Cocrico Inn**, a small motel with good local food. The walk from the fort provides a charming, superficial picture of village life, with cocks crowing and schoolchildren in neat blue uniforms running about, and pastel houses with neat yards up against wooden shacks overgrown with hibiscus, banana palms and other tropical plants.

The simple dining room at the Inn has linoleum floors and dinette tables, and the cook comes out to take orders. Read the local magazines provided while you wait.

North Road, one of the main streets in town, turns into a dirt lane and then ends in a narrow stretch of rough beach, good for a quick dip only, but refreshing if you're hot and a half hour's drive from the next beach!

The Mot-Mot Trail: The gently curving road out of Plymouth leads inland for some time, with **Arnos Vale Hotel** about a mile away. Terraced along a small hillside with winding paths through botanical plantings, Arnos Vale offers some of the best snorkeling and bird-watching on Tobago. Even if you don't stay there, it's worth the trip for those attractions.

The original English owners covered the hillside with scarlet ixora, pink oleander, pastel bougainvillea, rosy hibiscus, multi-hued foliage bushes, many flamboyant trees with their deep green leaves and orange flowers, and other sweet-scented tropical plants. The stunted trees with rubbery leaves on the beach are Indian almonds. Take the Mot-Mot Trail early in the morning for bird-watching, or follow other little paths to their summits overlooking the bay.

Because the cove is so protected, with sharp rocky outcroppings stepping down into the water, there are myriad places for brilliant tropical fish to live and hide. Rent snorkeling equipment from the hotel, and swim out to see barracuda, brain coral, sea fans, the blue-green parrot fish, male stoplights, the multihued angelfish with their pendant "whiskers," yellow and black rock beauties, hawkfish, electric blue tangs and surgeonfish, rays, trumpetfish and the waves of small silver blue grunts which miraculously surround you in shallow water.

Fishing off the rocks can yield Caribbean salmon, kingfish, bonita, or albacore, though offshore your chances are improved. To the left of the main beach, a short hike over the rocks or a brief swim,

Bovine bug repellent.

is a secluded triangle of sand; to the right, carved into rocky cliffs, are caves. There is even a very dark Indian man living in one, and you can tell his particular cave by the Hindu flag outside!

Creole Coteaux: The Arnos Vale Road past the hotel continues to curve upwards through rolling countryside planted with the short, leafy banana palms which are, strictly speaking, large herbs. A half mile or so past the hotel is a sign on the right for Franklyn's Road, a hilly, bumpy trace which eventually emerges in the hill town of **Les Coteaux**.

But just after the turn onto the trace, on the right practically hidden by thick undergrowth, is the original **Arnos Vale water wheel**. Its deep red bricks now covered with creeping vines, the wheel dates back to colonial times.

The trace leads past Franklyn's Estate, now a modern vacation home surrounded by a high pink wall and wrought-iron gate, with an unlikely stand of pine trees. Past that are small houses with neat yards, and many deep ruts.

The Arnos Vale Road continues through low dry hills reminiscent of Indonesia or Africa, past the ubiquitous tethered livestock, and into the village of Les Coteaux, a crossroads of comparatively goodly size in this area of Tobago.

The sounds of crowing roosters and klaxon horns make every day sound like Sunday, and the friendly residents will happily offer directions, whether or not they know the way, and whether or not you can interpret their dialect.

The name of their home, an obvious leftover from the days of French colonization, is pronounced by locals as something more akin to "Leckito." If you give it a French pronunciation, you risk misunderstanding.

At Les Coteaux three roads meet: to the left the road leads up north along the shore; to the right down through lush hills and streams to Scarborough, and straight ahead (sort of) it twists off toward the Hillsborough Dam. Keep left to explore the northern shore.

A Tropical Amalfi Coast: The bad mountain road leads over rocky terrain with ravines crowded with the immortelle, vivid orange in the dry season, and terraced hillsides fringed by the pale pale green of bamboo stands. Little iridescent lizards, like baby dinosaurs, dart across the road, which is often washed out in places, and periwinkle-blue morning glories carpet the

Ramshackle house near Les Coteaux.

road banks.

For **Culloden Bay**, take the Culloden Road at the fork, leading south through the tiny hamlet of **Golden Lane**. There are beautiful vistas out to sea across hills dotted with palm and breadfruit trees. Take a sharp right at the Moriah/Arnos Vale junction in Golden Lane and an extremely rocky dirt road leads to the bay. (Beware; the map can be confusing.)

Culloden Bay is a pebbly fisherman's cove with the charm of the utilitarian. The fishermen here catch redfish, bonito and albacore, among other things, and if you care to venture down (there are some amazing trees along the way), you might convince one of them to take you fishing some very early Sunday morning for a lot less than the organized tours will charge. The boats are fiberglass dinghies, and their methods uncomplicated — trolling with heavy line and massive hooks — but the fishermen know how to read the waters and skies for schooling fish.

Return the way you came, past the small settlements of pastel houses on stilts, some with flags that resemble those of the Hindus but signify a shango house, and small groceries marked by Carib beer signs. North of **Moriah** the coastal road traverses

steeper and steeper hills as it climbs toward the small fishing villages and perfect beaches of Castara and Parlatuvier.

Here are some of the most spectacular views and stunning shores on the island, glimpsed around hairpin turns, as the glittering navy sea shades into turquoise near the shore hundreds of feet below. At the height of the road you might simply dive into the clouds like an unbroken expanse of the sparkling water. **King Peter's Bay**, on the way, named for a Carib monarch, is not particularly good for swimming.

The **Sisters Rocks** appear offshore surrounded by white foam, right before the road spins down headily to Castara Bay. On the beach you might imagine yourself on the Amalfi Coast, with sharp, dark green cliffs enclosing the town and bay, and the blue water glittering like diamonds. **Castara**, like most of the north coast towns, is a fishing village, and most of the 500 or so residents support themselves by a combination of fishing, farming and government work: road repair. It is a Tobago conundrum that a great number of island men work on the roads, yet aside from a few main thoroughfares, most are deeply potholed, and quite a number in the further reaches simply don't exist or are not

passable.

Castara has the usual changing rooms, showers and toilets, but mostly you'll find fishermen liming in their shed while they mend nets and line and wait for the tide to change. The long wide beach, edged by low thick palms, often has green nets laid out to dry, and wooden dinghies float offshore with their bamboo rods balanced like insect antennae.

If you're hungry, visit Henry Jackson's "First and Last" roti stand just up the road from the beach, where he sells goat, chicken and potato roti, cold drinks, liquor and such sundry items as bay rum, hard balls and toothpaste. Sit on the shaded bench and watch shy smiling children pass while friendly bony dogs beg for scraps. Or there's the "No Problem" food supply store nearby.

North of Castara the views are equally stunning, as the road winds inward through jungle, up and down steep hills and back out toward the coast. The second rocky bay past Castara is **Englishman's**, below the railing on the coastal side. Drive down to where the road is straight and then find the path to this secluded beach.

Next is **Parlatuvier**, about a leisurely thirty minutes' drive from Castara. Parlatuvier has a perfect crescent beach curving away toward pastel houses and palm fringed hills, a little elementary school shaking with the noise and concentration of children, a tiny store or two, and not much else. Teenage boys lounge under palm trees, burly fishermen drag in their seines, and the sea rolls quietly on the sand. Parlatuvier is village life at its heart.

Beyond the beach, the North Road crosses a small bridge over a reedy estuary and heads up the hill toward the left. Beyond, the road is often impassable but it does provide quiet green views and perhaps motmots or cocricos in roadside bushes until the lane peters off entirely on a curve above a mossy green ravine.

The right fork leads to a crossroad, after a bumpy ride on a wide dirt road, and a right at the cross leads to **Roxborough**, over the top of the mountain.

Beyond Parlatuvier is Charlotteville and the south side, but the road between the two towns hasn't been passable in a long time. When and if it is, it will be a beautiful drive through jungle past **Bloody Bay**, the site of a long-ago battle which stained the waters red, and **Man of War**, where pirates secreted their booty.

Interior Idyll: There are a number of

A fisherman brings in his seine.

overland routes to the south side. The Parlatuvier-Roxborough road is wide, smooth and lovely, only a half hour's drive. There are sweeping curves through jungle above steep ravines filled with bamboo and birds, until a low cocoa grove and a school signal the Windward Road.

Another overland route is via the **Hillsborough Dam**, in the heart of the **Tobago Forest Reserve**. This is a much longer and rougher ride, taking almost two hours. At the north end of Les Coteaux, go straight onto the **Mason Hall Road.** After the bridge bear right down a dirt road and you're on your way.

This area, like much of Tobago, was for years cocoa and coffee estates and is still cultivated for those crops, though on a much smaller scale. You can still see coffee drying houses with their corrugated roofs that slide on rafters to expose the beans when it's sunny and cover them when it rains. The huge iron pots in some yards used to be (and still sometimes are) used for boiling sugar. Neighborhood dogs were allowed to lick them clean and so are called "pot hounds."

Local connoisseurs claim that coffee and cocoa have been debased by "clonal" varieties, bred for reasons other than their excellent taste. The original strain of cocoa on Tobago was called Alligator or Caracas, and it is a lucky and rare person who can find the few women who still preserve that strain.

The bumpy dirt road passes soft hills and isolated houses where young girls walk three miles a day just to fetch water and do the family laundry. At the pavement, take a left, past neatly tended gardens and small glades and you are at the dam.

A surprising mixture of pines and palms surrounds the quiet lake, and if you walk out across the dam you might see a cayman alligator nosing about the reeds. The dam is a good place from whence to begin a hike or a hunt, but don't set out without a guide who knows the area well. Check with your hotel or the Tourist Board in Scarborough for suggestions and permits.

The road from the dam down to the **Windward Road** at **Studley Park** takes about an hour. First pass the lush growth of palms and bamboo supported by streams trickling through mossy beds, and stop the car to listen to the loud noise of balisier leaves rubbing together. Pass a gravel quarry and then wind down through the small town of Studley Park, only five minutes above the water.

View from Moriah to King Peter's Bay.

Back to Civilization: The interior on the west side of the island is more populated and less wild, situated as it is between Plymouth and Scarborough. Near **Patience Hill** is the **National Fine Arts Centre**, a small stucco building housing a permanent exhibition of old maps of Tobago alongside changing modern exhibits by Tobagonians or about Tobago. The ride between the two towns is only twenty minutes or so, providing you don't stop to pick up hitchhikers or have a roti and beer along the way.

Scarborough is Tobago's largest and most important town, a market center and port where 17,000 of the island's 40,000 inhabitants live. Compared to some of the more European cities in the Caribbean, Scarborough is ramshackle and provincial, with little of interest to buy, duty-free or otherwise, and few remnants of a grander age. It is a town for Tobagonians, not visitors, and is interesting as such but certainly overshadowed by the more striking natural and rural beauty of the island. But as a center for island life it's worth an afternoon's perusal.

Ranged up and down a steep hill overlooking **Rockley Bay**, Scarborough became the capital in 1779. The town is divided into Upper and Lower Scarborough, the latter having been a Dutch depot in the 17th Century. Nowadays, the ferry from Port of Spain docks here, as do fishing and cargo boats, though over the years ship captains have cursed the sharp red rocks of the harbor which give the bay its name. The town consists largely of tin-roofed shops, shacks selling a variety of clothing and local produce, and some more solid cement buildings housing well-known emporia like Stecher's, Kirpalani's, and Phillips.

A diminutive town square sits below government buildings and the Tourist Bureau on Jerningham Street, and the narrow streets crawl with slow moving traffic, schoolchildren and professional limers. On Fridays, an open fruit and vegetable market brings villagers to town.

Any number of undistinguished and sometimes unnamed bars and restaurants serve fried chicken, beer, roti, fish and chips. **The Old Donkey Cart House** restaurant, on the road east toward Bacolet, has more expensive Creole food and a relatively extensive German wine list. In an old Victorian house overlooking Bacolet and Rockley bays, the restaurant is gussied up with Christmas lights and

Scarborough from Rockley Bay.

taped music.

In Lower Scarborough there is a modern mall encompassing a school and the local library, among other buildings, and though the brick and concrete modern architecture seems out of keeping with the rest of town, it houses a number of useful resources.

The library offers a periodical section on the main floor with a wide selection of Caribbean magazines and newspapers. The Caribbean book section upstairs contains many British and American books on Trinidad and Tobago, some impossible to find elsewhere, as well as all monographs and books written by T&Ters on Tobago. This is a cool, quiet (until school lets out and kids come here to flirt) and different place to spend the hot midday hours.

Scarborough also boasts a **Botanic Garden**, near the approach highway, where you can stroll amid cultivated versions of plants and trees which grow wild on the island, but are sometimes difficult to find.

Fort King George, high above Scarborough, was built by the English in 1779 to protect the town, and was later captured by the French. Like Tobago, it changed hands a number of times, and now lies in partial ruins above the hospital, surround-ed by palms, ferns and lawns. The views, particularly at sunset, are breathtaking.

Bacolet and Coconuts: From the Fort, continue on the Windward Road, past the Old Donkey Cart House between low hedges and neat palm groves, a tropical version of rural England, to within 100 yards of the Windward Road junction, at the Bacolet River. Continue down a small paved lane on the right and at the intersection take a left, then another left to the end of the road. Walk fifty feet toward the water, and you are on **Bacolet Beach**, one of Tobago's most famous.

A long, rough, beautiful crescent fringed with tall palms and littered with coconut husks and tree trunks, Bacolet was the setting for the movie version of "The Swiss Family Robinson." The dark sand beach is set in a residential area of large seaside homes with well-groomed yards, though a deep coconut grove separates it from nearby houses. Pounding surf creates a misty spray of rainbows and haze around the palms, and the beach is often deserted.

In the grove you might see coconut pickers and their rickety ladders balanced on the beds of old rounded-line pickup trucks. Their ability to launch themselves into the fronds 40 feet above an absolute-

Left, Scarborough schoolboys at recess and, right, woodcarvings of Tobago dancers on exhibit at the National Fine Arts Centre.

ly straight trunk is astounding and rare. Coconut sellers used to climb the trees in search of the best fruit, but now, lament old-timers, most wait until the nuts drop of their own accord.

Winding Up the Windward: The drive from Buccoo to Charlotteville at the far end of the Windward Road would probably take three or four hours without stops. But as it passes some of the most enchanting beaches in the Caribbean on the way, there's little chance you'll make the trip in three hours.

Ideally, one could take two or three days and take the road in stretches, returning home each night by a slightly different route, or staying at one of the hotels or guesthouses on the Windward Road.

The Windward is also one of the most used roads on the island, much more so than the northside road, and so you may encounter mild inter-village traffic which, combined with hair-raising turns over breathtaking prospects, slows one's progress considerably yet pleasurably. East of Scarborough, it is a tropical combination of California's Highway One and Italy's Amalfi Coast.

Beyond Bacolet, the Windward Road curves to and from the shoreline, offering glimpses of long misty beaches or sparkling water, with coconut and cocoa groves and watery estuaries between the road and the beaches.

You can swim pretty much anywhere and if you spot an inviting beach, be assured that there is at least a footpath leading to it. **Hillsborough** and **Barbadoes Bay** offer many bathing sites.

Between the two, the terrain gradually becomes hillier and the road begins to climb, offering panoramic views of Barbadoes Bay, rocky coves, or across palm forests to wide rough beaches. Here Tobago becomes more the tiny rural tropical island and less the idyllic vacation retreat.

There are only a few lodging places up this end, and all are small, and most, unassuming. Village life reigns supreme here, and the roads are traversed by strong Tobago women, renowned for their broad shoulders and ample girth, with bundles on their heads or umbrellas unfurled against the sun and passing showers.

The ubiquitous schoolchildren are sassier here and boys may shout unintelligible but highly amusing remarks to the sightseer passing through. In time-honored Tobagonian (and African) tradition, these

King's Bay waterfall.

light-hearted verbal assaults are meant as much for amusement as energy releasers and an acceptable means of criticism. Though the *picong* may make the visitor feel slightly uncomfortable, generally it's not meant terribly seriously.

Towns are small and perched precariously on cliffs overlooking stunning seascapes, and on those days when light rain comes and goes, there may be three or four rainbows at once, stretching from shack to sea, from treetop to pastel house. There are few roti stands or restaurants, and those that exist are closed on weekends, after 4 p.m. or any other time the owner would rather be elsewhere.

Richmond Restored: Just outside the hamlet of **Belle Garden**, keep an eye out for the wooden sign to **Richmond Great House**. One of many old estate houses, Richmond Great House is one of the few to have been restored.

An 18th-Century plantation house, it was bought in a state of great disrepair by a Professor Lynch of Columbia University in New York City. Professor Lynch was unable to spend a great deal of time on Tobago, so his friend Rita, an Aruban who lived in the United States and in Trinidad, put her own considerable labor and work into the house, with the dream of providing a guesthouse with a sense of history and local atmosphere for a small number of visitors.

The square whitewashed brick house sits on top of a knoll overlooking rolling land to the sea, with mountains behind and palm trees and jungle as far as the eye can see. The Great House's chief charms are its location — isolated yet civilized, and a short ride or fifteen minutes' walk from the beach; its design, which permits cool breezes to blow through the rooms even on the hottest of days; and its knowledgeable manager, who provides both an insider's and an outsider's view of island life. It is also a good place for nature lovers, with an abundance of birds and plant life all around.

Continue on to the village of **Delaford**, and right outside look for a sandy parking lot on the left side of the road. This is the entrance to the **King's Bay Waterfall**. One hundred feet high, the highest in the Republic, in the rainy season the falls are full and active with rain and stream water, and it can be excitingly treacherous to climb the ledges above the main pool.

In the dry season, it is much calmer and somewhat tame. The Tourist Board pro-

Bird of Paradise Island from the Windward Road.

vides changing rooms and a neat path to the falls, alongside a cocoa grove. High overhead, in the branches of some tall trees, look for the pendant nests, resembling socks filled with sand, of the crested orapendula. These birds permit rice grackles to live in the nests alongside them, as they eat parasitic insects off the chicks' bodies.

Royal Sands and Birds of Paradise: Down the road (the King's Bay Depot road) is the approach to **King's Bay Beach**. This sheltered beach has deep gray sand and a soft pebbly bottom. The usual facilities are provided, though most beachcombers are townspeople from Delaford, or local fishermen.

A small restaurant next to the beach is a comfortable place for an informal meal, when it's open. Private sailboats sometimes dock offshore for a week or so to avail themselves of the protected harbor and peaceful, verdant scenery. Enclosed by the jungle-covered hills as it is, King's Bay seems cooler and wilder than more westerly beaches.

After King's Bay, the Windward Road turns inland until **Speyside**, the jumping-off point for trips to **Bird of Paradise Island**. This small, almost barren little island a mile or so off the coast is the only place in the western hemisphere where Birds of Paradise can be seen, as they are indigenous to New Guinea and were brought to this island at the beginning of the 20th Century, when they were threatened with extinction in their native habitat. (See Above and Below the Water, p. 220)

Recent hurricanes have diminished the bird population so that it is unclear how many birds remain. You might want to check with the game warden about the bird count, since tour boatmen will all tell you there are plenty to be seen. It's a twenty-minutes' boat ride to any of the three offshore islands, and you can swim at the beach in front of the playing field before and after you go.

Blue Waters at Batteaux Bay: Beyond Speyside, toward the tiny enclave of **Lucyville,** is the remote and romantic **Blue Waters Inn**, a small hotel on its own bay, across from **Goat Island**. After climbing a side road for a few hundred feet, you'll see on your right the entrance to the Inn, a small dirt lane. Drive toward it and you'll think you're about to fly off into the blue, the declivity is so steep.

It is a thrilling vista, and one that makes you want to jump right into the ocean once

An old water wheel on the grounds of an abandoned estate in Speyside.

you arrive. Blue Waters is run by its owners, the Zollnas, and their manager, Mr. Baptiste, all of whom have a great love and respect for wildlife, birds and the relatively simple life.

Renovated in 1985, it consists of 11 rooms, really separate cottages along the small beach, and an airy, open dining room for meals and drinks. The narrow beach is confined by sea grapes like natural cabanas, and bird-watching is almost unavoidable.

The End of the Road: Between Speyside and Charlotteville the road winds across the mountains through dense, wet, deep green jungle. Curving and mountainous, it can be treacherous during sudden heavy downpours, and though it is only about four miles between the two towns, the drive takes a good half hour. Midway is a scenic vista from a metal lookout tower placed at Tobago's highest point. Bird of Paradise Island is distinctly visible across forest and water.

Charlotteville is the most picturesque of many picturesque towns on Tobago. Isolated by the mountains to the south and the impassable road to the west, it sleeps undisturbed on sharp, steep cliffs above a deep blue bay.

Some of the best fishing on the island can be found offshore, and most male inhabitants are fishermen. There are beach facilities and a beach club offering local music at night, and you may rent cabins on the beach, with simple interiors and porches from which to watch the sunset.

More extensive than it seems at first, Charlotteville is made up of numerous dirt and paved lanes winding back and up along the mountainside. Beyond and to the west is the continuation of the north road, in 1986 a dirt lane impassable after a few miles. But it's worth a bumpy ride for its sheer fecundity.

Everything is covered in a carpet of soft green vegetation, with orchids and bromeliads growing from trees, guy wires, telephone poles or anything else that provides a small foothold. Tree frogs chirp ceaselessly and small perfect waterfalls edge the roadside here and there. You might even see parrots flying above. The effect is of being in an enormous misty terrarium. It makes the south end of the island seem positively arid!

If there are too many deep muddy potholes, do turn back, because it might be hours until someone else passes, and days before a tow truck can come.

Charlotteville tumbles down the hill to Man of War bay.

ABOVE AND BELOW THE WATER

Its native Indian inhabitants called it Ieri, "land of the hummingbird," and even today Trinidad and Tobago is home to about 15 different species of these brilliant fluttering creatures, amongst the over 420 species of birds, 617 species of butterfly, and a wealth of flora and fauna matched only by the South American continent itself. Unlike other Caribbean islands, which are volcanic in origin, as recently as 11,000 years ago Trinidad and Tobago was a part of the coast of Venezuela. Thus despite their small size, the two islands are graced with a diversity of environment which includes four mountain ranges, four major rivers, mangrove swamps, tropical savannahs, numerous streams and small rivers, and a marine environment influenced by Venezuela's Orinoco River as well as the Atlantic and Caribbean.

The Rich Rain Forest: The Northern Range of Trinidad is only minutes away from downtown Port of Spain, yet is almost primeval in its unspoiled richness of life. In the dry season, December to March, the cultivated valleys and slopes glow with the deep orange blossoms of the tall mountain immortelle tree, *erythrina micropteryx,* introduced to the islands over 150 years ago as shade for cocoa and coffee trees.

At the end of the dry season, around the beginning of April, the yellow poui tree blooms spectacularly, its leaves dropping to present the yellow flowers in solitary splendor. It is a popular belief that the rains arrive with the third burst of blooms.

In the early months of the year, when forest trees are in flower, honeycreepers and hummingbirds, as well as other nectar feeders, are visible in profusion. This is nesting time for many of these birds.

With the coming of the rains in April and May and thus the seeding of the numerous grasses, finches and other seed-eaters bring forth their young while there is an abundance of food.

In August the hundreds of butterflies that have lain dormant during the dry season emerge to paint the islands in vibrant colors. In short, there is no bad time for nature watching in Trinidad and Tobago and every season offers its particular beauties and wonders.

Although the Republic has hundreds of

Preceding pages: seining at Castara; and an elusive parrot. Left, oilbirds roosting in a Northern Range cave; and right, a mountain immortelle in the Northern Range is garlanded with epiphytes.

species of birds, there are few native bird watchers, the greatest number of that species being migratory visitors from the United States and Europe. Many vacationers to the islands come simply to bird-watch because in an area slightly smaller than the island of Bali and about the size of the state of Delaware (not quite 2,000 square miles), Trinidad and Tobago offers a unique opportunity to see over 400 species of birds in a manageable area.

Victorian Nature Retreat: There is perhaps no better place to begin than at the Asa Wright Nature Centre and Lodge, in the Northern

Range's Arima Valley 1,200 feet above sea level. The winding, mountainous drive from Port of Spain to Asa Wright climbs through a tropical rain forest comprised of several tiers of lush vegetation.

The uppermost tier is that of the spreading branches of trees growing up to 150 feet. Orchids, bromeliads called "wild pines," and liana vines grow in profusion on their trunks and limbs and even telephone wires. Various species of ferns, heliconias and philodendrons are common below, and huge stands of bamboo and small mossy waterfalls line the road.

Along the way are glimpses of sliding-roofed sheds used for drying coffee on the big estates; Asa Wright was originally a private cocoa, coffee and citrus plantation, and is surrounded by working estates.

The Centre still retains the aura of a civilized country retreat. At the end of a bumpy driveway is the "Great House," constructed in 1906-1908 as a Victorian estate house and perched over a forest valley alive with birds and butterflies.

Since the turn of the century the 197-acre estate has changed hands a couple of times, ending up, in 1947, in the possession of Dr. Newcome Wright and his Icelandic-born wife Asa, who came to Trinidad from England.

In 1950, Dr. William Beebe, a famous explorer and naturalist, established the Tropical Research Station of the New York Zoological Society in the Arima Valley close to the Wrights' property. Dr. Beebe and many of the research staff at Simla, as it was called after a sister station in India, befriended the Wrights,

perty—230 acres and several small buildings—to Asa Wright Centre as a gift. Today researchers and students of natural history are housed at Simla, while amateur naturalists can stay in the colonial comfort of the Great House and enjoy nature hikes guided by experts.

Little Devils of Eternal Darkness: One of the most renowned species to be observed at Asa Wright is the *Steatornis caripensis,* or nocturnal oilbird. In hiking distance of the world's most accessible colony of these birds, Asa Wright offers a rare opportunity to see them in their strange natural habitat.

Guacharos—"he who cries," to the Spanish-speaking people of South America—oilbirds are known in French patois as diablotin, or "little devils," and Jon Lindblad, the famous nature photographer, described them as "the bird of

and it was not long before the Wrights were host to visiting naturalists and bird watchers who wished to take advantage of the rich flora and fauna of the valley.

Among these early visitors was Donald Eckelberry, an American bird artist and naturalist who came to paint the species of the Arima Valley. It was Eckelberry who, after the death of Mr. Wright, persuaded Asa to sell the property in order that a non-profit Trust might be established to preserve that part of the Valley in perpetuity as a conservation, study and recreation area.

And thus in October 1967 the Asa Wright Nature Centre, the first of its kind in the Caribbean, was established. Following the closing of Simla in 1970, the Society donated its pro-

eternal darkness."

The medium-brown oilbird can be as much as 15 inches long with a wing span of three feet, and lives deep in caves, leaving only at night to forage for food in the forest. The only known nocturnal fruit-eating bird, oilbirds prefer the fruit of the palm, laurel and incense trees, which they pull off in flight.

The young birds become very fat on this diet, and at about 70 days are approximately two pounds: one and a half times the weight of the adult bird. The Amerindians and other inhabitants of Caribe chose this time—mid-June—to collect the fat young nestlings, which they then boiled and rendered for their oil, which never went rancid. They ate the flesh and used the oil for lamps and torches—thus the name.

In Trinidad there are eight known nesting colonies of oilbirds: some in the limestone caves of the Northern Range, and some on Huevos, an offshore island. The colony at Asa Wright has increased from 22 birds in 1967 to 170 in 1980, but since then there has been an annual migration to a more remote cave. In December 1985, during the annual Christmas bird count, only 48 birds were recorded at the cave near the Centre. However, a cave about 10 miles east of the Arima Valley, at Cumaca, supports a colony of approximately 600 birds.

High Level Birds: For a chance to see such birds as the yellow-legged thrush, the nightingale thrush and the blue-capped tanager, which only occur at elevations above 2,000 feet, the intrepid must make an all-day trip to the heights

macaws and orange-winged parrots, which feed on the fruit of the Moniche palms growing abundantly at the fringes of the grasslands. The drooping fronds of that palm also provide a home for the uncommon fork-tailed palm swift and, during the rainy season, the rare white-tailed golden-throated hummingbird may be found nesting in the shrubbery of the savannah.

The area is interesting for its plant life as well. Sundew, or *Drossera capilaris,* a kind of Venus's-flytrap, covers the surface of the grasslands, waiting for insects upon which to feed. These plants have little competition here because a layer of impervious clay just beneath the surface keeps the soil very dry in the dry season and water-logged when the rains come. Because its soil is therefore very poor in nutrients, many of the plants found there must

of Aripo, slightly south and east of Asa Wright. With luck, you might also see a poui or piping guan, the only bird endemic to Trinidad and Tobago but very rarely seen even here.

A less strenuous trip is one to the Aripo Savannah and the Arima forest, which may provide sightings of up to 70 species. A short stop at the Government Cattle farm on the road to the savannah can yield a glimpse of the savannah hawk, the southern lapwing and flocks of jacanas. In the savannah are many colorful and easily spotted species including red-bellied

Left, the tangled roots of mangrove trees in Nariva Swamp and, right, Scarlet Ibises roosting at dusk, Caroni.

capture insects for food.

Flying Sunset: Another fertile area for bird-watching is the Caroni Swamp, where the white, red and black mangrove trees sink their spidery support roots into the brackish water. The entire swamp comprises over 12,000 acres of mangrove forests, tidal lagoons and marshlands which are subject to daily tidal fluctuations. It is in the Caroni Swamp that the beautiful scarlet ibis, one of Trinidad and Tobago's national birds, makes its home.

In flocks that number up to 100, the scarlet birds Trinidadians call flamingos fly in from all directions and perch on the top branches of the mangrove islands. During the rainy season as many as 12,000 birds will arrive in the twilight hours, but in the earlier part of the year, there are fewer, as most migrate to the mainland to nest.

The neo-tropical cormorant, red-capped cardinal, common pottoo, clapper rail, tri-colored heron, boat-bill heron, anhinga, and the greater ani are some of the 140 species in the Caroni Swamp. And if your guide points out a ball of blonde fur in the fork of a tree, he has found a nocturnal silky anteater.

While you are waiting to see the birds you might want to drop a line, as the swamp waters are thick with fish, including tarpon, grouper, snook, salmon and mangrove snapper, and 100-pound groupers are not a rarity. The blue crab used in crab and *callaloo*, a popular soup-like dish, and in curried crab and dumplings, traditional in Tobago, are also caught in the mangrove swamps of both islands. During their

egg-laying season, hundreds of crabs leave the mangroves and "run" to the sea to release their eggs. (For details on arranging tours to Caroni, see the "Trinidad" chapter, p. 162.)

Tobago's Tropical Pheasant: For most of T&T's wildlife, life hasn't changed for thousands of years. So with the cocrico, or rufous-vented chachalaca, a turkey- or pheasant-like bird indigenous to Tobago, and one of the Republic's national birds.

When Hurricane Flora struck Tobago in September of 1963, she inflicted severe damage on the elevated forests. With their original habitat destroyed, many birds and beasts, including the cocrico, had to seek food in the lowlands close to the human habitation.

Aware of the birds' predicament, Eleanor

Alefounder, the owner of the 400-acre Grafton Estate on Tobago's north shore, along with a number of other residents began to feed the birds regularly. By 1970, the cocricos at the Grafton feeding tables were so tame that they could be fed from the hand. In a short while, racquet-tailed blue-crowned motmots began to swoop from their perches to take bits of cheese from between the fingers of visitors as well.

The verandah of the Grafton Great House became a popular rendezvous for visitors to Tobago, who joined the birds at teatime. Nowhere else could cocricos, motmots, red-crowned woodpeckers, blue-gray tanagers and many more species be seen and photographed at such short range and such leisure. Since the death of Mrs. Alefounder the house has fallen into disrepair and the bird feedings have become less of a tradition, but it is still possible to see a goodly number hovering around the estate.

Sea Birds and Sanctuaries: In 1968, Charles Turpin, proprietor of Charlotteville Estate in northeast Tobago, presented a group of islands known as the Melvilles to the Government of Trinidad and Tobago for the establishment of a wildlife sanctuary.

The largest of these islands, which are situated about a half mile off the northeast coast of Tobago, is the 72-acre St. Giles Island. Thick masses of cacti, low shrubs and deciduous trees cover the steep slopes which rise from the water to a height of 350 feet.

Due largely to their inaccessibility to man and other beasts, these islands are able to support one of the most important seabird breeding grounds in the southern West Indies. Noddy terns, brown boobies, the beautiful red-billed white tropic birds, red-footed boobies, magnificent frigate birds and several other species feed and nest on the rocky shores.

Little Tobago, or Bird of Paradise Island, is another fertile place for bird watchers, situated about one mile off the northeast coast of Tobago near the village of Speyside. In 1909, Sir William Ingram, a former owner of the island, became concerned about the threat posed to Birds of Paradise in their native New Guinea by trade in their plumes. So he arranged to have forty-eight greater Birds of Paradise captured in the Aru Islands off the coast of New Guinea and released on Little Tobago. The birds, along with their new home, were presented to the Government in 1928 as a sanctuary by Sir William's heirs. (Also see Tobago, p. 210)

Hurricane Flora ravished the smaller island as well, and since then there has been a constant decline in the number of Birds of Paradise. Nevertheless, Little Tobago offers the naturalist and nature photographer an opportunity to see at least 58 other species, including brown boobies, brown noddies, sooty and bridled terns, laughing gulls, Audubon shearwaters and red-billed tropic birds.

At Charlotteville and Speyside boats are available for trips to these islands, but prior permission must be obtained from the Conservator of Forests and Chief Wildlife Warden to land at the St. Giles Wildlife Sanctuary.

From March to July, sooty terns and brown noddies nest in considerable numbers on the two-acre rock called Soldado. Six miles west of the extreme western point of Trinidad, only seven miles from Venezuela, Soldado was declared a sanctuary in 1934. Brown pelicans, royal terns, sandwich terns and brown boobies are also to be found there, attracted by the abundant fish around the island. Boats may be hired for fishing around Soldado, but be careful not to pass the rock into Venezuela's territorial

but they are also put to work "cockbulling." In this sport the caged birds are placed about ten feet apart and during the space of a half hour or so the number of bars or rolls that each gives is counted. Several hundreds, or even thousands of dollars can be wagered on the birds' output.

Elusive Forest Dwellers: The forests of Trinidad and Tobago also abound in mammals, the most beautiful of which is arguably the ocelot, *Felis pardalis*. Although fully protected by law, ocelots are often shot by farmers who consider them pests, and consequently are confined to forested areas and rarely seen.

Relatively more common are brocket deer, white-collared peccary or quenk, tattoo or nine-banded armadillo, manicou or opossum, and two members of the rodent family—the agouti, and the lappe or paca.

waters.

A Gilded Cage: In rural areas it is not uncommon to see, during open season, caged birds hanging from the eaves of houses. Songbirds especially are enticed into cages with decoys and "laglue" or "laglee," a honey-like substance made from the sap of the breadfruit tree. As a result, there has been a steady decline in the songbird population, and the Twa-twa, or large-billed seed finch; the Chickichong, or lesser seed finch; and the Tobago picoplat, or variable seedeater, are in great peril.

Most often, these birds are sold to dealers,

Trinidad and Tobago has a rich birdlife. Seen here are just some of what's available: the cocroni at far left, and the motmot, above left.

Afficionados maintain packs of well-trained beagle hounds to hunt with, but mongrels can be taught the job as well. Though protected by law, manicou, tamandua, ocelot and other mammals are much sought-after by gourmets and are sold for as much as twice the price of the best tenderloin. From October to March these are all in season and can be hunted with a permit. Hiking in the Forest Reserves is another good way to see wild animals.

Below the Water: The swamps and rivers and streams of Trinidad and Tobago support over seventy species of fish. Perhaps the most familiar is *Lebistes reticulatus,* or the guppy. Locals call the prolific wild guppy "millions"; they appear everywhere, even in roadside drains and provide the welcomed service of eating mosquitoes. Selective breeding has also produced the beautiful delta-tailed varieties so popular for aquariums.

Many streams and rivers are replete with the South American plated catfish, *Hoplosternum littorale,* dubbed cascadura or cascadoo. Considered a delicacy despite its external covering of bony plates, legend has it that anyone who eats of the cascadoo must return to Trinidad to rest his bones.

Another common freshwater fish is the Tilapia Mossambica, a species of the Cichlid family which was imported from Africa with a view to farming the fish in ponds and rice paddies. While experiments were being conducted in the Government fish farms at Valsayn, several slippery specimens escaped into the nearby St. Joseph river and found their way to

to Nariva Swamp may provide sightings of these charmingly ugly sea mammals.

Rarer still are the otters which live in the Paria and Madamas rivers on Trinidad's north coast. These rivers teem with life and, through the swamps, effect the life in the ocean as well.

But the river that most greatly affects Trinidad's marine life is the Orinoco in Venezuela. Its fresh, turbid floodwaters prevent any major coral growth on Trinidad's coast. Tobago, on the other hand, is relatively free from the Orinoco's influence and its marine fauna are more like that of an oceanic island.

Reef Life: The turquoise waters of Buccoo Reef lie just off the southwestern corner of Tobago. A shallow fringing reef made up primarily of stag and elkhorn coral, Buccoo swarms with electric-colored French angels,

Caroni Swamp.

Now, twenty-five years later, tilapia is so plentiful in the shallower parts of the swamp that it has become a popular sport to catch one- to 1½- pound fish with bare hands. Unfortunately however, the tilapia has destroyed the feeding grounds of the thousands of migratory ducks which used to visit Trinidad every year.

But the swamp still provides much food for man and beast. Tree oysters sold on the street as oyster cocktails grow on the roots of the red mangrove, just below high water mark. Embedded in the muddy bottom one can find Trinidad's indigenous mussels, which, steamed in garlic sauce, make their way onto the menus of local restaurants. And although manatee are not common, a boat trip up the Ortoire or in-

grunts, trigger, butterfly, surgeon and parrot fish, all of which are accustomed enough to the snorkeler to remain unconcerned with his investigations.

The Buccoo Reef ecosystem is complex and includes not only the reef crest and flats where the tourist boats anchor, but also the Nylon Pool, an area where the white sand of broken coral fragments has settled into an offshore sandbar, creating a swimming-pool-like area. The mangrove-fringed Bon Accord Lagoon which is home to the vohites or cone shells so prized by collectors serves as the nursery for many of the reef-dwelling fish.

During World War II, Buccoo Reef and the Nylon Pool first gained popularity as sister attractions after Dillon and Cecil Anthony, two

Buccoo village residents, located the more beautiful areas and identified the channels which led to the reef crest. But over the years the popularity of the area has resulted in serious destruction of the coral heads. Boats, anchors, walking on the coral head and the removal of the corals, conch, lobsters and fish by visitors and boatmen have all contributed to the reef's demise.

Under the Marine Preservation Act Buccoo was declared a protected area, but unfortunately this legislation is not enforced. The destruction continues and has resulted in a reef which is a poor cousin to the less spoiled environments of some other Caribbean tourist islands. (Also see p. 196–198 for more about Buccoo Reef.)

A deep area of the reef called the Marine Gardens is still undamaged and supports a

plentiful during their breeding season, as is albacore.

Professional fishing expeditions will supply comfortable motorboats, rods and reels, and knowledgeable guides at a price. The impecunious might try to persuade a local fisherman to take them out some early morning, for a fraction of the cost. Tobagonian fisherman, though, tend to use small outboard motorboats and heavy handlines with massive hooks, but they can read the waters as if their lives depended on it, as to a great extent, they do.

On Turtle Beach: Perhaps the most mysterious marine phenomenon is the nesting ritual of the leatherback turtle. These are the largest (up to seven feet long and weighing up to 1,200 pounds) of the five species of sea turtle (of seven in the world) which nest on the beaches of

variety of coral formations. It is alive with star, fire, brain, staghorn, elkhorn, and soft corals, as well as sea fans, sea ferns and sea whips. This area and the less popular reefs of Tobago's northeast coast can provide a memorable experience for the scuba diver, protected as they are from the heavier waves of visitors. PADI instructors are available to conduct tours, and can be found through the major hotels.

Tobago also provides variety in abundance for the fisherman. Spanish mackerel, locally carite, is the most abundant food fish, with king mackerel and red snapper present in lesser numbers. Crevalle and bluefish, or ancho, are

Right, a leatherback turtle lays eggs, unperturbed by observers and, left , a rock beauty underwater.

Trinidad and Tobago. The green, the loggerhead, the hawksbill, and the olive ridley (smallest at around three feet) turtles all visit the beaches at Matura on the east coast of Trinidad; Toco, Tacarib and Las Cuevas on the north coast; and on Tobago at Courland (or Turtle), Grafton, Bloody, Speyside and Charlotteville bays.

There the females climb up on the beach to lay anywhere from 100 to 150 eggs at a time. They dig relatively deep holes, lay the eggs within, and cover them with sand. They then return to the sea to continue their annual farflung (sometimes as far as Australia) migrations. The turtles seem unconcerned with the humans who observe them at their labors.

Legislation protects turtles during their

nesting season from March to July, but from September to February when the turtles are at sea, the season is open and turtle steak is a delicacy and local favorite. Every year since 1965 the Trinidad and Tobago Field Naturalists' Club has organized regular night trips to see the turtles nesting; inquiries can be made at 809-624-3321.

Local Flora

It would be virtually impossible to list all the species of plants and trees the visiting naturalist is likely to see on a tour of the two islands, and even the simple beach-loving tourist is certain to notice tens upon tens of tropical plants. But certain ones crop up over and over again, whether for their ubiquity or their beauty, and

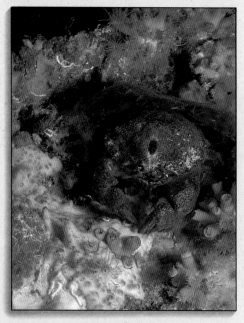

the following is a list of some of those species with a brief, un-scientific description of each, designed to make it easy to name those trees and shrubs the visitors notice.

Palms

Coconut Palm: The groves of tall, graceful palms with smooth trunks and fronds emanating in a circle from the top which line the beaches of Trinidad and Tobago are groves of money-producing coconut palms.

Royal Palms: They look similar to the more common coconuts, but their trunks are white and tend to be straight, and often have a few feet of green trunk below the frond ball at the top.

Banana Palms: Fun facts to know and tell: the banana tree is not really a palm but rather the largest member of the herb family. Low, squat plants about six feet high, the banana trees are also planted in groves, though not usually along the beach. They look like miniature palm trees, about six feet tall, with their trunks peeling thick pieces of bark, and their wide, flat fronds whose edges look as though they'd been ripped, unevenly, by hand. There are numerous groves on the Arnos Vale Road towards Les Coteaux and the road that passes the Turtle Beach Hotel, both in Tobago.

Traveler's Palm: A gray trunk holds long stems standing straight up and ending in regular fronds. It grows two-dimensionally, and looks like a wonderfully huge fan.

Other Trees

Almond: On resort beaches you will notice low trees with dark green, rubbery round leaves, often trained into umbrella shapes. These are Almond trees, though not the kind that produces the delectable nut — their fruit just looks like almonds. The flat leaves turn red before they fall, and the branches grow horizontally from the trunk.

Banyan: The Banyan is hard to mistake; its enormous trunk looks like hundreds of woody vines growing down from the upper branches.

Breadfruit: This evergreen tree has glossy dark leaves with deep lobes, and its round fruits are yellowish and covered with small, pointy puckers. The Breadnut tree can be distinguished by its fruit which is similar but covered with sharp points, like a medieval mace.

Cocoa: With their deep red pods and ovoid leaves in various stages of green, these low trees have a bush look. They, too, grow in groves, and are often shaded by the rusty-blossomed immortelle. There are numerous groves in the Northern Range, and one small one on the path to the King's Bay waterfall in Tobago.

Flamboyant: This umbrella-shaped tree is crowned all over with bright red flowers from February through August, or longer. It can be distinguished from the immortelle because it retains its leaves when in flower.

Mango: Tall and glossily deep green, it has slender, waxy dark green leaves. The fruits are purply-brown and round and are ripe from March to October. The leaves smell like turpentine when broken.

Papaya: At the top of a palm-like trunk are a cluster of large, green melons, from which extend deeply lobed leaves at the end of long stems. Looks a little like a windmill.

Left, a crab blends into the coral polyps and, right, diver encounters a scorpion fish.

MUSICAL NATION

On a Saturday afternoon walk through the streets of any working-class neighborhood of Port of Spain, you may well run into a steel band rehearsal underway in one of the many tin-roofed, dirt-floored pan yards that dot the city. These sessions are a study in discipline and determination. Though the majority are unable to read music, the thirty to one hundred members of a steel band practice for hours, week after week, without pay, until they have memorized an astonishing repertoire. Steel bands pride themselves on being able to play any kind of music—from Mozart to the Mighty Sparrow.

When the rehearsals are through and the band takes the stage, stand back. This is a revolution in sound. The steel drum, an entirely new concept in musical instrument invented in the last one hundred years and having impact on the musical mainstream, was first fashioned in Trinidad from cast-off oil drums in the 1930s. Only Spree Simon, Ellie Manette and a few other musicians in Port of Spain originally saw their potential as music makers, but now steel bands move young and old, Trinidadians and foreigners, and their sound symbolizes Caribbean culture all over the world.

Music in Trinidad is not a spectator sport. Calypsonians and pan (as steel drums are familiarly known) players do not perform for a politely quiet audience. The risqué lyrics of musician Sparrow, pretending to report the Queen of England's point of view regarding the intruder who entered her bedroom—"he was longer...stronger"—are conducive to free-spirited involvement. The insistent rhythms of an impromptu party band, beating dustbins, bottles, and tin cans demand that you participate.

Audience response and involvement is a characteristic of black music all over, and the ultimate source of this aesthetic is Africa. Though no one ethnic group can claim exclusive credit for Trinidad's musical heritage, it is from Africa that much of Trinidad's music springs, evolving over the past five hundred years into a spicy international potpourri.

Afro-European Synthesis: In Trinidad, as in the rest of the West Indies, music and culture are dominated by an Afro-European synthesis. The first musical result was *parang*, Spanish Christmas carols introduced during Trinidad's days as a Spanish colony (1498-1797). In towns

Preceding pages: pan men play Panorama. Left, Carnival musicians and, right, an America calypso record from the '50s.

like Lopinot, Arima and Rio Claro the descendants of the first Spanish-speaking peoples in Trinidad maintain the parang tradition, and the continual movement between Trinidad and Venezuela, 10 miles (16 km) away, helps reinforce the tradition. Recently, many young people, searching for their roots, have become involved with parang, sparking a renaissance of the old tradition. The lyrics and stringed instruments used in parang—guitar, cuatro, mandolin—are the Spanish contribution, while Africa adds the call-and-response performance style and the incredible rhythms which

transform maracas into a solo instrument.

The parang season stretches from the last week of November through the first week of January. At night, groups of musicians and singers show up unannounced on friends' and relatives' doorsteps, playing music, singing and asking to be let in. Once admitted, the music continues, African style, until dawn, with breaks only for rum, food and coffee.

Parang is only one of several Afro-European syntheses in Trinidad, the best known of which hybrids is calypso. Like African folk songs, calypsos are repositories of history, reminders of moral values, and broadcasts of social commentary and news. Calypso combines the African traditions of lively rhythm and an improvised, tell-it-like-it-is attitude sung with European languages, scales and musical instruments.

Steel drums, another Afro-European synthesis, originated when African-style percussion bands, beating brake drums, bottles and other odds and ends, switched to oil drums, which had the potential for sounding more notes. Steel drums are tuned to a chromatic, European scale and, from the beginning, their repertoire has included calypso and classical music. A steel band is an orchestra of many moods. It retains its rhythmic punch when playing calypso, but shimmers like steel when tackling Tchaikovsky.

Purists might recoil at the thought of classical music being played on instruments for which it was never intended, but that doesn't bother Trinidadians. In fact, steel bands have popularized the classics, transforming them into music with mass appeal unmatched in many

Tassa drumming, which accompanies the street parades of Hosay, a Muslim festival, is one of the most important contributions Indians have made to Trinidadian music. Its rhythms knock down the walls between Muslim and non-Muslim Afro-Trinidadians, who are drawn to the drumming and join the processions through Port of Spain. Many non-Muslims have become excellent tassa drummers, creating an Afro-Indian style of music.

The common point which made such a synthesis possible is the integral nature of drumming to many religious celebrations and social activities, both in Africa and India. The felt need for drumming is so strong that in the 1880s, when the British banned drumming, both Africans and Indians rioted, fighting the police on several occasions.

European countries. Furthermore, when steel bands play classical music, they do not feel bound by the European ideal of faithfulness to the score. Instead, steel band arrangers, like jazz musicians, see the score as a point of departure and strive to put their personal stamp on a composition. Bertie Marshall explains:

I felt that when I was arranging a particular classic that I was imposing myself on the composer. It was like taking the foundation he had built for his tune and building an entirely new house.

After influences from Africa and Europe, the most important musical traditions come from India. East Indians are now the most populous group in the country, having in the 1970s surpassed those of African descent.

Even today, drumming is an integral part of many social activities in Trinidad and Tobago, from the rites of the African Shango religion to boxing matches. In 1985 when a boxer from the tough Laventille Hills area fought for the Commonwealth light-heavyweight crown, his fans of all races were at the ringside, urging their man to victory by singing and beating drums and ringing cowbells.

Pervasive Pan: A ride in a Port of Spain taxi is more than a trip across town. Most cab drivers have expensive, almost disco-quality sound systems in their cars, making a ride a musical journey through calypso, steel band, reggae, soul, or the classical traditions of India and Europe. The music never stops. As necessary as a full tank of gas, these contemporary work songs fulfill the same function that the singing of the cane cutters did one hundred years ago.

In Trinidad, good musicians can be found in unlikely places. For example, in the United States, insurance agents are not known as a musical lot, but every year in Trinidad the staff and management of the American Life and General Insurance Company draw hundreds to their talent show. In dazzling costumes, they perform the songs and dances of a host of countries: Trinidad, Africa, India, Spain, Mexico, Venezuela and the Caribbean. Obviously, they know about a lot more than underwriting.

Steel bands exist in countless countries around the world — even the U.S. Navy has one. In the 1960s, when Chubby Checker urged his

itself. Some argue that the correct name for calypso is *kaiso* — a Hausa word meaning "bravo" and this name is used in Trinidad today alongside calypso. Some trace the word to the French *carrousseaux*, a drinking party, the Spanish *caliso*, a topical song, or the Carib *carieto*, also a topical song. The Greek goddess Calypso was "she who conceals," and calypso songs excel in shrouding their point in cleverly double- or triple-edged lyrics.

The situation is complicated by the fact that several ethnic groups in Trinidad had song forms which merged to create calypso. What is clear is that the roots of calypso reach deep into Trinidad's past and that calypso resulted from a synthesis of the songs of several different ethnic groups, although the dominant elements are African.

listeners to "limbo lower now; how low can you go?" he made the limbo, a Trinidadian folk dance that has been in the repertoire of many American dance companies. Jazzman Andy Narrell popularized the steel drum in the United States. More recently, Lionel Richie's "All Night Long" continued the tradition of borrowing from Trinidadian sources. And any time an American advertiser wants to conjure up images of sun, sea and Caribbean romance, steel drums appear on the score.

Calypso's Roots: Calypso put Trinidad and Tobago on the world music map, but controversy surrounds its origins and even the word

Left, a parang group at practice and, right, old folk songs.

The slaves that French planters brought in the 1780s carried with them a tradition of improvised song which is the main ingredient in what we now call calypso. From the beginning of slavery in Trinidad and Tobago, slaves were assigned land on which they cultivated their own food in a communal fashion. Gangs competed with one another to accomplish the most, led by singers with such names as Elephant, Trumpeter, and Thunderer, the forerunners of today's Growling Tiger, Lord Invader, Mighty Duke and Black Stalin. The job of the early slave singers was to improvise songs of praise or scorn to inspire their work gangs to surpass all others.

At night, after the day's work was completed, the lead singer of the most productive group exalted his group's achievements and condemned the inadequacies of other gangs.

These songs of self-praise and scorn for others gave rise to the *picong* (or *mépris*) tradition of improvised verbal dueling which is a respected talent in calypsonians today. Africa, where songs of ridicule are a powerful mechanism of social control, where royalty never appears in public without its praise singers, is the source of the highly respected art of extemporizing song texts and music.

In Trinidad these traditions were adapted to local conditions. In the 1780s, a famous French slaveholder, Pierre Bergorrat, held court like a king in a cave near Diego Martin and had several slaves sing his praises and damn his enemies in verbal duels. Bergorrat crowned his favorite singer "Gros Jean Master of Kaiso," the first calypso king.

Forced to censor their songs and behavior during slavery, the freed Africans made songs of praise, scorn and social comment a Carnival institution. *Kalenda* and masquerade bands, with their lead singers praising their own members and denigrating the opposition, roamed the streets ready to do verbal and physical battle.

In this period just after Emancipation, Carnival tents of bamboo and thatch were first erected to provide practice space for the neighborhood bands at the beginning of the Carnival season. These tents became local night spots where anyone was free to drop in and observe the performances. The Carnival tents and masquerade bands forged a link between calypso and Carnival that is still strong today.

Freed slaves for the most part remained landless, and therefore flocked to the cities in

Similar verbal duels were an essential part of the music accompanying the *kalenda*, an acrobatic dance with sticks popular with slaves from Trinidad to New Orleans. The *kalenda* is really a thinly-veiled version of the African martial art of stick fighting, and it is always accompanied by singing. The *kalenda* songs became a major force in Trinidad culture, especially after Emancipation.

Carnival and Kalenda: The 1838 Emancipation changed the country's cultural life forever. No longer confined by slave society, the creativity of the Africans blossomed. They expropriated Carnival, transforming it from a series of bourgeois balls to a raucous street party, enlivened by African drumming and filled with ribald masqueraders mocking high society.

search of employment. At the same time, the colonial government encouraged immigration from other Caribbean islands, and continued to do so until well into the 20th Century. The competition for the necessities of life intensified. People divided themselves along ethnic lines and attempted to hold onto what little they had. Gangs arose to protect territory to which the inhabitants had no clear title.

The *kalenda* bands institutionalized gang warfare at Carnival. For 40 years, until they were suppressed in the 1880s, bands of stick fighters roamed the streets of Trinidad's cities, especially during Carnival. Every band had its chantwell, or lead singer. When two bands met, their chantwells traded insults in song, anticipating the actual battle. Calypso was stigmatized by its association with violence and the life-style of those on the margins of society who did not have steady enough employment to be considered working-class. This stigma remained with Carnival until well into this century.

The songs of the chantwells were not mere entertainment but powerful and magical talismans that could put a stick fighter into a state of mind where he would not feel the blows of his opponents. The simple lyrics expressed this magical state of mind and body:

Rain can't wet me,
When I have my poui [fighting stick] in
*   my hand.*
Rain can't wet me,
I advancing on the foe like a roaring lion!

Even in this basic chant, the blended elements of Trinidad and Africa are seen in the singer's

cariso!"

In bringing Moore's business to the streets, Surisima fulfilled an important social function, ridiculing behavior offensive to society. Calypso in one sense is a poor man's newspaper, one part *New York Times* and one part *National Enquirer*, extremely important to have in the 19th Century when illiteracy rates were high. Calypso is a cultural record of events as seen from the perspective of the people, and as a result, the whole course of Trinidad's social and political development can be traced through its calypso songs.

Censoring the Newspaper: By the mid-19th Century, Trinidad had been a British colony for more than 50 years, but its culture was anything but British. Its language, for example, was not English but Creole, a French-African mixture.

invocation of a thoroughly African beast, the lion.

Calypso and Carnival were the centerpieces of this synthesized culture, and Trinidadians guarded them against any attack. In 1859 an American named William Moore had the gall to state publicly that calypso, then called cariso, was merely a Trinidadian version of British and American ballads. In the streets outside Moore's hotel, Surisima the Carib, an excellent calypso singer, ridiculed Moore, singing, "Moore, the monkey from America," while a crowd answered, "Tell me wha' you know about we

Left to right, up-beat drummer at Carnival; discarded oil drums were amongst the first steel pans; and horns add a soca beat to a Carnival band.

The British were convinced of the need to Anglicize the natives for political stability, and Trinidadians, of course, resolved to resist. The struggle lasted more than 40 years.

First, calypso and Carnival came under attack from the press, the police, the church and the courts. The attacks focused on the obscenity and violence associated with them. For years, these aspects of calypso and Carnival had been denounced, but now the full power of the state was brought to bear. In 1884 drumming and *kalenda* bands were outlawed, despite the successful efforts of Carnival revelers to police themselves. Troops were called out to enforce the ban. In the 1890s, various masquerade characters were outlawed. Using police and army troops, the government was able to break the back of resistance.

Although masquerade bands continued to be led by calypsonians, the ban on drumming altered the sound of the music itself. Within a few years, tamboo bamboo bands replaced the outlawed drums. Tamboo bamboo consisted of tuned lengths of cured bamboo that when stamped on the ground produced a rhythmic percussion like that of drums, but without their carrying power. The highly skilled art of these instruments has a long history in Africa, Venezuela and the Caribbean.

The purge of the drummers cleared the way for the middle and upper classes to participate in both calypso and Carnival. Businessmen sponsored calypso and Carnival competitions to ensure that bourgeois standards of taste would not be violated. White and mixed race

string bands were eventually replaced by jazz bands in the 1920s. However, poor blacks continued to accompany their calypsos with tamboo bamboo until the steel drums replaced them in the 1930s and '40s.

In this period of rapid change, one event stands out as a symbol of the transformation of Trinidadian culture. In 1899 the first completely English calypso appeared sung by Norman Le Blanc, a white calypsonian:

Jerningham, the Governor,
He so fas' listening to you.
He so rude listening to you,
To break the laws of the Borough Council.

Following the tradition of the poor man's newspaper, it reported on the action of the British Governor, Sir Hubert Jerningham, who disbanded the Port of Spain Borough Council

calypsonians appeared in larger numbers than ever before.

Known as jacketmen because they wore jackets as a sign of their true status, they were nonetheless ostracized for their ventures into the social milieu of the poor blacks. They fought with sticks (individually, not in gangs), sang calypsos and chased women in poor neighborhoods; college students, seeking thrills, hired calypsonians for parties. All this activity tended to increase calypso's acceptance by broadening its audience, but of course, a price had to be paid. Bourgeois taste became much more important.

Soon the Venezuelan string bands, like those associated with parang, began to accompany the singing of the middle and upper classes. These

in a dispute between the Council and the Governor. Jerningham's heavy-handed response offended most Trinidadians, who saw it as further evidence of British arrogance.

Typically, the calypso does not explain all of the circumstances surrounding Jerningham's action. Instead, the song presupposes certain knowledge and is aimed at people already familiar with the issue. The implicit, almost cryptic quality of the lyrics is common in many African-American traditions, from soul to reggae. A pithy, four-line stanza characterizes the single-tone style of calypso, a style rooted in the verbal duels and acerbic comments of the *kalenda* and masquerade bands and work gangs of the 19th Century.

The fact that the song was sung in English

is a milestone in the cultural history of Trinidad. After one hundred years of British rule, the English language was finally understood widely enough to be used in a popular song. The Anglicization of Trinidad's culture was succeeding, and from 1899 on, Creole was increasingly replaced by English in calypso, marking the decline of French culture in Trinidad.

Anglophilia: In the early 20th Century, the country experienced a wave of Anglophilia inspired by the death of Queen Victoria (widely believed to have abolished slavery). Britain encouraged this feeling as a means to support its involvement in the Boer War and World War I, and the names of many calypsonians of that time—the Duke of Albany and Richard Coeur de Leon, for example, reflect the process of change.

May she rest in peace eternally.
Mourn, Trinidadians, mourn.

The oratorical style was preferred by jacketmen such as Atilla the Hun, Lord Executor and Chieftain Douglas, men who tried to elevate calypso by avoiding gossip and scandal in favor of more dignified subjects. These men fought long and hard to change the tastes of the common people, who still preferred the older single-tone style with its implicit meanings and spicy flavor.

In a *picong* battle early in this century, Lord Executor explained the requirements for success in oratorical calypso to his opponent, Atilla the Hun.

I admire your ambition, you'd like to sing,
But you will never be a kaiso king.
To reach such a height without a blemish

A new style of calypso was also emerging. Known as the double-tone or oratorical style, it featured eight-line stanzas, which gave calypsonians more room to present ideas in an explicit, step-by-step fashion, leaving much less to interpretation. Chieftain Douglas' "Mourn, Trinidadians, Mourn" is a good example.

Mourn, Trinidadians, mourn
For Queen Victoria who is dead and gone.
Mourn, Trinidadians, mourn
For Queen Victoria who is dead and gone.
It was she who abolished slavery,
And set our forefathers free.
So sing R.I.P.

Left, the Police band plays and, right, shimmering steel.

or spot,
You must study Shakespeare, Byron, Milton and Scott.
But, I'm afraid I'm casting pearls before swine,
For you'll never inculcate such thoughts divine.
You really got a good intention, but poor education.

By the 1920s, Trinidad's taste for things British had begun to go sour. Britain had fought wars for freedom, but the fruits of democracy eluded Trinidadians. In 1920, Patrick Jones, formerly a singer of pro-British songs, sang the following:

Class legislation is the order of the land.
We are ruled with an iron hand.

Class legislation is the order of the land.
We are ruled with an iron hand.
Britain boasts of democracy,
Brotherly love and fraternity,
But British colonists have been ruled in
perpetual misery.

Jones was nearly indicted for sedition.

By the end of the '20s, it was clear that the oratorical style would not replace the single-tone style any more than Venezuelan-style string bands would replace tamboo bamboo in street parades. But it was being converted into a voice for incipient nationalism and opposition to colonial rule. Poor blacks and even the middle class chafed under British dominance and calypsos expressed this discontent. As a result, police spies began to sit in the audiences of calypso performances.

cial value of Trinidad's indigenous culture — especially calypso and Carnival, which is in part why they were not completely destroyed in the late 19th Century. By sponsoring various competitions the business community was able to reform and influence calypso and Carnival.

Calypsonians themselves began to set up their own tents independent of masquerade bands, and for the first time charge admission. According to Atilla the Hun, King Fanto was the first calpysonian to do so, but others soon followed. By 1929, syndicates or cooperatives of calypsonians were setting up tents and competing for audiences. Frequently, the musicians secured the sponsorship of businessmen in return for advertising. The Toddy Syndicate, for example, took its name from a chocolate malt drink. Their jingle in praise of it seemed to

Despite surveillance and repression, the Anglicization of Trinidadian culture was not a complete success. Instead, Trinidad absorbed some British elements, adding to it a mixture that already contained a number of other ingredients. By the 1920s, calypso had proven that it could adapt and continue, capturing a wider audience by expressing the feelings of a majority. Furthermore, some were just beginning to realize how to cash in on calypso's popularity. The commercialization of calypso laid the foundation for its golden years.

Commercial Calypso: Between the '20s and World War II, calypso enjoyed its heyday, gaining both independence from Carnival and international recognition. Businessmen had long perceived the mass appeal and potential finan-

herald the transition from folk songs to professional entertainment.

As fewer and fewer Carnival bands could afford the services of the best calypsonians, mass media — radio and records — spread calypso's message at home and abroad, opening up new markets for musicians but changing the nature of their art.

The American band leader Paul Whiteman scored a hit with the calypso "Sly Mongoose" early in the '20s. In 1929, calypsonian Houdini became the first calypsonian to emigrate to the United States to perform. And by 1934, when Atilla the Hun and Lion left to record for Decca, the prestigious American record label, Trinidadians were beginning to realize the potential of the international market. A crowd of thousands jammed the docks to see them off, and it was obvious that calypso was something Trinidad could be proud of.

In the United States, calypso became the rage. Rudy Vallee and Bing Crosby attended Atilla and Lion's recording session, and Vallee included Lion's "Ugly Woman" in a coast-to-coast NBC broadcast. The show was picked up in parts of Trinidad, and thousands crowded around radios and public loudspeakers to hear it.

If you want to be happy and live a king's life,
Never make a pretty woman your wife.
If you want to be happy and live a king's life,
Never make a pretty woman your wife.
All you've got to do is just what I say,

Upon their return, Atilla and Lion received a hero's welcome. Crowds filled the streets and speeches were made in their praise. Distributors couldn't keep the stores stocked with the records Atilla and Lion recorded abroad. Atilla composed the following to commemorate the tour:

A prophet hath no honor in his own land.
The truth of the proverb I now understand.
When you sing kaiso in Trinidad,
You are a vagabond and everything that's bad.
In your native land, you are a hooligan.
In New York, you are an artiste and a gentleman,
For instance, take the Lion and me
Having dinner with Rudy Vallee.

Lords, Kings, Lions and Dictators: The first wave of professional calypsonians became

And you'll always be happy and gay.
From a logical point of view,
Always marry a woman uglier than you,

An ugly woman gives you your meals on time,
And will always try to console your mind.
At night when you lie on your cosy bed,
She will coax, caress you and scratch your head.
And she will never shame her husband at all,
By exhibiting herself with Peter and Paul.
So from a logical point of view,
Always marry a woman uglier than you.

Left, homage to musical history and, right, a calypso performance circa 1940.

known as the Old Brigade, and included singers such as Growling Tiger, Lord Beginner, Atilla the Hun, King Radio, the Roaring Lion, Lord Pretender and the Mighty Dictator.

King Radio's "Matilda" was a hit in the United States, but the influence of the recording industry was a mixed blessing. Since it required that the ensembles accompanying the songs resemble those current in popular music from the United States, tamboo bamboo bands were out, but string and wind bands, rooted in Trinidad's Spanish tradition, were in, as were jazz bands featuring trumpets, clarinets and saxophones. Also popular were ensembles derived from minstrel bands, consisting of piano, bass, woodwinds and violin.

The folk tradition of calypso was also moving in several different directions, developing new forms of instrumental music, since so many of the calypsonians had become professional entertainers. Radio and the record industry distributed jazz and other American popular music in Trinidad as well as calypso, and the calypso folk tradition accommodated itself to the influence of mass media. Masquerade bands parading through the streets at Carnival began to use jazz instruments such as the trumpet, clarinet and trombone which had already proven themselves to have the carrying power necessary for marching bands in the streets of New Orleans. So the Trinidadian folk tradition absorbed elements of the Afro-American jazz and marching band tradition in the United States as well.

Though most Trinidadians could not afford

slaughter house during the butchers' lunch break:

> They [the butchers] used to get into the old train carriages opposite the abbatoir and beat out a rhythm from old brake drums which they got from Kehela's scrapyard. They also used their knives, pieces of steel which all butchers carried, and oil tins into which they put their ends of meat....

By the late '30s, the new percussion ensembles were popular with masquerade bands at Carnival. In 1937 newspapers reported on the "terrific din set up by the clanking pieces of tin" in these bands. But in fact this was not an entirely new development, for percussion of one kind or another had been part of Carnival since the emancipation of the slaves.

Nineteenth-Century *kalenda* bands march-

these instruments, and tamboo bamboo bands and Venezuelan string and wind ensembles continued to provide music for calypso and masquerade bands in the countryside, these ensembles could not satisfy the tastes of the growing urban working-class. In the urban areas, tamboo bamboo bands were replaced by percussion bands which transformed the flotsam of industrial society—brake linings, trash cans, paint cans and biscuit tins—into musical instruments. These cast-off metal products had more carrying power than the tamboo bamboo.

Tin Pan Alley: The development of the new percussion bands was a collective process in which many participated without necessarily knowing where their innovations would lead. Bertie Marshall describes the scene outside a

ed to the beating of drums and the blowing of horns. When drums were not available, substitutes were improvised from tin kettles, salt boxes and almost anything else. When drums were banned in 1884, tamboo bamboo bands replaced them. The ancestors of all these percussion bands are the ensembles of drums, bells and rattles that dominate West African music, but what is interesting is that the percussion bands of the '30s satisfied the African preference for percussion by using the materials available in an industrial environment.

At first, the metal objects in these new bands produced only rhythm, and bugles were used to provide a melodic line. But by chance musicians discovered that the metal tins they had been beating on could produce more than one tone if the surfaces struck were shaped in certain ways. They began a process of experimentation, heating and pounding out the metal containers to produce several notes. A few claim to have been the first to discover the possibility of producing several notes from a metal tin and the conflicting claims probably indicate that a folk process was in operation, with many moving in the same direction at the same time.

Gradually, musicians began to use oil drums because their larger surfaces could accommodate more notes than paint cans and biscuit tins. From this process of experimentation, the steel drum was born. It was during the golden years of calypso that the steel bands started on the rocky road to international acclaim. Since steel bands were musically and

1937, King Radio expressed the calypsonian's reaction to this repression.

They want to licen' me foot,
They no want me to walk.
They want to licen' me mouth
They no want me to talk

Calypso was still under attack, but it held its own by expressing the experience of a colonized nation. The period between 1920 and World War II had seen disillusionment with British concepts of democracy, the growth of militant trade unionism in response to the Great Depression, and the growth of a Trinidadian middle class anxious to lead the country to independence.

As always, calypso accurately reflected the feelings of the people and the British could not ignore its ridicule of their failures. Its mass

socially the direct descendants of *kalenda* bands, at first they were perceived as lower class gangs and not musical ensembles. It is, perhaps, the great effort to overcome the stigma of its social origins which has caused steel bands to develop a broad musical repertoire.

Steel Band Struggle: Although calypso flourished in the '30s and '40s, opposition to it had far from disappeared. The Theatre and Dance Halls Ordinance of 1934 gave the English officers within the police the power to censor song texts, and the Colonial Secretary had the right to ban any record. Furthermore, calypsonians had to obtain licenses to sing in tents. In

Left and right, the music of Trinidad and Tobago flooded the American market after the War.

appeal and commercial value made calypso difficult to suppress, and so the colonial government fought a holding action, muzzling calypsonians to keep them in line. A.A. Cipriani and other nationalist leaders rose to their defense, and the battle raged back and forth. But the calypsonians' achievements became harder and harder to deny, especially after World War II brought the Yankee soldiers to Trinidad in large numbers.

The Yankee Dollar: World War II affected Trinidad deeply although no fighting took place there, and most Trinidadians who enlisted never saw combat. The War ushered in a new era — one characterized by the influence of the Yankee dollar. The colonial government signed a 99-year lease granting the U.S. government land for a major naval base at Chaguaramas, in northwestern Trinidad. The U.S. Airforce and Army also built bases, and work there provided jobs paying 10 or 20 times the 40 cents an hour previously earned by the average laborer. The influx of thousands of soldiers fueled the economy and in particular the entertainment industry.

The number of calypsonians grew as nightclubs opened to entertain the troops: in the words of Chieftain Douglas, "all the little ducks are bathing." Steel bands suddenly found themselves in demand to entertain soldiers at the bases, and wartime shortages of imported goods, including musical instruments, increased their popularity. The more foreigners at the bases expressed their enthusiasm for calypso and steel band the harder it was for the detrac-

They have the young girls going mad.
The girls say they treat them nice,
And they give them a better price.

They buy rum and Coca Cola.
Go down Point Cumana.
Both mother and daughter
Working for the Yankee dollar.

But "Rum and Coca Cola" came to symbolize the difficulties faced by Trinidadians in another respect. The song became one of the greatest calypso hits of all time, but Invader had to fight to receive any financial rewards. Americans on the bases had heard the tune and taken it back to the States, where the calypso craze of the '30s was not forgotten. The Andrews Sisters then released a cover version which sold more than 4 million copies around the

tors of Trinidad's indigenous culture to be heard. This wartime boost was important, especially for the calypsonian, as during the War the record industry experienced a slump worldwide and in Trinidad all Carnival and street processions were banned.

Soon a boom mentality set in, and for a while everyone was happy. It did not take long, however, before the presence of so many soldiers with money to spend caused an increase in prostitution and promiscuity. Trinidadians of all social classes were shocked by the sudden increase in light-skinned, fatherless children, and Trinidadian men felt their wives and daughters had betrayed them. Invaders' 1943 "Rum and Coco Cola" summed it all up:

Since the Yankees come to Trinidad,

world, paying Invader nothing since he had no copyright.

Invader sued and almost lost, but Lion and Atilla had included the lyrics in a copyrighted booklet of calypso lyrics before the Andrews Sisters released their version. In the end, Invader prevailed, narrowly avoiding the plight of many calypsonians: fame and poverty.

The Young Brigade: By 1945 a new challenge faced the Old Brigade. During the War, calypso's foreign audience had grown, but although these fans loved the music, lyrics referring to local Trinidadian events were irrelevant to them. To increase calypso's share of the international market, calypsonians and their musicians needed to change their lyrics, gain greater technical facility with Western musical instruments, and

240

incorporate more elements of American jazz and popular music. American G.I.s and Trinidad's middle and upper classes, who supported calypso in nightclubs and tents, wanted entertainment, not political satire and news reports.

A new generation of singers rose to meet the demand, de-emphasizing *picong*, satire and politics in favor of sex and fantasy, describing events not linked to a particular time or place. Killer's "Green Fowl," which concerns itself with a priapic rooster, is a good example of the prevailing style.

These more commercially oriented calypsonians called themselves the Young Brigade, and although the style was new, in many ways they continued calypso traditions, adopting names symbolizing power: Lord Kitchener, Mighty Killer, Mighty Spoiler, Mighty Dictator and

these measures were soon circumvented, as the Young Brigade opened their own tent, and, having gained a forum, soon became the people's choice. In 1945 Lion released "Mary Ann," which showed his acceptance of the new concern with love and sex. "Mary Ann" has since become a calypso classic.

Calypso's audience broadened, and the music became more of a national art, something with which all classes and ethnic groups identified. It was a creative, experimental period, and musical styles proliferated, as calypsonians incorporated elements of many ethnic styles. Killer sang "Grinding Massala," using Indian rhythms and speech patterns, and Kitchener's "Double Ten" celebrated the founding of Sun Yat Sen's republican China with Chinese rhythms. Like Trinidad itself, these songs repre-

Lord Wonder. Lord Melody was one of a few exceptions, and his name may reflect the importance of expanded melodic techniques in the new style.

The Young Brigade boldly announced their intentions:

Everybody knows or have been told
That the young bound to conquer the old.
So tell them we are not afraid.
We're going to mash up the Old Brigade.

To defend themselves from the challengers, the Old Brigade began to monopolize the tents, refusing to allow the Young Brigade to sing. But

Left, an American book taught calypso dance steps and, right, vacationers enjoy their version of island life.

sent a synthesis of elements drawn from Africa, Europe and Asia. A new national consciousness had begun to emerge, and the indigenous culture of Trinidad gained new respect.

National Recognition: There was such joy after the Allies' victory in Europe that the creativity of the Trinidadian people could hardly be restrained. And as a part of the 1946 Carnival, a special concert was organized to showcase steel drums. In the first solo concert of steel drum music, Winston Spree Simon demonstrated the versatility of pans, which now had up to 14 notes apiece. He selected a program which included all kinds of music: a hymn, "I Am A Warrior"; Schubert's "Ave Maria"; Kitchener's "Tie Tongue Mopsy"; and "God Save the King." Legend has it that at the sound of the last, the Governor sprang to attention, popping all the buttons on his coat.

That the Governor and other dignitaries attended at all was a sign of new respect and a major advance for steel band. The concert proved that pans could play even classical music, but skeptics were not completely silenced by the applause Simon received. An aura of violence was still associated with steel band, and this had to be removed before they could gain final acceptance. As in the clean-up of 19th-Century Carnival and calypso, the government took the lead.

In 1948, the Trinidad and Tobago Youth Council asked the government to establish a committee to identify the causes of violence among the steel bands. This committee, chaired by Canon Farquhar, made several landmark

recommendations, including the creation of the Trinidad and Tobago Steelbandmen's Association to provide a mechanism for resolving conflicts and promoting steel band music. The Association was successful and soon radio stations began to broadcast programs of steel band music.

Changing attitudes toward steel band and calypso were part of a general shift in support of indigenous culture. The British government had come to realize that the colony would not be so forever and that it would be best to prepare Trinidadians to rule themselves. It had become increasingly clear to middle-class Trinidadians that they could not hope to lead the common people to independence if they didn't respect their culture.

Acclaim! In 1948 Beryl McBurnie opened the Little Carib Theatre to promote indigenous music and dance. There were other dance groups at the time, but they presented ballet and other European forms. The very first performance by McBurnie's company was attended by prominent people in government, the church, academia and the press. The movers and shakers in Trinidadian society had finally decided that the limbo, bongo, bel air and other local dances were art, along with calypso and steel band.

Within a few years, Dr. Eric Williams, who later led Trinidad to independence, was praising McBurnie, saying that "the Little Carib Theatre teaches our people that their hands are capable to build a temple and nothing can hide its nobility." Things had changed since the days when, as one observer noticed, "[all] one had to do...[was] to walk the streets with a pan stick in his pocket and a beebop cap on his head to be recognized as a curse to our society."

In 1950, the first national steel band competition was held in Trinidad, and in the same year, the "Concerto in Pan" was held at the prestigious Trinidad Turf Club. Casablanca performed last and its versions of "The Bells of St. Mary" and Chopin's "Nocturne in E-Flat" were well received. Still, some were amazed that illiterate musicians could perform these compositions. Significantly, Casablanca's members were of African, East Indian and Venezuelan descent—a cross-section of the Trinidadian nation, strugggling for identity through pan.

Soon steel bands were being asked to perform abroad. In 1951 the Trinidad and Tobago All Steel Percussion Orchestra, comprising the best musicians from all bands, represented Trinidad at the Festival of Britain. At first, skepticism and sarcasm greeted "the tin can boys from Trinidad" but British audiences went wild when they heard the music. The success of this tour opened the door for steel band at home. They now became indispensable at national festivals, dances, parties, weddings and even church services.

Calypso Campaign: During the '50s, the bands grew larger and larger, as more pans were added for sound and melodic possibility. Eventually, steel bands rivaled the costumes of the masqueraders as a Carnival attraction. Pan became a national obsession. Bands were formed in the best schools, and people of every race and class joined in a celebration of their common culture. The tremendous popularity of steel bands during the '50s created the opportunity for calypsonians to compose specifically for pans.

In 1950, Atilla the Hun, one of the Old Brigade who never gave up political calypso, was elected to the Trinidad Legislative Council. In true calypso fashion, Atilla ran his campaign from the calypso tents, and apparently, his songs were more eloquent than the speeches of his opponent. Once elected, Atilla attacked the 1934 Ordinance which required calypsonians to secure licenses to sing and forced them to submit their songs to the censors. Never before had the voice of the calypsonian been heard in legislative debate. In the same year, the colonial government created a new post, Director of Dance in the Ministry of Education, specifically for Beryl McBurnie. This was the first time performers had been elected or appointed officials in government.

Calypso tents were now packed with mainly white audiences: Trinidadians, tourists and G.I.s., continuing a trend begun in the mid-'40s. In the United States and England, many nightclubs now featured calypso, and Kitchener, perhaps the best of the Young Brigade, lived and

many Trinidadians. Actually, calypso was only part of what Belafonte did, the key to his popularity being that he tailored West Indian songs to suit the tastes of the supper clubs.

Sparrow Sings: The most successful Trinidadian musician of the '50s was a newcomer to the Young Brigade, the Mighty Sparrow. The record industry was working hard to supply enough records to meet the international demand, and the pressure was on calypsonians to develop greater marketability. Sparrow, with his music talent and business acumen, responded to the challenge more successfully than most.

Blessed with a better voice than most calypsonians, Sparrow could sing a wider range of material and he had the versatility to update his style, incorporating elements of jazz, rock, or Latin styles to match international trends in

performed in England, though he sent a steady stream of records back home.

Kitchener was one of several calypsonians who migrated to England or the United States to pursue their careers, a trend begun in the '20s and '30s reflecting both the international appeal of calypso and the limitations of its Trinidadian market. The Mighty Terror sang at the Young Brigade's tent until 1953, when he left for England to sing in the nightclubs, and in 1957, was crowned Calypso King of Britain.

In America, a Jamaican became King of Calypso when RCA released Harry Belafonte's calypso album. His success was resented by

Left, basic rhythms and, right, horns add a modern beat.

popular music. But he had the strength as a performer to put his own stamp on his songs whatever their style.

In the mid-'50s, long-playing records began to compete with 45s, and recording artists needed to produce an LP regularly to remain popular. Calypsonians could no longer rely on the stock of about 50 melodies that had served so well up to that point. Sparrow produced a new album every year and has continued to do so since 1957. The singles released by other artists were no match for Sparrow's LPs, which he produced at his own record company while at the same time maintaining his own calypso tent outside Port of Spain.

In 1956, Sparrow's "Jean and Dinah" won the first calypso king competition sponsored by the Carnival Development Committee (CDC), a government agency which still sponsors competitions for calypsonians, steel bands and masqueraders. Established after Eric Williams' People's National Movement won the '56 elections and formed a government, the CDC's support of Trinidadian culture meant official recognition by government.

But even professional calypsonians with international reputations continued to produce songs on local topics, encouraged by the progress Trinidad was making toward independence. Although these did not sell well abroad, at home they still carried weight. And in 1958, Striker won the Road March with "Don't Blame the PNM."

Fame, No Fortune: In 1962, Trinidad finally gained its independence under a government led

high hopes for the new government, believing it would reverse years of underdevelopment and colonialism. Specifically, calypsonians and panmen hoped that Williams' new government would actively promote indigenous music and dance, in keeping with Williams' stated appreciation and respect for them. And the government did continue to send calypso and steel bands abroad to represent the country, and to organize competitions like Best Village, and Panorama, a competition for steel bands.

But once-a-year competitions and engagements at occasional international festivals are not enough to sustain performers. Too many talented calypsonians or panmen returned home to obscurity, after a moment of fame on a foreign stage, without the ongoing support necessary to sustain interest: something which

by Williams, whose People's National Movement has so far enjoyed 24 years in power. Calypsonians helped elect the new government with songs such as the following by the Mighty Wrangler:

> *Who built the schools in George Street for us?*
> *Nobody but the Doctor [Williams].*
> *And the North Coast road going Las Cuevas?*
> *Nobody but the Doctor.*
> *And the Housing Scheme we have in Morvant?*
> *Nobody but the Doctor.*
> *And who do you think build the bridge we call the Flyover?*
> *Nobody but the Doctor.*

Like most Trinidadians, calypsonians had

could be as simple as playing the music on the government controlled radio. Even today, Trinidadian radio inundates listeners with calypso and steel band during the Carnival season, but during the rest of the year they comprise less than a fourth of the programming.

There are other basic steps that could and can be taken, such as joining a copyright convention so that musicians can protect their recordings. Even today, pirated tapes are sold openly on the streets, in hotels and in record stores. Musicians can hardly recover their recording costs under such conditions.

Unfortunately, commercial sponsorship and the music industry itself also fail to fill the gap. Commercial sponsors often made minimal financial commitments to the band bearing their names, and royalties from recordings often amounted to pennies per song for each copy sold. The only hope for commercial success as a recording artist still lies in marketing large numbers of recordings overseas, but this depends on the popularity of calypso fads in the United States and Britain.

Scrunting and Sex: In the 1960s disillusionment set in as Trinidadians realized that, despite independence, pan and calypso were still scrunting—struggling for survival. And dissatisfaction with the results of the cultural policies of the Williams government paralleled disappointment with economic and social conditions.

For example, blacks could not secure employment as tellers in banks, despite the fact that their Prime Minister was a black himself!

They raise up on the taxi fare.
No, Doctor, No.
And the blasted milk gone up so dear.
No, Doctor, No.
But you must remember
We support you in September.
You better come good
Because I have a big piece of mango wood.

Although the Young Brigade concentrated on lighter themes, political calypsos never really died out in Trinidad. They resurfaced in the mid-'50s, as independence neared, and with the discontent of the '60s, there was again incentive to speak out. But still relationships between men and women and especially the sexuality at Carnival were the most popular themes. Written after his return to Trinidad from England, Terror's 1966 hit "Last Year's Happiness" won

It seemed that institutionalized discrimination was being tolerated. Several calypsos addressed to the Williams government voiced this discontent with the status quo. Sparrow's "No, Doctor, No" is typical.

Listen, listen carefully.
I am a man does never be˙sorry,
But I went and vote for some Councilmen.
They have me now in a pen.
After promising to give so much tender care,
They forget me as they walk out of Wood-
ford Square.

Left, pounding out a pan and, right, the finished products.

him the Calypso King's title.

Yes, I enjoy meself last year
That's the reason why I come back down here
I say, I enjoy meself last year
That's the reason the Mighty Terror come
*   back here.*
Carnival is really amusing
Don't leave off your mask Jour Ouvert
*   morning.*
For any woman inside the band
Is your woman in the land.

That is real happiness.
Not a soul prejudice
Play your mas' as you like
But don't interfere,
Don't look for fight.

When the steel orchestra
Blast the rhythm in your ear,
Grab a girl and start wining
from Monday 'til Ash Wednesday morning.

By the mid-'60s, the CDC's calypso competition had fallen into a predictable pattern. The calypsonian sang a serious song of social commentary and a lighter, catchy tune good for wining (moving your hips) through the streets. Some calypsonians began to complain, and the Mighty Chalkdust put his complaints into a song.

If you want to win the crown,
Sing about wine, women, and song.
Sing about your neighbor's wife.
Sing about your own sex life.

When Terror won his title in 1966, his second tune was "Steelband Jamboree," touting the international reputation of steel band and noting its recognition by John Williams and other prominent foreign musicians. The song lauds the transformation of the oil drum into a musical instrument—"When you think of it, it is excellent"—and mentions Neville Jules and Ellie Manette as steel band leaders we cannot forget. But with cruel irony, Terror notes that many steel band heroes are out of work and have joined the police force "to lock up the panmen, of course."

Panorama: Steel bands went into decline for a variety of reasons in the '70s. They lost touch with the masquerade bands, no longer concentrating on providing music for them, and became totally absorbed in the CDC's Panorama competition, becoming so large and so expensive that they priced themselves out of the masquerade market. They also began to play more and more classical music, perhaps in an effort to legitimize themselves. In any case, classical music does not go over well in the streets of Trinidad at Carnival time. In 1975, Maestro expressed the feelings of many:

Masqueraders bawling
I hear them complaining,
Steel bands playing too slow.
They say they want tempo.
Playing too much classic.
Too much Yankee music.
Straying from the beat,
And they leaving we in heat.

To recapture their proper place in Carnival, steel bands needed to amplify their sound and ride on flatbed trucks to move through the

streets alongside the mas' players. They also needed to expand their repertoire to include more rhythmic music, and in the mid-'80s there are indications that some bands are moving in these directions.

From the late '60s on, while pan has been having its problems, calypso has moved in a very different direction. Absorbing the impact of the Civil Rights and Black Power movements from the United States, it has responded to the deteriorating economic conditions of the working-class. Out of the social ferment of 1970 and the Black Power Movement came a new generation of calypsonians: Mighty Chalkdust, Black Stalin, Explainer and Valentino, who once again concentrated on political calypso. In the '60s, calypsonians like Sparrow, Kitchener and

Terror sang a range of material which included political calypsos as but one aspect of their repertoire.

A Schoolteacher Speaks: The most important of these new calypsonians is the Mighty Chalkdust, who dominated the '70s as far as political calypso is concerned. A schoolteacher, Chalkie's lyrics are always well-constructed as, according to Chalkdust, the calypsonian is "...not only an articulator of the population, he is also a fount of public opinion. He expresses the mood of the people, the beliefs of the people. He is a mouthpiece of the people."

Chalkdust's first album, released on the 10th-anniversary of independence, included "We're Ten Years Old":

> It's true our people enjoy a high per capita income,

tion does not have its own steel band. This album also includes "Ah 'Fraid Karl," a reference to the Attorney General, Karl Hudson-Phillips, who could charge dissidents with sedition and had, in fact, jailed government opponents under the State of Emergency declared after the rebellion of 1970.

Chalkdust was never indicted, but various attempts were made to muzzle him. In 1969, the Ministry of Education tried to prevent him from singing because, as a Ministry employee, he needed its permission before accepting outside employment. In true calypso fashion, Chalkdust took his case to the people through a calypso which pointed out that other Ministry employees worked part-time in journalism, the military, the theater and other occupations. The Ministry dropped its case.

> But we share the national cake and thousands only get crumbs.
> Living standards have risen,
> We have no money to buy.
> But taxation choking us dry
> While the cost of living is sky high.
> Change that because
> We are ten years old.
> Remember, we are ten years old.

This first album also contained "Our Cultural Heritage" wherein he encourages the use of indigenous food and music, and wonders why the Port of Spain Hilton serves American, not Trinidadian, food, and why every institu-

Left, the Mighty Sparrow at Panorama 1986 and, right, floor show, Carnival 1986.

Calypso Rose: The women's movement of the '70s also had a major effect on calypso. Until then, calypso had been a male bastion, but when women claimed their right to sing, the Calypso King Competition was renamed the Monarch Competition, reflecting the fact that it now included woman. In 1978, the competition was won by a woman for the first time. Calypso Rose had already won the Road March title in 1977, and then captured it again in 1978. Since Rose's success, the ranks of female calypsonians continue to grow with peformers like Singing Francine, Twiggy and others.

Soca Fever: While politics were the lyrical focus for calypso, another force, the international pop music industry, was about to change its sound. As professional entertainers, calypsonians have always had to accommodate changes in the music industry. And in the late '70s, a new style of calypso emerged which shook calypso to its foundations.

Called soca, the new style is much more than a simple blend of soul music and calypso, as its name seems to suggest. The new style incorporates technological advances that changed the nature of the pop music industry in the United States as well. By the mid-'70s, the U.S. music industry was producing dance music heavily dependent on synthesizers and advanced production techniques.

The disco craze was only one manifestation of the changes going on. As electronic gadgetry grew in sophistication, musicians depended more and more heavily on arrangers and producers to create the final product. Faced with

the need to expand their share of the pop music market, calypsonians began to incorporate the new technology into their recordings. The result was soca.

Soca features furious tempos, funky, fractured bass lines, hot horn sections with plenty of riffs, independent rhythms on bass drum and snare, and assorted percussion to fill out the sound. Soca is an electronic big band assembled in the studio to create sounds nearly impossible to duplicate on stage.

The first to master the new style were Maestro and Lord Short (now Ras Shorty I). Although he was a creator of the new style, Maestro seemed to have mixed feelings about its effect on calypso.

I did not intend to lose control,

To promote my calypso through soul,
But it seems it is the only way
To survive in this business today.

In any case, soca has been released and shows no signs of yielding ground. The rage of the '80s in Trinidad, every calypsonian must pay homage to the new style or face failure in the marketplace. The demand for soca has placed new burdens on the calypsonian, who must travel to New York or other recording centers because Trinidad lacks adequate facilities to manufacture the new sound. In "Soca Fever," Sparrow almost makes catching the disease a patriotic duty:

You say you could wave the flag.
You say you could wine.
You used to boast and brag.
You could do the grind.
But this is a new era.

People getting soca fever.
If you want to make it sister,
wine faster, grind faster.

Don't drop the tempo.
Don't stop the tempo.
Keep up the tempo.

The new style includes songs on all topics; sex, politics, religion and more. Penguin's 1985 "Freedom Road" celebrates the government's decision to declare August 1st a national holiday, Emancipation Day, in honor of the day the slaves were freed. Previously, August 1st had been celebrated as Discovery Day, the day Columbus first visited the island. Blue Boy's "Soca Baptist" landed him in hot water with the Spiritual Baptists, who felt they were being mocked. Sparrow's "Vanessa" reveals that the poor man's newspaper is still in circulation. In it he takes Vanessa Williams, the first black Miss America, to task for appearing nude in a magazine, but Sparrow softens his criticism at the end of the song:

Sexy Vanessa, I hope you understand
I love your pictures and I'm still your greatest fan.
I'm upset with you, and jealous I'll admit.
Not for what you do
But because it's not me you do it with.

Today, calypso lives in soca. Soca is not the end of calypso, as some have feared, but a new creative avenue for the mind of the calypsonian. Through it, calypsonians continue to express themselves on the range of issues that concern them—unemployment, inflation, politics, scandal, or sex.

Left, never too young to soca and, right, not just a male province.

ROTI ON THE RUN

Like Trinidad and Tobago's rhythmic soca music, island food and drink are a sensual blend of many continents and countries. A mouth-watering melange of African, East Indian, Amerindian, Chinese, Middle Eastern and European flavors combines in recipes that have survived conquest, slavery and indentureship, offering a staggering variety of the most exotic foods in the Caribbean.

The *joie-de-vivre* that people of these two islands demand as a birthright is as concentrated in their culinary culture as it is in their Carnival. Good eating is an important part of what Trinidadians and Tobagonians enjoy about living in a part of the world where food is plentiful and fresh, though sometimes expensive. And islanders like to cook and love to eat, so they do both in abundance. The streets of Port of Spain are crowded with food vendors, bars, snack shops and open markets, and every little hamlet has at least a roti stand. T&Ters are quick to have a "cookup" the minute friends drop by, and any social event, like playing All Fours — a card game — or watching a video, is a respectable pretense for a meal. At parties, a full dinner is more the rule than hor d'oeuvres. The style of food you find in private homes depends to a good degree on the ethnic background of your hosts, but a certain blurring of culinary borders has occurred so that Trinidadian cuisine might be said to be made up of unique variations on other people's themes.

Some Local Names: The names of local specialities reflect their mixed and exotic sources, encouraging even the jaded to experiment. Who wouldn't be curious about *callaloo*, *coocoo*, *pelau*, *roti*, *buljol*, *accra* and "oil down" or *san coche*, a recent import from the smaller islands of the Caribbean? And there are unfamiliar and delicious fruit punches — soursop, shaddock, barbadine — and rum drinks to cool off the heat.

Creole food, which with Indian is most prevalent, is an amalgamation of dishes with an African past that incorporates contributions from French settlers who brought slaves here two centuries ago. *Pelau*, *callaloo* and *coocoo* are all Creole dishes whose likenesses can be found in other Caribbean islands. The country's former Spanish colonists have also left their enduring influence. *Pastelles* and *arepas*, spiced corn patties filled with meat or chicken,

for example, are purely Spanish, although they taste less of olive oil than their Latin American counterparts.

Curries, roti and other exotically spiced dishes brought here by indentured East Indian laborers in the 19th Century add to the already singular potpourri. Indian foods, like those of other cultures commingling in Trinidad and Tobago, sometimes take completely new forms, so that many no longer bear resemblance to their originals.

The Chinese, who also came under indentureship, brought a crisper, fresher version of their cuisine than that usually found in the Chinatowns of the world. *Chow mein* in Trinidad, for instance, is quickly stir fried, without the cornstarch that gives it the gooey consistency familiar to North Americans and others. Like some Indian dishes, many Chinese foods have been "creolized." Their fried rice borrows spices and flavor from *pelau*, a rice and peas dish, and many Chinese meat and poultry dishes look suspiciously as if they've been "browned down," the Creole process of cooking in caramelized sugar.

The Syrians, Lebanese and Portuguese have also contributed to the Trinidad and Tobago menu, though to a lesser degree, since their arrival here is more recent. Middle Easterners spread the use of vermicelli, and influenced the already popular potato salad, augmenting it with beets, carrots and peas.

The Rafters on Warner Street is a small restaurant with a typically Trinidadian atmosphere and menu. It used to be an old rum shop and the exterior and interior have been left virtually unchanged. For Creole cuisine there is Villa Creole on the Western Main Road, Veni Mange on Lucknow Street, and Pot Luck on Dondonald street. If you are downtown around lunchtime, eat at L&J Caterers at 53 Park St., where the proprietor and his family provide a changing daily menu for office workers and storekeepers much like what you might eat if you had lunch at their home. The Mango Tree and The Outhouse are housed in converted private homes, and the imaginative Creole cooking at The Outhouse is favored by a younger crowd.

The best place for Indian food is Mangal's, in an elaborately gingerbread mansion right off the Savannah. The authentic, hot curries and ample buffet are worth the expense. For good Chinese food and a romantic view, Tiki Village is on the roof at the Kapok Hotel. Shay Shay Tien also offers authentic Chinese cuisine.

Left, roadside menu in Port of Spain.

Roti on the Run: One of the most delicious and popular foods to be found anywhere and everywhere is the roti. A complete meal, roti consists of a delicate Indian flat bread filled with curried beef, chicken, goat, shrimp or vegetables. Curried potatoes and chick peas are added and the bread is folded over everything to create a portable crepe. The bread, called *dhalpourri*, is made of two flat thin layers of dough seasoned with ground split peas in between. In many shops the *dhalpourri* is still baked on iron rolling stones heated over coal pots. There are also other breads used with the curried meats, like *paratha*, *aloopourri* and *dosti*, more common in the homemade varieties.

Rotis are sold from roadside stands, bars and restaurants, and are practically the cheapest food you can buy. They are ideal for lunch, or are usually mustard or oil based, and may contain papaya (or pawpaw), lime, onions and plenty of the hot, yellow variety of pepper that grows all over the islands.

The hungry visitor must be an adventurous traveler to discover the out-of-the-way (and unassuming) places serving serious local food; *buljol*, salted codfish, onions, tomatoes and hot pepper, related to the Portugese dish *bacalao*; *coocoo*, a dumpling of cornmeal and okra; *callaloo*, pureed okra and spinach; and *pelau*, rice and peas spiced with cinnamon, allspice and any number of secret ingredients such as coconut milk or red wine, depending on the cook.

Rumshop Society: An aspect of city life that is sadly disappearing is the once vibrant rumshop, a liquor bar where working-class men

as an informal dinner. Specialty roti shops still do the briskest business of all food sellers, although American-style fast-food restaurants have mushroomed in recent years. In places like St. James along the Western Main Road, and Back Chain Street in San Juan you'll find what might be called "roti rows." The Hot Shoppe, near the Trinidad and Tobago T.V. station, and the new Breakfast Shed, near the Holiday Inn, are reliable and popular restaurants for roti lunches.

A day at the beach should include fried shark and hops, called *bake 'n' shark*, usual fare at beachside bars and restaurants. The deep fried roll and thick fish steak are doused with the ever handy hot pepper sauce, and downed with a number of Carib beers. These hot sauces used to gather after work for simple socializing and drinking at a cheap rate. Outside the rumshop on the pavement, vendors sold black pudding, a sort of blood pudding, and souse or pig's trotters. Akra and float, a salt-fish cake and pancake, and thick slices of fried shark in hops bread were also available. Inside, men (women never entered) sat at tables under ornate ceilings, or lounged, against equally ornate bars and drank their rum and talked. The potent effect of the spirit added considerably to the heat of the argument about every subject under the sun, voices raised so loudly they could be heard way down the street.

Outside, and side by side with the vendors, would be small Salvation Army bands and groups of Baptist preachers with lighted candles and ringing bells, conducting services.

There used to be a rumshop at the corner of Park and Tragarete Road, the walls of which were painted green, so the corner became known as Green Corner. It was a terminal for taxis commuting to and from the districts on the western outskirts of the city known as Carenage and Point Cumana, which were close to the U.S. Naval Bases at Chaguaramas, during World War II. With servicemen patronizing the shop, Green Corner grew notorious.

Today, only a few rumshops still remain, but wherever they are found, they provide the same atmosphere of friendship and lively conversation. Brooklyn Bar at Roberts Street, Woodbrook, still exists. So, too, do Broadway Bar on South Quay, the Empire at the corner of Prince and Henry Street, and the only all-night rum-

Carnival seasons, and much of the time in between, since there are 13 national holidays, and at least seven more religious holidays celebrated, drinking becomes a national avocation.

Street Sweets: During Carnival, food shacks spring up all around the Savannah, and even during the rest of the year street vendors offer a broad choice in one of the safest cities in the Caribbean to buy roadside food.

Doubles, saucy, curried chick peas spread between two (thus the term "doubles") lightly flavored breads called *barahs*, is another Indian-influenced street food widely eaten as a lunch on the run. Indian vendors also carry *aloo pies*, *katchowrie*, *sahina* and *poolouri*, all seasoned breads eaten with mango or tamarind sauces, and invariably, a touch of pepper sauce.

shop, Canton Bar, at the corner of St. Vincent and Duke, all of which retain the old character of traditional rumshops.

Trinidad produces over 4 million gallons of rum annually, but grudgingly exports only what the people can't drink themselves, so that Trinidadian brands are less familiar, though no less excellent, than Barbadian and Jamaican brands. Old Oak and Vat 19 are the best-sellers in a country where rum drinking is a national pastime, approached with more gusto than eating. During the Easter, Christmas and

Left, a Tobago food shack and, right, selling snocones and solo around the Savannah.

To cool the hot sauce, a nearby vendor will gladly offer coconut water, spilling from the fruit he has just opened with his machete. All around the Savannah in Port of Spain, and by the roadside in more rural areas, the coconut trucks dispense fresh coconuts from the full backs of their flatbed trucks. By merely shaking the fruit the seller knows if it is ready or not, and when he finds a ripe one a few deft, frightening strokes of his blade reveal the milk. It's also an opportunity to savor the jelly that remains after the milk has been drained, which, after hardening, provides the nut that is grated as flavor or main ingredient in numerous dishes.

Pastry vendors are also common, their little glass boxes filled with coconut and currant rolls, sweet cassava breads called *pone*, beef pies and even vegetable patties. Some vendors get fancier, including the less ethnic fare like sponge cake and fruit tarts. In recent years, many vendors have begun selling the Rastafarian-inspired "Ital" or vegetarian patty. Other forms of Ital food, some of which are delicious, have gradually found acceptance among the public.

Wherever sugar is produced, sweet tooths are rampant, and in Trinidad and Tobago confectionaries are to be found everywhere. The islanders use coconut in a variety of these sweets — mixing it with sugar and baking it into a sugar cake, or grating it into chips to be blended with molasses for *tooloom*, a sweet that was favored by slaves. The *tamarind ball* is a wicked idea invented to confuse the tongue. In this candy-like dumpling, sugar and salt collide with the tangy flavor of the tamarind fruit.

cherries are also preserved and sold widely by vendors.

Oysters are another roadside victual, feeding the islanders' belief in their aphrodisiac qualities. The oysters are very small in Trinidad, where they grow on mangrove roots in swamps. They are also more succulent than sea oysters. And while health codes now prevent vendors from selling the mollusks in their shell, oyster cocktails have become as popular as the oyster plate that once allowed the aficionado to suck them out. The oysters are dressed in a sauce of hot pepper, tomato ketchup and vinegar.

There are a number of other foods and drinks islanders claim have aphrodisiac powers. These include *sea moss*, a kelp drink; *babande*, made from a tree bark; bush rum or *mountain dew*; and *pachro*, sea urchin. Consumption of

Indian-inspired sweets include *kurma*, a sweet dough dropped in oil and fried until crisp, which is the candy of choice on the islands. Other Indian sweets like *jilebi*, *ladoo*, *maleeda* and *sawaine*, can only be found in the market stalls on Sunday mornings.

Sea Moss and Sorrel: Expectably, fruit is everywhere on these two lush islands. An endless variety of mangoes competes for shelf space with more exotic offerings like pomsitae, guava, sapodilla — the gum of whose bark is used to make chicle — soursop, kymet and sugar apple, in addition to vast quantities of banana and citrus fruit. Mango is curried and used as a side dish, grated and seasoned into chutney as a condiment, and preserved in varying degrees of sweet and sour. Tropical plums and

these and more obscure concoctions never seems to diminish. We offer no guarantees, but do encourage the adventurous to experiment and report findings, please.

The list of non-alcoholic drinks is long. Most popular are *sorrel*, a tangy, ruby-colored drink made from the petals of the sorrel flower; *ginger beer*, the spicy predecessor of ginger ale; *mauby*, a slightly bitter extract from the bark of the mauby tree; and *peanut punch*, a peanut butter-flavored thick shake. Of course, even non-alcoholic drinks are likely to be spiked with a drop of rum, and the world-famous Angostura Bitters, whose secret herbal ingredients are under lock and key in the company's offices in Trinidad.

Bitters is an important component of *punch-*

a-creme, a spiked eggnog that can lay out the light-headed when really potent. Bitters is also used heavily in a mixture of Guinness stout, milk and nutmeg called "the Bomb" and said to make one virile and other macho things.

The ultimate drink on an island that produces some of the finest rums in the world is the rum punch. In Trinidad and Tobago, this fruity drink finds a flavor more subtle and seductive than that found on the other islands. The best rum punches, needless to say, are more likely to be found at a private home than at the bars. Everyone's uncle or aunt adds some secret ingredient that makes his or her rum punch special—anything from whole spices to fruit slices might appear in homemade punch. The bottled variety put out by Angostura and offered in most restaurants is certainly an able

a time for substantial family meals. Sunday dinner might consist of rice, meat, fish, or poultry, and some kind of stewed peas or *callaloo*. Or it could be curried crab, gingered *bok choy* stir fried with pork or codfish, and roasted eggplant with garlic. Or *coocoo* and fish steamed with coconut milk in a thin gravy. Ground provisions—root vegetables—also find their way onto most tables. So, quite frequently, do a rich macaroni pie and a Lebanese-inspired potato salad.

Preparation for Sunday dinner sometimes begins Saturday evening, but really gets going with an early Sunday trip to the open market. A Sunday morning market scene begins before full dawn, as knowledgeable housewives seize the opportunity for first pick at the offerings. The largest market by far is in Port of Spain,

substitute until you can wangle a private invitation.

T&Ters consume beer like it's going out of style, blaming their bibacity on the heat. The sun and fresh trade winds seem to neutralize alcohol content, particularly during Carnival, making it easy to down four or five in a couple of hours. The two local beers, Carib and Stag, compete vigorously with that other universal favorite, Heineken.

A Meal at Home: As much on-the-run eating as islanders do during the week, weekends are

Left, colorful catch awaits a beach picnic and, right, pumpkin pelau.

which attracts both wholesalers and retail shoppers. But most medium-sized towns boast their own markets. Back at home, the entire family is conscripted for odd tasks like shelling pigeon peas, cleaning *callaloo* leaves and okra, or peeling the ground provisions. And by late Sunday morning, the entire country is a scented room of seasoned selections.

Callaloo is a mixture of the leaves of the dasheen plant, similar to spinach and called *taro* by the Latins, pureed with chopped okra and flavored with either crab or salted pork. Both the dasheen and okra were brought here by African slaves and were a big part of the slave diet. The *callaloo* can be cooked with a hot pepper for that little extra kick. Generally it is poured over rice, and served with meat or poultry. Gourmets, however, serve it as a soup, an appetizer for the meal to come. *Callaloo* is such an important part of Trinidad and Tobago that in 1984, band leader Peter Minshall made it the theme of his Carnival celebration!

Coocoo is a blend of cornflour and okra, steamed with coconut milk into a cake that hardens after it cools, akin to grits or the Italian *polenta*. The okra moisturizes the *coocoo*, although it must still be eaten with lots of gravy to be swallowed smoothly.

If you don't happen to know any Trinidadians to invite you for a home-cooked meal, the Port of Spain Hilton puts on a Creole spread by the pool once a week which is surprisingly good and close to homemade.

Bush Meat and Seafood: Seafood, not surprisingly, is plentiful and widely consumed. Be on

game that more adventurous islanders enjoy. Some people's eyes glaze over when they speak of *manicou stew*, made with fried iguana or possum. Others love the tender meat of the *tatoo*, a species of armadillo, or *quenk*, a wild boar.

More common meats and poultry are likely to be browned down, which has the added effect of making the food a tad sweet. There's also a habit of slipping bits of vegetables into the browned down meat or poultry. And some stew beans in the pot, but more often that's done separately, and frequently flavored with pumpkin.

Pelau is used either as a side dish or a main course. Variations of this dish are infinite, but always the intent is to produce a sweetly spicy mix of rice, pigeon peas and vegetables. Every-

the lookout for beach parties—open to the public—in Tobago, where beachcombers can quickly "season down" something from the day's catch for a peppery fish broth. The *cascadura*, an oily river fish, has gained almost mythical proportions, allegedly responsible for luring Trinidadians and Tobagonians back home no matter where they roam. Kingfish usually dominates the day's ocean catch. A meaty fish similar to swordfish, it's often fried, curried a lot, and a favorite in fish broth. Red snapper, shark, grouper, bonito, carite, yellow tuna and salmon also fill the fishermen's nets. There are also good shrimp, chip-chip (a tiny, clam-like crustacean), lobster and oysters. And a beach party is probably the most likely place to find "bush meat," the several varieties of

one adds this or that little something else for a particular taste—a whole green pepper, coconut milk, or a bit of wine.

But enough! There's but so much reading one can do about all this delicious food. The taste of the pudding is in the eating, and fortunately, there's even a chance to get a taste of some of these foods in North America and Britain. A roti shop or restaurant always springs up wherever T&Ters and other West Indians find themselves.

Left, eating curry crab and, right, chopping Cocos Bay coconuts to sell in town. Following pages: liming ladies in St. Joseph; and, heliconia near Blue Basin.

TRAVEL TIPS

GETTING THERE

BY AIR

Almost touching the coast of South America, **Piarco Airport** in Trinidad is a good 6 hours from New York by plane. Tobago's **Crown Point Airport** is just 12 minutes flying time further, on one of the national carrier, **BWIA's** six daily flights.

Regular airfares to Trinidad and Tobago run relatively high. There are fewer air-plus-hotel packages than for some of the more heavily advertised and touristed Caribbean countries, but several airlines do offer them occasionally. Also, there are a number of specialized travel agencies, catering to the large Trinidadian populations of New York, Toronto, and Miami, who retain a reserve of charter seats on BWIA, familiarly known as Beewee. These round-trip fares are much lower than regular fares, making airfares to the Republic competitive with other islands. To find one of these neighborhood agencies, which often do not advertise, ask the people in the BWIA offices or the Tourism Development Authority (TDA) if they can suggest one. Another option is to make reservations for T&T during one of the airline price wars or discount periods, when carriers advertise low fares to "anywhere in the Caribbean." This can reduce fares by one-half to one-third; check the travel sections of the larger newspapers.

BWIA offers flights from Miami to Piarco Airport daily, from London and New York five days a week, Baltimore-Washington three times a week, Toronto twice, Stockholm and Frankfurt once a week. Most flights top briefly on one of the smaller islands like Barbados. When you buy your ticket to Piarco on BWIA anywhere outside of T&T, a round-trip connection to Tobago is included free of charge if you request it when you make your reservation. Otherwise, the round-trip fare is approximately TT$125.

American Airlines has daily nonstop service from San Juan, linked to cities throughout the US. There are also daily flights from Miami and New York on **Pan Am**, and from London on **British Airways. Air Canada's** direct flights leave from Toronto; some are nonstop, depending on the day of the week. **K.L.M.** flies to and from Amsterdam once a week. There are also connections to other Caribbean islands and South America via BWIA, **LIAT** (Leeward Island Air Transport), **LAV** (Linea Aeropostal Venezolana), and **Guyana Airways**.

Air Canada, tel: 664-4065 (reservations and flight information, 8 a.m.–4.30 p.m.), 800-422-6232 (toll free in US and Canada).
American Airlines, tel: 664-4731 (Piarco), 625-1661/2/3/4/5 (ticket office, Port of Spain), 800-433-7300 (toll free in US).
BWIA International, tel: 625-1010/9 (Port of Spain), 639-3291/3 (Tobago), 800-327-7401 (toll free in US and Canada).
British Airways, tel: 625-1811/6 (reservations), 625-1349 (flight information).
Cruziero Brazilian Airlines, tel: 623-5610 (Port of Spain), 625-1010 (BWIA for reservations).
Eastern Airlines, tel: 625-1671/2, 625-1655 (Port of Spain), 664-5458 (Piarco).
Guyana Airways, tel: 625-1171 (reservations and information).
KLM Royal Dutch Airlines, tel: 625-1719 (reservations).
Leeward Island Air Transport (LIAT), tel: 623-1837/8 (Port of Spain), 664-4268 (Piarco).
Linea Aeropostal (LAV), tel: 623-8201, 623-6522 (reservations).
Pan American World Airways, tel: 664-4839 (reservations and information, Piarco).

BY SEA

Trinidad and Tobago is developing its assets as a cruise destination through large scale expansion of Scarborough Harbor and other improvements. This, combined with a boom in the cruise industry, means new options for travelers and more cruise lines with one or both islands on their routes. Check with a travel agent before booking.

The main problem with taking the sea route is the difficulty in extending your stay beyond the few hours the ship is docked. Most cruise ship tickets are sold for complete voyages and you'll probably want to avoid the logistical maneuvering involved in a change.

The ships from the following cruise lines stop at Trinidad and/or Tobago.

Cunard Cruise Lines, tel: 800-327-9501.
Epirotiki Lines Inc. (World Renaissance), tel: 800-221-2470.
Princess Cruises, tel: 800-421-0522.
Windjammer Cruises, tel: 800-245-6338.

TRAVEL ESSENTIALS

VISAS & PASSPORTS

All visitors must have a return or ongoing ticket and a valid passport for entry into Trinidad and Tobago. Citizens of the UK, US and Canada do not need visas unless they are doing business in T&T. Visitors from certain European countries do need visas, however, so check with authorities in your own country before you go.

MONEY MATTERS

The TT dollar is the basic unit of currency in Trinidad and Tobago. At press time, the exchange rate was TT$4.25 to US$1. Since many TT$ prices are the same as they were before devaluation, Trinidad and Tobago is a more reasonably priced destination than it once was, especially if you buy goods and services geared to locals or West Indian travelers.

Currently, the TT dollar is classified as a "restricted currency," as a result of policies aimed at curbing inflation. For visitors, this means you should reconvert all the TT$ you have not spent before you leave Trinidad and Tobago, because you probably won't be able to do so in another country. Also, be sure to get a receipt for all cash and traveler's checks you change into TT$. You must show it in order to change your money back. There is no limit to the amount of foreign currency you can bring in, but TT$1,200 (worth about US$280) is the maximum you will be able to reconvert on departure.

The National Commercial Bank of Trinidad and Tobago has a foreign exchange branch at Piarco Airport (tel: 664-5281/5322), which changes British pounds, US and Canadian dollars and all Caribbean currencies for a small fee, but not Swiss or French francs or other European currencies. For these, you must go to a large bank in Port of Spain, so try to bring some US dollars or pounds sterling to change at the airport for initial expenses like a taxi to your hotel.

Major credit cards can be used at the larger hotels, restaurants and car rental firms throughout the islands, and at stores that cater mainly to visitors. However, many of the smaller hotels, guesthouses, restaurants and shops do not accept them, so it's wise to have an international brand of traveler's checks and a good supply of cash on hand.

HEALTH

Vaccinations for smallpox and yellow fever are not required for entry into T&T unless you have just passed through an infected area.

Throughout the Republic, the water is safe to drink and even street food is generally tasty and fresh for most of the year. However, during Carnival it's probably best to avoid the seafood and meat specials sold from numerous shanties around the Savannah. Often the food is cooked at the vendor's home in the morning, and stored without refrigeration throughout the day.

The National AIDS Program of Trinidad and Tobago also issues a timely remind for Carnival and all year round: "AIDS is preventable; don't give it to yourself." Avoid casual sex, any procedures which pierce the skin, and remember that alcohol abuse can affect your judgement.

The sun shines with dangerous intensity all year round. Wear ample sunscreen, built tanning time slowly up from 15 minutes in the early morning and late afternoon, and bring a hat or buy one.

WHAT TO WEAR

Casual clothes in lightweight fabrics are most comfortable for touring the countryside. In town, most men wear dark trousers and shirt-jacs, or more formal business suits. Women wear dresses or skirts and blouses for work and shopping. Note that skimpy clothing, particularly on women, will attract attention and probably occasion comment.

Even at the best restaurants there's not much call for evening wear. Casual clothes in lush colors and lavish fabrics prevail: in fashionable Trinidad a sense of style is what counts. On the beaches, anything goes. But, especially in Tobago, keep in mind that this is a small-town society, so the rules of small town propriety should be observed. Wear bathing suits on the beach only.

WHAT TO BRING

Don't forget your radio, especially as Carnival approaches, you won't want to turn it off. Also bring paperbacks, sunscreens, cosmetics, and any sporting goods you plan to use. Import duties raise the price of these goods, so it's probably better to bring them from home. If you plan to do much walking, either in the nature centers (bring insect repellent!) or to avoid the high private taxi fares, a pair of good tennis shoes will come in handy.

ON ARRIVAL

On the airplane or ship, just before you arrive, you will be asked to fill out an immigration form. Immigration officials collect one copy as you enter the country. Save the duplicate; you will need it for departure. Also be prepared to show your return ticket and give the address where you will be staying in Trinidad and Tobago. If you do not have a T&T address, Tourism Development Authority staff meet all flights and can provide information on accommodations available.

RESERVATIONS

Reservations will make your travels here run smoother. But you can probably find a room without advance reservations in Port of Spain or Tobago, though you may not get your first choice. The exception to this is Carnival season when reserving a room far in advance is essential, especially if you want to stay near to the Savannah.

CUSTOMS

What you can bring in: Personal effects are duty free, and adult visitors are allowed 50 cigars or 200 cigarettes or 1 pound of tobacco plus 1 quart (0.9 liter) of spirits, free of duty.

What you can take home: US Customs regulations allow each resident to take home purchases totaling US$400 without paying duty, provided that the resident has been out of the country at least 48 hours and has not claimed the exemption within the past 30 days. Family members living in the same household can pool their exemptions. You may also mail home any number of gifts worth up to $50 each, as long as one person doesn't receive more than $50 in one day. But these gifts may not include spirits, perfume or tobacco. For more information, write for the booklet *Know Before You Go* from the US Customs Service, Washington, DC 20229.

Returning residents of **Canada** who have been out of the country over 48 hous may bring back CAD$100 worth of merchandise without paying duty. The merchandise must accompany the resident, and the exemption, claimed in writing, may be taken no more than once per quarter. Canadians who have been abroad more than 7 days may also bring home duty-free goods worth up to $300 once each calendar year. These goods may be shipped separately, but must be declared when the traveler reaches Canada. Canadians are eligible to take *both* the $100 and $300 exemptions on separate trips, but the two cannot be combined. The duty-free totals may include up to 200 cigarettes, 50 cigars, 2 pounds of tobacco for residents over 16, 40 ounces of wine or liquor, or 24 cans of beer, if you meet the age regulations of the province where you arrive.

The total exemption for residents returning to the **United Kingdom** from outside the EEC is L32. This may include 9 fluid ounces (225 grammes) of toilet water, 2 fluid ounces of perfume (50 grammes), and for persons over 17, ½ pound (250 grammes) of tobacco, or 200 cigarettes, or 100 cigarillos, or 50 cigars. If you live outside Europe, double the tobacco limits. Duty-free alcohol is a liter of spirits or 2 liters of sparkling wine, plus 2 liters of still table wine.

It is better not to try to bring pets. Regulations are very strict regarding the entry of animals, requiring a 6-month period of quarantine.

ON DEPARTURE

If you are leaving by plane, plan to arrive at the airport 2 hours before your flight is due to depart. Last minute schedule changes are not unheard of, so reconfirm your reservation 24 hours in advance, and make sure the flight is on time before leaving for the airport. Allow extra time – at least an hour – to get to Piarco if you are going in a taxi or private car from Port of Spain during rush hour. Between about 6.30 and 8.45 a.m., and 3.30 and 5.45 p.m., traffic is horrendous and can cause frustrating delays.

Also note that there are some strict departure rules for business people: find out what regulations apply to you at least a week before your planned department, as they may necessitate a visit to various government offices that are not always open.

On leaving Trinidad and Tobago, you will be required to pay a TT$50 departure tax. You will also be asked to surrender the carbon copy of the Immigration Card you filled in on arrival. Beyond the customs and immigration checkpoint, the airport departure area has duty-free shops, refreshment stands, and telephones for overseas calls. Once you have entered this area you will not be allowed to leave it until your flight is called.

GETTING ACQUAINTED

GOVERNMENT & ECONOMY

Trinidad and Tobago became fully independent from Britain in 1962, and declared the Republic into being in 1976, when the President replaced the British Monarch as head of state. The government is a parliamentary democracy, headed by President, His Excellency, Noor Mohamed Hassanali, and governed by Parliament and the Prime Minister, The Honourable A.N.R. Robinson, who took office in 1986. Tobago's legislative body, the House of Assembly, sets domestic policy for that island.

Since gaining political independence, Trinidad and Tobago's leaders have also worked to achieve economic independence and stability. This goal seemed well within their grasp during the late 1970s, when prices for exported T&T oil were at an all-time high. But much has changed in the last decade. Oil prices declined precipitously, unemployment claimed more of the workforce, and a populace that had grown accustomed to prosperity began to experience harder times. Thirty years of uninterrupted rule by founding father, Dr. Eric Williams' People's National Movement (PNM) party came to an end. And the coalition of interest groups forming the National Alliance for Reconstruction, headed by Mr Robinson, began to fragment soon after the election. Beset by economic problems, the government has turned more attention to tourism, a source of hard currency that has remained uncultivated for many years, and encouraged light industries to diversify the country's economic base.

See the "History & People" section of this book for background on T&T's complex political and economic history.

GEOGRAPHY & POPULATION

Of all Caribbean islands, **Trinidad** is furthest south, just 7 miles (11 km) from the coast of Venezuela across the Gulf of Paria. Roughly triangular in shape, the island is about 50 miles (80 km) long and almsot 40 miles (64 km) wide, with three mountain ranges traversing the interior. These areas remain heavily forested and rich in wildlife. The east and west coasts tend to be swampy; the most popular beaches are in the north, over the mountains from Port of Spain, the capital. The south is very different, with its famous pitch lake, oilfields and several mud volcanos.

Fish shaped **Tobago** is 26 miles (41 km) long, 7 miles (11 km) wide and lies 21 miles (32 km) northeast of Trinidad. A central range of mountains forms a spine through the Tobago Forest Reserve in the north. Coral reefs surround much of the southern tip of the island. Several smaller islands lying off the coasts are wildlife sanctuaries.

As a nation, the population of Trinidad and Tobago is divided between roughly equal numbers of African and East Indian descendants, and much smaller percentages of Chinese, Europeans and Syrians. This diversity is mainly confined to Trinidad, however; in Tobago, over 90 percent of the people are of African descent.

TIME ZONES

Trinidad and Tobago operate one hour ahead of Eastern Standard Time, or the same as Eastern Daylight Savings Time.

CLIMATE

The weather is almost always perfect. Because of the trade winds, the sun's heat is mitigated by sea breezes. Average temperatures are 74˚F (23˚C) at night and 84˚F (28˚C) during the day. There are two seasons: the Wet and the Dry, from December to May and June to November respectively. All this means – except in late October and November, when hurricanes further north can create stormy weather – is that from June to December it rains briefly in the afternoon. June is the wettest month; February and March the driest. It never rains during Carnival.

CULTURE & CUSTOMS

The ambience on both islands is pleasantly relaxed, but good manners are important in Trinidad and Tobago. Visitors are expected to act like guests: to say "please" and "thank you," and to ask permission before taking anyone's picture. And although Trinidadians, in particular, have a disarming way of getting straight to the point in conversation, it's still inappropriate to launch right into a request for service or directions without a proper greeting – "hello, good morning," "good afternoon," or "good evening."

In T&T time tends to be enlarged. If your Trini friends say they'll pick you up at 8, they'll probably come closer to 9. Don't be insulted and don't worry about other appointments because the whole country is on the same schedule. "He's coming just now" may mean he'll be here any second or in the next day or two – often the latter. Slow down; it'll happen when it happens; "no problem." If you really need something done in a hurry, be polite and be persistent.

WEIGHTS & MEASURES

T&T uses the metric system. Given below are some standard equivalents of metric units:

1 inch = 2.54 centimeters
1 foot = 0.305 meters
1 mile = 1.609 kilometers
1 square mile = 2.69 square kilometers
1 gallon = 3.785 liters
1 ounce = 28.35 grams
1 pound = 0.434 kilograms

ELECTRICITY

Trinidad and Tobago operates on 110 volts and 60 cycles of electric current. If you need a transformer, most hotels can supply one.

BUSINESS HOURS

Monday through Friday, most shops and offices are open from 8 a.m. until 4 or 4.30 p.m. Some food stores stay open until 6 p.m., except on Thursdays when food and liquor stores close at noon. Saturday closing time is 12 noon or 1 p.m., except for food and liquor stores, which are open all day. Large malls like the Long Circular stay open late; other malls are open late on Friday and Saturday.

All banks stay open from 9 a.m.–2 p.m. Monday to Thursday, and from 9 a.m.–1 p.m. and 3 p.m.–5 p.m. on Fridays. Most of the major commercial banks have offices on Independence Square, as well as various branches.

HOLIDAYS

Public holidays when offices and most shops close are: **Good Friday, Easter Monday, Whit Monday** (8th Monday after Easter), **Corpus Christi, Labor Day** (June 19), **Emancipation Day** (August 1), **Independence Day** (August 31), **Eid-Ul-Fitr** (as decreed), **Divali** (as decreed), **Republic Day** (September 24), **Christmas Day** (December 25), **Boxing Day** (December 26).

In addition, Carnival, the raucous and unforgettable national party takes place on the Monday and (Shrove) Tuesday before Ash Wednesday – with the precise dates different each year. Though not a legally decreed holiday, it's safe to assume that a very relaxed attitude will prevail at any office that stays open.

FESTIVALS

Festivals include Carnival, the Steelband Music Festival (every 2 years), the Natural History Festival (in October), the annual Indian festivals of Phagwah, Divali Nagar, Eid ul-Fitr and Hosay, the Best Village Folk Festival (October–December), annual Flower and Orchid Shows (March and October), the Drama Festival (May, June), and Tobago's Heritage Festival (in July).

See the "Festivals" chapter for a closer look at T&T's many celebrations.

RELIGIOUS SERVICES

Many world religions and numerous denominations are represented in Trinidad and Tobago. The selection of religious groups and worship services below comes from a list compiled for visitor information by the Tourism Development Authority.

ANGLICAN
All Saints, 13 Queens Park West, Port of Spain, tel: 627-7004. Sunday 6 and 7.30 a.m., 6 p.m., daily 6 a.m.
St Andrew's Tobago, Scarborough, tel: 639-2485. Sunday 7.30 a.m.
St Paul's, Harris Promenade, San Fernando, tel: 652-2182. Sunday 6 a.m. and 7.30 a.m.
Trinity Cathedral, Abercromby Street, Port of Spain, tel: 623-7217. Sunday 6, 7.30 and 9 a.m., 6 p.m.

BAHA'I
Baha'i Meeting, Petra Street, Woodbrook. Sunday 8 a.m.

BAPTIST
Patna Baptist Church, Diego Martin. Sunday 10.30 a.m., 5.30 p.m.

BUDDHIST
Community Prayer, Methuen Street, Woodbrook. Sunday 10 a.m.

ROMAN CATHOLIC
Assumption, Long Circular Road, Maraval, tel: 622-5728. Saturday 6 p.m., Sunday 7 and 9 a.m., daily 6.30 a.m.
Cathedral of the Immaculate Conception, Independence Square, Port of Spain, tel: 623-5232. Saturday 7 a.m. and 7 p.m., Sunday 6.30, 8 and 9.15 a.m., 6.30 p.m.
Notre Dame de Bon Secous, Harris Promenade, San Fernando, tel: 652-2269. Saturday 7 p.m., Sunday 6, 7.30 and 9 a.m., 6 p.m., daily 6.15 a.m.

HINDU
Krishna Mandir, Todd Street, San Fernando. Sunday 7.30 a.m.
Port of Spain Mandir, Ethel Street, St James. Sunday 8 a.m., 6 p.m.

METHODIST
Hanover, corner of Duke and Abercromby streets, Port of Spain. Sunday 9 a.m. and 6 p.m.

MORAVIAN
Belmont, St Barbs Road. Sunday 8 a.m.

MORMON
8 Melville Lane, Port of Spain. Sunday 9 a.m.

MUSLIM
The Anjuman, Sunnat-Ul-Jamaat Assoc. Inc., Headquarters Jama Masjid, 2 Queen Street, Port of Spain, tel: 623-8963, 657-8373.

PENTACOSTAL
Chaguanas, Cumberbatch Street. Sunday 9.30 a.m.
Faith Center, 3–5 Prince of Wales Street, San Fernando. Sunday 8 a.m. and 6 p.m.
Pentacostal Cathedral, 29–31 Duke Street, Port of Spain, tel: 623-4335.

PRESBYTERIAN
Church of Scotland, 50 Frederick Street, Port of Spain. Sunday 8 a.m.
Church of Scotland, Scarborough, Tobago. Sunday 9 a.m. and 6.30 p.m.

COMMUNICATIONS

MEDIA

PRESS

There are two daily papers published in Port of Spain and distributed throughout Trinidad and spottily in Tobago. They are The Trinidad *Guardian* and *The Trinidad Express*.

A number of weekly tabloids are also available and popular. Though prone to lurid stories and bathing beauty photos, some also feature lively investigations and political debates. They include the *Bomb, Blast, Heat* and *The TNT Mirror* with its companion paper, *The Sunday Punch*. The Trinidad and Tobago Roman Catholic Church publishes *The Catholic News*.

The *Tobago News* is published daily in Scarborough, and is mainly concerned with news of the smaller island.

RADIO & TELEVISION

There are two national radio stations and one television station. The radio stations include **Radio 610** and **Radio Trinidad.**

The two television stations available without a satellite dish are **Trinidad and Tobago Television (TTT)** on Channel 2 and Channel 9. TTT is operated by the same board of directors as Radio 610. A number of hotels and individuals have satellite dishes enabling them to pick up American stations, cable networks and the like.

MAGAZINES & BOOKS

Several magazines devoted to local themes and/or the Caribbean are available on the islands. *People Magazine* is about local personalities, and *Carnival Magazine* is published around Carnival and features articles on the year's events. Souvenir magazines with profiles of various calypsonians also come out annually. Check record stores as well as bookstores for these.

There are several book and pamphlet publishers, and several interesting bookstores. (*See "Further Reading" for a listing of books*.) On a walking tour of bookstores in Port of Sapin, visit **Uptown Bookstore** on Oxford Street for general and scholarly reading; **Metropolitan** in the Colsort Mall and

R.I.K. in Frenchie's Arcade, both on Frederick Street, for good selections of magazines and bestsellers from overseas; and **Imprint Books**, specializing in local authors and its own publications, in the Express Building on South Independence Square. In Tobago, readers gravitate to Scarborough's attractive public library.

TELEPHONE & TELEX

The **area code** for Trinidad and Tobago is **809.**

Telco, the Trinidad and Tobago Telephone Company, Ltd., provides local and overseas calling. Their **International Calling Center** is located at 54 Frederick Street in Port of Spain. Direct dialing is available throughout T&T for both local and overseas calls.

Telco Service, Billing, and General Inquiries: 625-0515
Local Assistance: 6211
Overseas Assistance: 6311
Directory Inquiries: 6411

Charges for overseas calls are based on a 1 minute minimum for direct dialed calls, a 3 minute minimum for operator assisted station to station, and a 3 minute minimum plus 1 minute surcharge for person to person. A sampling of charges per minute to various countries in TT$ is:

Bahamas: $6
France: $6
Jamaica: $2.05
Japan: $10
Malaysia: $6.85
Sweden: $6.85

United Kingdom: Belfast – $5.50
London – $5.50

Canada: Alberta – $7.30
Ontario – $5.50

United States: Alabama – $5
Arizona – $8
New Jersey – $6
New York – $6

Inquiries for telegrams, cables and telexes can be made at post offices and hotel front desks. Cables may be handed in at the Tourism Development Authority on Frederick Street, Piarco Airport, post offices, hotel desks, or the offices of **Textel,** 1 Edward Street, Port of Spain. Textel also has branch offices in San Fernando and Scarborough.

POSTAL SERVICES

Located throughout the islands, Post Offices are open from 8 a.m.–4 p.m. Monday through Friday.

EMERGENCIES

SECURITY & CRIME

Wherever you travel, use common sense. Leave your hotel key at the desk when you go out, stay off deserted streets especially after dark, don't leave valuables unattended on the beach or in your room, and avoid conspicuously displaying money: a TT$20 bill may be a flashy sum when it's handed to a street vendor but not in a hotel restaurant.

Port of Spain is a big city, and big city precautions should be observed. Do not under any circumstances cross the Savannah at night, except during Carnival (and then only if it is well lit and full of people), watch for pickpockets, and compare taxi and other prices before you commit yourself. Generally even Port of Spain is relatively safe, compared to any big North American city, and one facet of Trinidadian hospitality is telling visitors when and how to be careful. Heed the warnings, but don't let them make you nervous.

TRINIDAD
Fire and Police: 990

TOBAGO
Police: 639-8888
Fire: 639-2108
Emergency: 990

MEDICAL SERVICES

For minor illnesses and cuts or bruises, some of the larger chain hotels have doctors or nurses on call. Major illnesses can be handled by specialists, most of whom are in or near Port of Spain. You might want to check with your hotel or embassy for recommendations.

Outlying areas are served by local Health Centers which offer free service to the public during specified hours. Major Hospitals include **The Mount Hope Medical Complex**, **San Fernando Medical Center**, and **Port of Spain Adventist Hospital**. Important phone numbers are:

TRINIDAD
Ambulance: 990

TOBAGO
General Hospital: 639-2551

GETTING AROUND

ORIENTATION

For advice before your trip, consult one of the **Tourism Development Authority** offices in Trinidad, New York, Miami, Toronto or London (*see "Useful Addresses"*). The **TDA Information Office** (tel: 664-5196) at Piarco Airport is open every day except Christmas from 6 a.m.–12 midnight. Here you will find friendly and efficient answers to questions about accommodations, transportation and events of interest to visitors. TDA staff also meet all cruise ships and arrange special activities like tours and calypso performances for the passengers.

The Trinidad and Tobago Hotel and Tourism Association is also happy to provide brochures on member hotels, and information about facilities and services. Write them at P.O. Box 243, Port of Spain; telephone or fax 624-3065.

FROM THE AIRPORT

TRINIDAD

Piarco Airport is located about 12 miles from Port of Spain. You can take a taxi into town; go by bus, which may involve carrying your bags some distance; or arrange to pick up a rental car, which will probably take a good bit of prior arranging. If you are traveling alone on a weekend, when the business districts of Port of Spain are fairly deserted, it is better to take taxi.

Go to the taxi dispatcher by the door of the Arrivals area, check the fare – it will probably be about TT$50 – and beware of the many drivers who rush up to offer their services; some are not above grossly overcharging. Driving time from the airport to the Savannah is about 30 minutes with minimal traffic; during rush hour it can take over an hour.

The bus stop is a covered walkway on the far side of a wide grassy traffic island (the scene of some sumptuous family picnics), directly opposite the Arrivals area. Buses run every hour on weekends, every half hour on weekdays. Buy a ticket just to the right of the Arrivals door or from the booth at the bus stop. Fares vary by distance – it's TT$1.50 to the terminal in Port of Spain – and the ride takes about 45 minutes via a special set of lanes reserved for buses. To go from the bus terminal to your hotel, you will have to take one of the route taxis which depart from stands several blocks' walk from the bus terminal. Depending on the location of your hotel, the fare will probably be a modest TT$2. Route taxis are discussed in the "Public Transport" section.

TOBAGO

When you make your reservation, find out whether your hotel has an airport transfer service and approximatley how long the drive is from the airport. Several of the hotels near Store Bay and Crown Point are in easy walking distance if you travel light. Others are a long and costly taxi ride away. Here too, if you take a taxi, consult the dispatcher, check the posted rates, and agree on the fare with the driver before setting out. Most of the drivers are well informed guides who will gladly take you on a tour later.

WATER TRANSPORT

Two ferries ply between Port of Spain and Scarborough, the *M.V. Tobago* and the *M.F. Panorama*. The trip takes 5 hours, and food and drinks are available on board. Cabins are available for TT$80, one way double occupancy, which might be a good idea if you take the 8 p.m. sailing. Tickets are sold only at the Port of Spain and Scarborough offices; passenger ticket sales close 2 hours before sailing time. For more information call 625-4906 in Port of Spain and 639-2417 in Tobago.

PUBLIC TRANSPORT

BUS

The **Public Service Transport Service (PTSC)** runs both buses and maxi-taxis. Buses go to every part of both islands, and are quite cheap. But because they are often hot and crowded, most tourists, and many locals, prefer the maxi-taxi which costs slightly more.

MAXI-TAXIS

These color-coded mini-buses follow particular routes on both islands. In Tobago, ask directions to the nearest stop. The table below provides information on some of the maxi-taxis departing from central Port of Spain.

ROUTE TAXIS

These cars carry up to 5 passengers along set routes from fixed stands to various destinations. Sometimes drivers will digress slightly for visitors if the car isn't crowded. Unless they render special services, drivers do not expect tips. In Scarborough, Tobago, route taxi stands are located across from the bus terminal and central shopping plaza. The table below states some routes and stands in Port of Spain

MAXI-TAXIS

From	To	Color	Fare
Charlotte Street, between Ind. Sq. & South Quay	Arima/Eastern Main Road	red	$1–3
Broadway	Arima/Highway	red	$3
Ind. Sq. South between Henry & Frederick streets	Chaguanas	green	$2.50
Chacon Street & Ind. Sq. South	Diego Martin/Petit Valley	yellow	$1.50
Ind. Sq. South between Henry & Frederick streets	San Fernando	green	$4

ROUTE TAXIS

From	To	Fare
Ind. Sq. South between Henry & Frederick streets	Arima	$4
Corner St Vincent & Park streets	Carenage	$2
Charlotte Street between Prince & Queen streets	Belmont/Gonzales	$1.50
Ind. Sq. North (facing East)	Long Circular via Wrightston Road	$2
Corner Duke & Charlotte streets	Maraval	$2
Corner Frederick & Hart streets	St Ann's	$2
Corner Frederick & Hart streets	St James	$2

HIRE TAXIS

Like route taxis, hire taxis have an **H** on their licence plates, but they are essentially private taxis, carrying only you and your companions exactly where you want to to. Hire taxis do not have meters and are rather expensive: at press time, a 30-minute ride from the Queen's Park Hotel to the airport was TT$50, from the Holiday Inn to Asa Wright TT$120, and from the Hilton to downtown – a briskly walkable distance – TT$20. In Tobago the fare from the airport to Speyside is approximately TT$100, to Scarborough TT$30. Usually rates are equivalent between drivers, but you can sometimes strike a bargain if you use the same driver for a number of trips or as a guide for a narrated tour: something most do with enthusiasm. Always agree on fares in advance. Also note that fares in Tobago double after 9 p.m.

Hire taxis wait near most large hotels. Below are a few taxi services:

Kapok Taxi Service, 16–18 Cotton Hill, St Clair, tel: 622-6995.
Himraj Taxi Rental Service, St Helena Village, Piarco, tel: 622-3566.
Queen's Park Taxi Stand, Queen's Park West, tel: 625-6005.
St Christopher Taxi Co-op Society, Ltd., tel: 624-3560, 624-3111 (Hilton, main office), 625-4531 ext. 1514 (Holiday Inn), or 625-3361, 625-1694.
Tobago Taxi Cab Co-op Society Ltd., tel: 639-2659 (Carrington Street), 639-2707 (Milford Road).
Tobago Taxi Owners and Drivers Association, tel: 639-2659 (Crown Reef Hotel), 639-2692 (downtown Scarborough).

DRIVING REGULATIONS

If you have a valid driver's licence from the US, Canada, France, UK, Germany or the Bahamas, you may drive in Trinidad and Tobago for a period of up to 3 months – but only the class of vehicle specified on your licence. (China, South Vietnam and South Africa are excluded from this privilege.) If your stay exceeds this limit, you must apply to the Licencing Department on Wrightston Road in Port of Spain. If your country has not signed the Convention on International Driver's Permits, check with the Tourism Development Authority to determine what rules apply.

While driving **stay to the left**, and at all times carry both your driver's licence and a document (such as a passport) certifying the date of your arrival in T&T.

RENTAL CARS

Car rental in T&T is handled by numerous local fleets. Many take credit cards for both rental fees and the substantial deposit (up to TT$1,000) that is often required. (Caution: Remember that there is a limit to the amount of TT$ you can reconvert on departure. If you expect the refund of a large TT$ deposit when you turn in your car, make sure it won't put you over the limit, or allow time to spend it.) Day rates for unairconditioned cars with manual transmission begin at about TT$120; weekly rates start at TT$725. The difficulty with car rental is that business clients engage many of the cars for long periods, so a short term rental can be hard to find. Plan to shop around well in advance and consult a travel agent for suggestions. A few rental firms follow.

TRINIDAD

Carr Rentals, Ltd., 34 Sydenham Avenue, St Ann's, tel: 624-1028.
Wong's Rentals, 114 Belmont Circular Road, Port of Spain, tel: 624-5385.
Econo-Car Rentals, Ltd., La Puerta Avenue and Diego Martin Main Road, Diego Martin, tel: 637-6891.
Premier Auto Rentals Ltd., St Ann's Village (at the Normandie), 10 Nook Avenue, tel: 624-7265.

TOBAGO

R.L. Rattan Car Rental Service, Shirvan Road, tel: 639-8271.
Tobago Travel, Ltd., P.O. Box 163, Tobago, tel: 639-8778, 639-8105.
Spence Rental Service, Crown Point, tel: 639-8082, 639-8781/4.
Banana Rentals, c/o Kariwak Village, Store Bay, tel: 639-8441, 639-8545.

SCOOTERS

You must be certified to ride a motorcycle or scooter on your driver's licence in order to rent one.

Banana Rentals, c/o Kariwak Village, Store Bay Road, Crown Point, Tobago, tel: 639-8441/8545.

HITCHHIKING

When driving in the country, you might see hitchhikers, particularly in Tobago. Everyone from schoolchildren to grandmothers hitch (though visitors shouldn't) and it's only friendly to "give a drop" to children, the elderly, and mothers with babies. Exercise more caution with young men.

WHERE TO STAY

Trinidad has a limited number of hotels, compared to the Caribbean's resort islands, and nothing that could be called a resort, American-style. As beautiful as the beaches are here, visitors come for music, culture, business, and Carnival, then retire to Tobago for relaxation. Many business travelers stay at the **Hilton** or the **Holiday Inn**, which have facilities for business people. The **Kapok Hotel** and **Hotel Normandie** also have large business clienteles and popular restaurants. Facing the Savannah within walking distance of downtown, the **Queen's Park Hotel** attracts value conscious Europeans and West Indians.

In the listing below, based on winter rates and subject to change, "inexpensive" generally means costing below US$30 per night, "reasonable" $30–$50, "moderater "$50–$80, "expensive" over $80 per night for a standard single room.

HOTELS

TRINIDAD

Bel Air International, Piarco Airport, tel: 664-4771/3. Moderate to Expensive.
Cactus Inn, Coconut Drive, Cross Crossing, San Fernando, tel: 657-2657/8. Reasonable.
Charconia Inn, 106 Saddle Road, Maraval, tel: 629-2101. Moderate.
Errol J. Lau, 66 Edward Street, Port of Spain, tel: 625-4381. Inexpensive.
Farrel House Hotel, Southern Main Road, Claxton Bay, San Fernando, tel: 659-2230, 659-2271/2. Reasonable.
Hilton International Trinidad, P.O. Box 442, Port of Spain, tel: 624-3211. Expensive.
Holiday Inn, P.O.Box 1017, Wrightston Road, Port of Spain, tel: 625-4531/8, 625-3361. Expensive
Hotel Normandie, P.O. Box 851, Nook Avenue, St Ann's, Port of Spain, tel: 624-1181/4. Moderate.
Kapok Hotel, 16–18 Cotton Street, Port of Spain, tel: 622-6441/4. Moderate.
Queen's Park Hotel, 5–5A Queen's Park West, tel: 625-1060/1. Reasonable.

TOBAGO

Arnos Vale, P.O. Box 208, Scarborough, tel: 639-2881. Expensive.

Blue Waters Inn, Batteaux Bay, Speyside, tel: 660-4341. Moderate.
Cocrico Inn, Plymouth, tel: 639-2961. Moderate.
Crown Point Beach Hotel, Crown Point, tel: 639-8781. Expensive.
Crown Reef Hotel, Store Bay, Tobago, tel: 639-8781. Expensive.
Grafton Hotel, Black Road.
Jimmy's Holiday Resort, Crown Point, tel: 639-8292. Reasonable to Moderate.
Kariwak Village, P.O. Box 27, Scarborough, tel: 639-8545. Moderate.
Man-O-War Cottages, Charlotte, tel: 639-4327. Reasonable.
Mount Irvine Bay Resort, P.O. Box 222, Scarborough, tel: 639-8871. Expensive.
Sandy Point Beach Club, P.O. Box 223, Crown Point, tel: 639-8533. Moderate.
Tropikist Beach Hotel, Crown Point, tel: 639-8512. Reasonable.
Turtle Beach Hotel, Courtland Bay, tel: 639-2851. Expensive.

GUEST HOUSES

TRINIDAD

Alicia's House, 7 Coblentz Gardens, St Ann's, Port of Spain, tel: 623-2802. Reasonable.
Kestour's Sports Villa, 58 Carlos Street, Woodbrook, Port of Spain, tel: 628-4028.
Monique's Guest House, 114 Saddle Road, Maraval, Port of Spain, tel: 629-2233. Reasonable.
Mount St Benedict Guest House, The Abbey of Mount St Benedict, Tunapuna, tel: 662-4084. Reasonable.
Zollna House, 12 Ramlogan Development, LaSeiva, Maraval, tel: 628-3731. Reasonable.

TOBAGO

Coral Reef Guest House, Milford Road, Scarborough, tel: 639-2536. Reasonable.
Della Mira Guest House, Bacolet Street, Scarborough, tel: 639-2531. Reasonable.
Richmond Great House, Belle Garden, tel: 660-4467. Reasonable.

BED & BREAKFAST

The **Bed and Breakfast Association of Trinidad and Tobago** publishes a leaflet listing a number of private homes with one or more rooms to spare. All have been inspected and many have extra features like television and access to kitchens. Breakfast is included in rates which range from US$17–$40, slightly higher during Carnival. TDA offices have information or write the Association at Diego Martin: P.O. Box 3231, Diego Martin, Republic of Trinidad and Tobago; or phone Miss Grace Steele (809) 637-9329, or Mrs Barbara Zollna (809) 628-3731 or 660-4341.

SPECIAL ACCOMMODATIONS

Asa Wright Nature Center, Blanchicheuse, tel: 667-0493. For reservations call in the US (212) 840-5961.

FOOD DIGEST

Travelers from the budget conscious student to the business executive can find food to suit their tastes and pockets, though food prices on the whole are relatively high. The more expensive hotels tend to serve a kind of bland continental cuisine, but some offer special creole meals.

Restaurants run the gamut from roti shops frequented by work people to sophisticated restaurants housed in restored Victorian mansions, serving the best French, creole, Indian, and Asian cuisines. Roadside stands proliferate, as do American-style fast-food outlets.

WHERE TO EAT

PORT OF SPAIN & VICINITY

Cafe Savannah, Kapok Hotel, tel: 622-6441. French cuisine.

Chaconia Inn, Saddle Road, tel: 629-2101. Varied cuisine, barbeques.

Chequers, 100 Saddle Road, Maraval, tel: 628-7007. Grilled meats and seafood, live entertainment.

China Palace, 5 Maraval Road, tel: 628-6439. Chinese cuisine.

Copper Kettle Grille, 66–68 Edward Street, tel: 625-4381. Grilled meat and seafood, creole specialties.

Cricket Wicket, 149 Tragarete Road, tel: 622-1808. Pub fare.

Cuisine Creole, 31 Abercromby Street. Homestyle creole.

The Hott Shoppe, Murcurapo Road and Maraval Road. Roti.

House of Buss-Up-Shut, Upper Edward Street. Roti.

House of Chan, 83–85 Picton Street, Newton, tel: 622-1304. Chinese cuisine.

JB's Restaurant, Valpark Shopping Plaza, tel: 662-5837. American cuisine.

L&L Caterers, 53 Park Street, tel: 625-9807. Creole lunches.

La Boucan, Hilton Hotel, tel: 624-3111. International and West Indian specialties.

La Fantasie, Hotel Normandie, tel: 624-1181/4. International.

La Ronde, Holiday Inn, tel: 625-3361. French cuisine.

Le Chateau Creole, 3 Herbert Street, St Clair, tel: 622-2353.

Mangal's, 13 Queen's Park East, tel: 624-4639. Indian cuisine.

Rafters, corner of Warner and Woodford streets, Newtown. Steak and seafood.

Seabelle, 27 Mucurapo Road, St James, tel: 622-3594.

Singho, Long Circular Mall, tel: 628-2077. Chinese cuisine.

Tiki Village, Kapok Hotel, tel: 622-6441. Chinese and Polynesian.

Veni Mange, Lucknow Street, St James. French creole specialties.

ELSEWHERE IN TRINIDAD

Cactus Inn, Coconut Drive, Cross Crossing, San Fernando, tel: 657-5665.

Farrell House, Claxton Bay, San Fernando, tel: 659-2271.

Horace's Garden Restaurant, 6–8 Farah Street, San Fernando, tel: 657-8331.

Soon's Great Wall, 97 Circular Road, San Fernando, tel: 652-2583.

TOBAGO

Arnos Vale Hotel, Arnos Vale Road, Plymouth, tel: 639-2881/2. Creole and Continental.

Blue Crab, Main and Robinson streets, Scarborough, tel: 639-2737. Specializes in local food and drink.

Blue Waters Inn, Speyside, tel: 660-4341. Creole and International food.

Cocrico Inn, Plymouth, tel: 639-2961. Tobagonian cooking.

The Flamboyant, Crown Point, Store Bay, tel: 639-8793.

The Golden Rooster, Sangster's Hill, tel: 639-5557. Pizza, burgers and dinners; delivers.

Grandma's Kottage, Burnett Street, Scarborough, tel: 639-3259. *Coocoo, calalloo* and other local dishes.

Jemma's Seafood Kitchen, Speyside, tel: 660-4066. Local and seafood specialties.

Kariwak Village, Store Bay Road, Crown Point, tel: 639-8545. Authentic Caribbean and homemade pastry.

Old Donkey Cart, Bacolet Street, Scarborough, tel: 639-3551. Creole and International dishes, German wine list.

Papillon, Old Grange Hill, Mount Irvine Village, tel: 639-0275. Seafood.

Pidgeon Point Restaurant and Bar, Pigeon Point, tel: 639-8141. Open 8 a.m.–6 p.m., sandwiches and local food.

Sugar Mill, Mount Irvine Bay Hotel, tel: 639-8871. Local seafood and creole dining.

DRINKING NOTES

Mixed drink specialties in Trinidad and Tobago revolve around rum, and it's not hard to find a rum punch that will infuse any time of year with a bit of Carnival. Trinidad is also home to Angostura Bitters, a secret concoction that has been adding zest to mixed drinks for generations. Two popular brands of beer are Stag and Carib. And don't forget to sample local soft drink favorites like sorrel, ginger beer and mauby.

THINGS TO DO

You'll find information and phone numbers for Trinidad and Tobago's main visitor attractions in the walking and driving tours that make up the "Places" section of this book.

OTHER VISITS

If your main stop is Trinidad, don't leave without spending some time in Tobago – or vice versa. BWIA has one-day packages to Tobago at a cost of TT$130, including transfers to the beach at Pigeon Point and a trip to Buccoo Reef. Tickets are sold only at BWIA offices and must be bought at least 24 hours in advance.

Nealco Air Services (tel: 664-5416, Piarco; 625-3426, Port of Spain) can arrange plane and helicopter sightseeing trips within Trinidad and Tobago and to other islands.

Pan American's daily flights from New York's John F. Kennedy Airport stop first in Caracas before landing at Piarco. If you've never visited South America (or even if you have), you can easily arrange a stop-over which includes a hotel, or make reservations yourself.

CRUISES

Jolly Roger, Point Gourde Road, just beyond the Small Boats Jetty, tel: 634-4334. Wednesdays, Calypso Cruise; Fridays, Heart to Heart Cruise. Boarding time 8.30 p.m., cruise 9 p.m. to midnight.

TOUR GUIDES

Caroni Bird Sanctuary, tours daily from 4.30 p.m.– 7 p.m.
Mr Winston Nanan, tel: 645-1305.

Mr David Ranasahai & Sons, tel: 663-2207, 645-4705.

TOUR OPERATORS

Bruce/Ying Tours, 99 Queen Street, Port of Spain, tel: 628-1851.
Trinidad and Tobago Sightseeing Tours, 10 Fitt Street, Woodbrook, Port of Spain, tel: 624-1984.
Eastman Tours, 1 Herbert Street, Newtown, tel: 628-1851.
Tobago Travel Ltd., Storebay, tel: 639-8778.

CULTURE PLUS

In addition to Carnival and the indigenous arts of calypso and steelband, Trinidad and Tobago boasts a number of theaters, museums, art galleries and festivals. T&T has also produced some of the region's best known and finest writers and performers, and much of the current crop of plays, verbal art and choreography is performed regularly. Check newspapers for special events during your visit.

ART GALLERIES & MUSEUMS

Aquarela Galleries, 1A Dere Street, Port of Spain, tel: 625-5982. Open Monday–Friday 9.30 a.m.– 5.30 p.m; Saturday and Sunday 10 a.m.–2 p.m.
Art Creators, Flat # 402, 7 Queen Ann's Road, Port of Spain, tel: 624-4369. Open Monday–Friday 10 a.m.–1 p.m., 4 p.m.–7 p.m; Saturday 10 a.m.–12 noon.
National Museum, 117 Frederick Street, Port of Spain, tel: 623-7166. Open Tuesday–Saturday 10 a.m.–6 p.m.
National Fine Arts Center, Orange Hill Road, Scarborough, tel: 639-6897.

CONCERTS

Queen's Hall, 1–3 St Ann's Road, St Ann's, Port of Spain, tel: 624-1284. Music, fashion shows and other events.
Hilton International, Port of Spain, tel: 624-3211, 624-3111. Check for periodic concerts in the Ballroom.
Spektakula Forum, 111 Henry Street, Port of Spain, tel: 623-2870, 623-0125, 625-0652. Venue for a number of leading calypsonians.

THEATERS

Astor Theater, French and Baden Powell streets, Port of Spain, tel: 628-7407.
Central Bank Auditorium, 1 St Vincent Street, Port of Spain, tel: 625-4921 ext. 2665.
Little Carib Theater, Corner Roberts and White streets, Woodbrook, Port of Spain, tel: 622-4644.

MUSIC

For those who want to hear steelband music, panyards dot the city: open lots where the bands practice regularly – particularly in the weeks leading up to Carnival. They do not stage shows, since this is truly practice space, but there is something about hearing the sparkling sound of a steelband at night that is more thrilling than staged events. This way you can decide on your favorites before the competition begins. Following is a randomly selected list of panyards around the country. Usually, the music starts around 7 p.m.

NORTH

Neal & Massy All Stars, Duke Street, P.O.S.
Blue Diamonds, George Street, P.O.S.
Witco Desperados, Laventille Community Center, Laventille.
Ebony, Lange Street, Gonzales.
Humming Birds Pan Groove, Fort George Road, St James.
Trintoc Invadors, Tragarette Road, P.O.S., opposite the oval.
Juba Youths (Pan Round Neck), Majuba Cross Road, Petit Valley.
Kool, 25–27 Baneres Road, St James.
Music Makers (Pan Round Neck), Picton Road, Laventile.
Pan Genesis, 1 Car Lane, Belmont.
Phase II Pan Grove, 13 Hamilton Holder, Woodbrook.
T & TEC Power Stars, 14 Western Main Road, St James.
Amoco Renegades, 17A Oxford Street, P.O.S.
Laventile Sound Specialists, Eastern Quarry, Laventille.
Trinidad Syncopators, Upper Duke Street, P.O.S.
Carib Tokyo, 1 St Joseph Road, P.O.S.
Valley Harps, Morne Coco Road, Petit Valley.

SOUTH

Tropical Angel Harps, Enterprise Village, Chaguanas.
Antillean All Stars, 8–10 Carib Street, San Fernando.
Siparia Deltones, Railroad Road, Siparia.
Hatters, Lady Hailes Avenue, San Fernando.
Jah Roots, Warden Road, Port Fortin.
Couva Joylanders, Railway Road, Couva.
Mooseians Pan Soca, Erin Road, Siparia.
Pan Patriots, Charlo Village, Penal.

Skiffle Bunch, (Pan Round Neck), Lambie Street, Vistabella, San Fernando.

EAST

Tunapuna All Stars, Railway Road, Tunapuna.
Bethel Gospel Tones, 2 Amorall Avenue, Arima.
National Quarries Cordettes, Moonoo Street, Sangre Grande.
Hometwon Facinators, La Pastora, Santa Cruz.
Klondykes Pan Sounds, Macoya Road, Tunapuna.
Melodians, Bellamy Street, Cocorite Road, Arima.
Potential Symphony, Upper Sixth Avenue, Malick Bataria.
Textel Pantastic Sounds, Old Southern Main Road, Curepe.

NIGHTLIFE

If an evening of theater or steelband music doesn't excite you, your best bet is probably dinner and dancing at one of the hotels, or a disco. At the Hilton's **Aviary Bar**, dancing and live music begin at 9 p.m. The Holiday Inn's **Calypso Lounge** also features live performers. **JB's Disco** at the Valpark Plaza shopping center is a neighborhood favorite; ask someone local for directions. On weekends the **Chaconia Inn** is a hotspot for the younger generation. Or dance until you drop at **Bedrock City** on Ariapita Road in St Ann's.

Tobago nights tend to have a heavy tropic darkness that calls for cool, rich sounds. You may find them when **Kariwak Village** follows its dinner buffet with a smooth and mellow brand of live music. The most sophisticated spots are the larger hotel bars at **Arnos Vale** and **Mount Irvine Bay**.

SHOPPING

The T&T mix of ethnic backgrounds provides a wide variety of shopping possibilities, particularly in Asian and East Indian goods. Silver filigree is an Indian specialty sold at Piarco as well as in Port of Spain and San Fernando at large stores. Fine silks and fabrics are sold in many fabric stores on **Frederick Street** and **Long Circular Mall**. Ask your hotel or local friends to recommend a tailor, and take home a made-to-order version of the casual clothes Trinidadians are famous for.

Traditional crafts have been largely supplanted by better paying jobs, but straw baskets, hats, and handbags are still available from street-corner vendors, and some young craftsmen have added new twists to old ideas – the handsomely carved calabash handbags sold on lower Frederick Street, for example. **Handicraft Co-Op** at the Hilton and the **Trinidad and Tobago Blind Welfare League** shop (118 Duke Street) have large selections of traditional and not-so-traditional work. **The Market** at the Hotel Normandie is home to **We Make It** and **Village Craft**, along with the specialty shops of **Gillian Bishop**, a noted jeweler, and **Josie's** hand-dyed fabrics. **Les Soeur** in the Galleria Shopping center features crafts that include copper work by Jacqueline Leera. Steelpans are expensive and cumbersome, but for serious musicians the real thing is available chromed and unchromed from **Lincoln Enterprises**, 18 Gallus Street in Woodbrook. Or take home one of the tourist versions producing a few notes that department stores sell.

Though not a duty-free shopper's mecca, Trinidad and Tobago does have its fair share of tempting jewels and scents. The largest selections are at **Y. de Lima** and especially **Stecher's**, with its main store on Frederick Street in Port of Spain and branches at the Hilton and in Tobago. Here you will find china, woolens, watches, crystal, perfume and other duty-free staples. Your bargain hunting will be enhanced if you know what you want and check prices at home for comparison.

SPORTS

SPECTATOR

Trinidadians love to play games of all sorts, especially cricket, and there are numerous opportunities to watch a game on a neighborhood or international level. There's also horseracing at the Savannah, among other places. For information about spectator events, check the newspaper or call the **Jean Pierre Sports Complex** (tel: 623-0305) and **Queen's Park Cricket Club** (tel: 622-3787).

PARTICIPANT

With the perfect climate and diverse geography of the islands it would be difficult to avoid participating in some form of physical activity, whether it's joining the parade of morning joggers circling the Savannah or cycling over back roads in Tobago. Golf, fishing, tennis and running are a few of the sports featured in special tournaments and competitive events; check with the TDA for more information. The following list notes some facilities for the more popular sports.

DEEP SEA FISHING

Pigeon Point: check with Mr Lennox Park at Pigeon Point Resort Restaurant for information on boat charters in Tobago, or inquire at your hotel.

DIVE OPERATORS

TRINIDAD
Scuba Shop Ltd., 120 Kajim Street, Union Park West, Marabella, tel: 658-2183.

TOBAGO
Tobago Scuba, Ltd., Speyside, tel: 660-4066, 660-4327.
Dive Tobago, Pigeon Point, tel: 639-2266, 639-2385, 639-8533/4, 639-8309.
Tobago Marine Sports, tel: 639-8571.
Paradise Seas Sports, Speyside, tel: 639-8545, 660-4360.
Tobago Dive Experience, Blue Waters, Speyside, tel: 639-0343, and in Trinidad 639-0343.

GOLF

TRINIDAD
St Andrews Golf Club, Moca, Maravali,
tel: 629-2314.

TOBAGO
Mount Irvine Bay Hotel, tel: 639-8871.

SQUASH

TRINIDAD
Long Circular Mall, tel: 622-3470. Advance booking required.
Valley Vue Squash Courts, St Ann's, tel: 627-8046.

TENNIS

TRINIDAD
Hilton Hotel

TOBAGO
Arnos Vale
Mount Irvine Hotel
Turtle Beach Hotel
Crown Reef Hotel

FURTHER READING

Anthony, Michael and Andrew Carr. *David Frost Introduces Trinidad & Tobago*. London: Andre Deutsch, 1975.

Bickerton, Dereck. *The Murders of Boysie Singh*. London: Arthur Baker Ltd., 1962.

Boomert, Arie. *"Our Amerindian Heritage."* Port of Spain: Trinidad Naturalist, 4:4, 1982.

Boomert, Arie. *"The Arawak Indians of Trinidad and Coastal Guyana, ca 1500–1650."* Journal of Caribbean History 19:2. University of the West Indies, 1986.

Borde, Pierre Gustav. *History of the Island of Trinidad under the Spanish Government*. Vols. I & II. Port of Spain: Paria Publishing Co., 1982.

Braithwaite, Lloyd. *Social Stratification in Trinidad*. Jamaica: Institute of Social and Economic Research, 1975.

Brereton, Bridget. *Race Relations in Colonial Trinidad 1870–1900*. Cambridge: Cambridge University Press, 1979.

Brereton, Bridget. *A History of Modern Trinidad 1783–1962*. London: Heinemann, 1981.

Calder-Marshall, Arthur. *Glory Dead*. London: Michael Joseph, 1939.

Carmichael, Gertrude. *The History of the West Indian Islands of Trinidad and Tobago*. Port of Spain: Columbus Publishers, 1986.

Ffrench, Richard and Peter Bacon. *Nature Trails of Trinidad*. Trinidad & Tobago: S.M. Publications, 1982.

Gomes, Albert. *Through a Maze of Colour*. Port of Spain: Key Caribbean Publications, 1974.

Hargreaves, Dorothy and Bob. *Tropical Tree*. Kailva, Hawaii: Hargreaves Co., 1965.

Hill, Errol. *The Trinidad Carnival: Mandate for a National Theatre*. Texas: University of Texas Press, 1972.

Jacobs, Richard. *Butler Versus the King*. Port of Spain: Key Caribbean Publications, 1975.

James, C.L.R. *Life of A.A. Cipriani*. Lancashire: Nelson, 1932.

James, C.L.R. *Beyond a Boundary*. Jamaica: Sangsters, 1963.

Jones, Anthony, Mark. *The Winston "Spree" Simon Story*. Port of Spain: Educo Press, 1982.

Lewis, Gordon K. *The Growth of the Modern West Indies*. New York: Monthly Review Press, 1968.

Lewis, W.A. *Labour in the West Indies*. London: New Beacon Books, 1977.

Martin, Tony. *The Pan African Connection: From Slavery to Garvey and Beyond*. Massachussets: The Majority Press, 1983.

Naipaul, V.S. *The Middle Passage*. Harmondsworth: Penguin Books, 1962.

Naipaul, V.S. *The Loss of El Dorado*. Harmondsworth: Penguin Books, 1973.

Naipaul, V.S. *Finding the Centre*. London: Andre Deutsch, 1984.

Newson, Linda. *Aboriginal and Spanish Colonial Trinidad*. London: Academic Press, 1976.

Nunley, John W. *Caribbean Festival Arts: Each and Every Bit of Difference*. London and Seattle: Saint Louis Art Museum in association with The University of Washington Press, 1988.

Oxaal, Ivar. *Black Intellectuals Come to Power*. Cambridge, Mass.: Schenkman Publishing Company, 1968.

Quevedo, Raymond. *Atilla's Kaiso: A Short History of Trinidad calypso*. St Augustine: University of the West Indies, 1983.

Ramdin, Ron. *From Chattel Slave to Wage Earner*. London: Martin Brian & O'Keefe, 1982.

Robinson, Arthur N.R. *Mechanics of Independence*.

Ryan, Selwyn. *Race and Nationalism in Trinidad and Tobago*. Toronto: University of Toronto Press, 1972.

Ryan, Selwyn. *The Politics of Succession*. St Augustine: University of the West Indies, 1979.

Sander, Reinhard W., ed. *From Trinidad: An Anthology of early West Indian Writing*. London: Hodder & Stoughton, 1978.

Warner, Keith. *The Trinidad Calypso*. London: Heinemann, 1982.

Williams, Eric. *History of the Peoples of Trinidad and Tobago*. Port of Spain: PNM Publishing Co., 1962.

Williams, Eric. *Inward Hunger: The Education of a Prime Minister*. London: Andre Deutsch, 1969.

Williams, Eric. *Forged From the Love of Liberty: Selected Speeches*. Port of Spain: Longmans Caribbean, 1982.

The books listed above are non-fiction, historical or biographical accounts. By themselves they will give the reader a general outline of the facts of Trinidad and Tobago's history. However, to get a feel for the experience of that history, the reader must turn to the country's creative writers, for only they can transform knowledge into understanding. A short list must include:

Boissiere, Ralph de. *Crown Jewel*. London: Pan Books, 1981.

Burnett, Paula, ed. *The Penguin Book of Caribbean Verse in English*. Harmondsworth: Penguin Books, 1986.

Lovelace, Earl. *The Dragon Can't Dance*. London: Andre Deutsch, 1979.

Mittelholzer, Edgar. *A Morning at the Office*. London: Heinemann Educational Books, 1974.

Naipaul, V.S. *The Mystic Masseur*. Harmondsworth: Penguin Books, 1964.

Naipaul, V.S. *The Suffrage of Elvira*. Harmondsworth: Penguin Books, 1969.

Naipaul, V.S. *A House for Mr Biswas*. Harmondsworth: Penguin Books, 1969.

Naipaul, V.S. *The Mimic Men*. Harmondsworth: Penguin Books, 1969.

Resistance, Brother. *Rapso Explosion*. London: Karia Press, 1986.

Selvon, Samuel. *A Brighter Sun*. London: Longman Books Ltd., 1979.

Walcott, Derek. *Sea Grapes*. London: Jonathan Cape Ltd., 1976.

Walcott, Derek. *The Star Apple Kingdom*. London: Jonathan Cape Ltd., 1980.

Walcott, Derek. *The Fortunate Traveller*. London: Jonathan Cape Ltd., 1983.

Finally, the reader is invited to listen, if possible, to the wit and wisdom of Trinidad and Tobago's calypsonians, for their range of oral history and poetry, social commentry and bawdiness, nonsense rhyme and satire, scandal mongering and fantasy has no parallel in any other art form.

USEFUL ADDRESSES

TOURISM DEVELOPMENT AUTHORITY OFFICES

Trinidad: 122–124 Frederick Street, Port of Spain, tel: (809) 623-1932/4, 623-1142

Tobago: Division of Tourism, Tobago House of Assembly, Scarborough Mall, Scarborough, tel: (809) 639-2125.

New York: Forest Hills Tower, 18–35 Queen's Blvd, New York, NY 11375, tel: (212) 838-7750/1.

Miami: 330 Biscayne Bay Blvd, Suite 310, Miami, Florida 33122

Toronto: 40 Holly Street, Suite 102, Toronto M4S 3C3, tel: (416) 486-4484, 486-4470.

London: 48 Leicester Square, WC2H 7QD, London, England, tel: (441) 930-6566/7.

CONSULATES

Austria: 27 Frederick St., P.O.S., tel: 623-2586, 623-6170.

Barbados: 13A, Pembroke Street, P.O.S., tel: 622-0866.

Belgium: c/o Co-operative Citrus Growers Association, Eastern Main Road, Laventille, tel: 623-4195.

Colombia: 67 Independence Square, P.O.S., tel: 623-6601, 627-7385.

Costa Rica: 9 Knightsbridge Road, Cascade, tel: 624-1217.

Denmark: 72–74 South Quay, P.O.S., tel: 623-4700.

Dominican Republic: 9 Knightsbridge Road, Cascade, tel: 624-1217

El Salvador: 58 Ellerslie Park, tel: 622-6247.

Finland: 14 Rookery Nook, Maraval, tel: 622-1061.

Guyana: 51–53 Dundonald Street, P.O.S., tel: 625-5117/3.

Italy: 47 Rockdale Road, tel: 637-3275.

Liberia: 64 Lorndale Road, Glencoe, tel: 637-3730.

Norway: c/o Melville Shipping Company, 18–20 London Street, P.O.S., tel: 625-1933, 625-2384.

Peru: 23 Frederick St., P.O.S., tel: 623-1366.

Portugal: 11–13 Milling Avenue, P.O. Box 283, Sea Lots, P.O.S.

Spain: 78 Wrightston Road, P.O.S., tel: 625-4324.

Senegal: 110 Frederick Street, P.O.S., tel: 623-2833, 623-2117.

Switzerland: 18–20 Pembroke Street, P.O.S., tel: 623-2897.

Turkey: 88–90 Abercromby Street, P.O.S., tel: 623-5565.
Venezuela: 42 Murray Street, Woodbrook, tel: 638-2452/3/4.

EMBASSIES

Argentina: 16, Victoria Avenue, P.O.S., tel: 623-4445.
Brazil: 6 Elizabeth Street, St Clair, tel: 662-5779.
China: 39 Alexandra Street, P.O.S., tel: 622-6976.
Colombia: 67 Independence Square, P.O.S., tel: 623-6601, 623-7385.
France: 3 Rapsey Street, St Clair, P.O.S., tel: 622-7446.
Germany: 7–9 Marli Street, P.O. Box 828, P.O.S., tel: 628-1630.
Japan: 5 Hayes Street, St Clair, tel: 625-5838.
Mexico: 84–86 Independence Square, P.O.S., tel: 625-3439.
Royal Netherlands: 90 Independence Square, P.O.S., tel: 625-1722.
United States of America: 15 Queen's Park West, P.O.S., tel: 622-6371.
Venezuela: 6 Mary Street, St Clair, tel: 622-2468/9.

HIGH COMMISSIONS

Barbados: 82 Long Circular Road, Maraval, tel: 622-0866, 622-0492.
Britain: 90 Independence Square, P.O.S., tel: 625-2861/2/3/4/5/6.
Canada: 72–74 South Quay, P.O.S., tel: 623-7254/8.
India: 87 Cipriani Blvd, P.O.S., tel: 627-7480.
Jamaica: 2 Newbold Street, St Clair, tel: 622-4995/6/7.
New Zealand: Resident Acting High Commissioner, 12 St Andrews Terrace, tel: 628-3754.
Nigeria: 3 Maxwell-Phillip Street, St Clair, tel: 622-6834/6.

ART/PHOTO CREDITS

Photography by

Page 16/17, 20, 21, 38, 39, 41, 42, 44, 46, 49, 50, 51, 52, 53, 55, 56, 57, 63, 71, 73L*, 79, 99, 102/103, 104*, 106, 108, 110, 111, 118, 126, 134, 136, 145, 155, 161R, 165, 166, 167L, 168, 175R, 176, 198, 200, 202, 203, 204, 207R, 208, 209, 210, 211, 214/215, 219, 221R, 229, 230, 234, 235, 237, 242, 243, 244, 245, 246, 247, 248, 252, 253, 256	Junia Browne
12/13, 105, 109, 112/113, 114/115, 167R, 169, 186, 194/195, 201, 255	Courtesy of T&T Tourism Development Authority
60, 68, 70, 86/87, 88, 89, 90, 91, 96, 98, 137L, 164, 228, 232, 233, 249, 250	Edmond Van Hoorick Fotograf
223, 224, 225	Stephen Frink
48	Harper & Row Publishers
107L&R	John Hill
216, 220, 221L, 222	Ian Lambie
47	Luis Marden/Courtesy of National Geographic Society
14, 212/213	Norman Parkinson
18*, 22*, 23*, 24*, 25*, 26*, 27*, 29*, 30*, 33*, 34*, 35*, 37*, 40*, 45*, 58*, 81, 97, 207L, 231*, 236*, 238*, 239*, 240*, 254	Elizabeth Saft
10/11, 61, 83, 94, 140L, 183, 196	Richard Spence
241	Travel Holiday, New York
Cover, 3, 5, 6/7, 8/9, 54, 64/65, 66/67, 69, 72L&R, 73R, 75, 76, 77, 78, 80, 82, 84/85, 92/93, 100/101, 116/117, 120/121, 122, 127L&R, 128, 129, 131, 132, 133, 135, 137R, 138, 139, 140R, 141, 142, 143, 146/147, 150, 152, 153, 154, 156, 157, 158, 159, 160, 161L, 162, 163L&R, 170, 171, 172, 173, 174, 175L, 177, 178, 179, 180, 181, 182, 184, 185, 187, 188/189, 192, 197, 199L&R, 205, 206, 218, 226/227, 257, 258/259, 260	Bill Wassman

Illustrations Klaus Geisler

Visual Consulting V. Barl

* Courtesy of the New York Public Library

INDEX

Prada, Dr. Henrique 140
Prince Albert 144, 185
Prince George (King George VI) 144, 185
Princes Town 185
Prince Street 126
Puerto de los Hispanoles 125
pujas (Hindu prayer meetings) 78, 107, 181
Punto de la Playa (now Erin) *see* Erin

Q

quarrying, gravel 176, 205
"Queens of the Bands" *see* "Magnificent Seven"
Queen's Park Hotel 140
Queen's Park Savannah *34*, 96, 100, 110, 130, 136,
     142, 157, 177, 253
     Carnival King and Queen competitions 99
     military parade on Republic Day 109
Queen's Royal College 140
Queen Street 126, 132
quenk (wild boar) 155, 256
Quevedo, Raymond 46
     also see Atilla the Hun

R

racial conflicts
     between Africans and Indians 33, 76–77
     between British and French Creoles 34
Radas 32
radio 82
Rafters 251
railway service, Port of Spain to San Fernando 175
Raleigh, Sir Walter *20*, 21, 179
Ramadan 78
Ramgoolie Temple *77*
Ramleela 78
Ramsaran Park 171
Rancho Quemado 174
Ras Shorty I (calypsonian) 248
Rate Payers Association (RPA) 38
"Raymoo" (a current at Staubles, phonetically spelt)
     167
Red Army (steel band group) 47
Red House 38, *38, 39,* 133, 134, 135
     burning of (1903) 38, 133
religion, official (Christianity) 72
Renegades (steel band group) 47
Republic Day (September 24) 109
resorts 168–169
     also see swimming spots *and individual listings*
rice, as staple food to the local blacks 71, 80
rice and peas (local dish) 71, 251, 252
     also see pelau
Richmond Great House 209
Ridgewood Tower Apartments 171
Rienzi, Adrian Cola 42, 45, *45*, 175
Rienzi Kinton Highway *see* Kirton (Rienzi) Highway
Rio Claro 44, 182, 229
Rio Santa Ana 126
River Estate 171
Riverside Plaza 131
Roach, Eric 43
Road March *81*, 99, 100
     in 1958: 244
     in 1977: 247

Roaring Lion 47, 48, 236, 237, 240, 241
Robinson, A.N.R. 56, 57, 59, 60, 62
Rock 169
Rockley Bay 206
Rogers, De Wilton 50
Rojas, John 43, 48, 59
Roman Catholic Cathedral of the Immaculate Conception
     130–131
Roodal, Timothy 42, 140
Roomer 140
Roosevelt, Franklin Delano 168
Rose (calypsonian) 247
Rostant, Philip 34, 36
roti (a flat supple bread) 73, 78, 80, 172, 251, 252
"roti rows" 252
Rousillac 39, 180
Roxborough 78, 194, 204
Royal Cedula of Population 160, 180
Royalists, the 24, 34
Rudder, David 144
rum 27, 251
     annual output 253
"Rum and Coca Cola" (calypso) 240
rum punch 99, 255
rumshops 252–253
Rushville 186
Rust, Randolph 39

S

Saddle Road 153, 155, 157, 170
St Andrews 153
St Ann's 126, 127, 144
St Augustine Campus, University of West Indies 157,
     158
St Bede's School 159
St Clair 144
Ste. Madelaine *see* Usine Ste. Madelaine
St Finbar 179
St Francis of Assisi 142
St George 186
St Giles Island 220
St James 105, 127, 128, 129, 142–143, 166, 183, 252
St James Barracks 143
St John the Baptist Church 134
St John's Road 158
St Joseph 21, 125, 159, *258–259*
St Joseph's Convent 135, 176
St Joseph Village, San Fernando 173
St Mary's College 135
St Peter
     chapel, Maracas 154, 166
     church, Carenage 166
     Feast Day 154
Salybia Bay *163L&R*, 165
Samaan 136, 153, 159, 161, 173
San Antonio nursery 155
san coche (local dish) 251
Sandy Point Beach Club 195, 196
San Fernando 36, 44, 78, 100, 158, 162, 171, 172,
     173, 174, 175, 176, 177, *177*
San Fernando Gazette 36
Sangre Chiquito 78, 186
Sangre Grande 78, 164, 186, *187*
San Juan 127, 157, 252
San Rafael 78
San Salvador Estate 181

288

Y